SPLITS IN THE SOUL

Integrating Traumatic Experiences

Professor Dr. Franz Ruppert is Professor of Psychology at the University of Applied Sciences in Munich, Germany. He gained his PhD in Work and Organisational Psychology at the Technical University of Munich in 1985.

Since 1995 he has focused on psychotherapeutic work and specifically on the causes of psychosis, schizophrenia and other forms of severe mental illness. He has combined with this his interest in bonding and attachment theories and modern trauma work to understand better the effect of traumatic events, not just on those who suffer the event but on entire bonding systems.

His publications include: *Verwirrte Seelen* (2002, Kösel, Munich), (*Confused Souls,* not available in English), followed by *Trauma, Bindung und Familienstellen: Seelische Verletsungen verstehen und heilen* (2005, Pfeiffer bei Klett-Cotta, Stuffgart) translated into English as *Trauma, Bonding & Family Constellations: Understanding and Healing Injuries of the Soul* (2008, Green Balloon Publishing, Frome, UK).

Ruppert facilitates workshops in Germany and many other countries, furthering his insights into the deeper transgenerational effects of trauma in different cultures, and researching the methodology of constellations as a means of better understanding and refining its powerful effects on patients.

This is Ruppert's second book available in English.

About this Book

Psychological problems can often be traced back to traumatic experiences that we have suffered. One of the most powerful types of trauma, which affects the whole process of our personality development, is that of bonding trauma, when a child feels powerless to create an emotional bond with his mother, who is herself traumatised from some prior event. The natural way that human beings manage traumatic experiences involves a splitting of the psychological and emotional structures of the person. While this splitting helps the person survive the traumatic experience, the required strategies of avoidance, control, compensation and delusional thinking will in time cause much stress and discomfort to the life of the sufferer. The author shows in numerous examples how unconscious splits in the personality can be brought to consciousness, their origins indentified and therapeutic solutions developed. A crucial part of this is the development of the methodology of family constellations into a constellation of these 'inner parts', known as trauma constellations.

This book opens up new avenues, not only for psychotherapists and professionals working in the psychotherapeutic field, but also for those affected by traumatic experiences and the subsequent effects on those they love.

Dr. Franz Ruppert is a Professor of Psychology at the

Catholic University in Munich and a practising psychother-apist. He specialises in working with the severely mentally ill. He runs workshops on his application of the constellations method in many countries around the world.

Other publications in English language by the author: Trauma, Bonding and Family Constellations published by Green Balloon Publishing, UK (originally published in German by Klett-Cotta Verlag). www.franz-ruppert.de

SPLITS IN THE SOUL

Integrating Traumatic Experiences

Franz Ruppert

Translated from German by Samuel Onn
and Alexandra Chalfont

English language version edited
by Vivian Broughton

Green Balloon Publishing

First published in the United Kingdom in 2011
by Green Balloon Publishing

First published in Germany in 2007 under the title
Seelische Spaltung und innere Heilung by Klett-Cotta
© 2007 J.G. Cotta'sche Buchhandlung Nachfolger GmbH Stuttgart

For the English language translation:
© 2011 Franz Ruppert

Green Balloon Publishing
Steyning, West Sussex BN44 3GF
www.greenballoonbooks.co.uk

ISBN 978-0-9559683-2-7

Book production by The Choir Press, Gloucester

Contents

Contents

Editor's Foreword to the English Edition

Editing a translation is a challenging task, and the quality of the translation has a great bearing on how difficult or easy this can be. The translators, Samuel Onn and Alexandra Chalfont, presented me with meticulous work in this case and I am extremely grateful to both.

My contact over the last 6 years with Professor Ruppert has changed much of my thinking, and my work is strongly influenced by his approach. So editing a book such as this provides me with a unique opportunity since editing requires a careful consideration of the author's ideas and their exposition for an English-speaking audience, a word by word and sentence by sentence scrutiny. This benefits me as a writer myself and as a worker with what Franz now calls "trauma constellations".

I want also to thank John Mitchell of Green Balloon Publishing, Miles Bailey of Action Publishing for his invaluable support in bringing this book to press, and John McClean for his careful proof-reading.

Vivian Broughton, 2011

A Word of Thanks

When *Trauma, Bonding & Family Constellations* was originally published in Germany in 2005, I did not expect two years later to be writing another book about my psychotherapeutic work. However, I had acquired so much new knowledge and so many new insights during those two years that I felt the need to put them down on paper, not least as a way of ordering and systematising my own thoughts.

On the one hand, I was encouraged by my discovery and understanding of the splits in the soul that are caused by trauma, and the distinction between the different ego-states (the healthy, traumatised and survival ego-components). On the other, during the last two years I was also inspired by the idea that the phenomenon of bonding, the mirror neurons discovered by neuroscientists, and the constellations method fit very well together. To my mind, this opens up two important new dimensions, allowing us to look deeper into the nature and foundations of the human soul.

I would first of all like to thank the many people who opened their souls during my seminars. In doing so they are also helping many other people. Besides the numerous constellations sessions I have conducted and witnessed, I was also able to deepen my knowledge and widen my perspective through an empirical research study I performed in Munich.

The people who contributed to this research as a team were Katharina Anane, Eva Baier, Christina Freund, Carla Kraus, Liesel Krüger, Sabine Metz, Cäcilia Pänzinger, Monika Stumpf and Josef Telake. Claudia Härter was responsible for coordinating the collection of empirical data and ensuring that the data were available for analysis. I extend my heartfelt thanks to the members of this team for their outstanding work, which was performed with great consistency and dedication.

My thanks also go to Dr. Christine Treml from Klett-Cotta Verlag for once again their helpful support in editing the original German text and Roland Knappe who is responsible for the fluid cooperation between Klett-Cotta, the German publishers, and Green Balloon Publishing, the English language publishers. I am especially grateful to Vivian Broughton, who has organised my lectures and seminars in Bristol and London since 2005 and has excellently managed all the necessary steps to translate this text from German into good English. Also I say a big thank you to John Mitchell for managing the publishing of this second book of mine for the English speaking community.

Franz Ruppert (October, 2010)

I have varied gender references in order to balance usage.

Editor's note: The term 'seelische' in German presents difficulties in translation, meaning as it does both the deeper sense that we have in English with the word 'soul', but also the more common meaning that we have in the word 'psyche'. The word psyche of course in its original does mean soul, but we in the west have co-opted it to cover by general consensus the mental and emotional aspects of the self, as evinced in our use of the word psychological (of, affecting or arising in the mind, related to the mental and emotional state of a person, Oxford Online Dictionary), and tend not to attribute the more spiritual dimension that we find in the German word 'seelische'. So I have decided in general to stay with the author's usage of the term 'soul', but would like to indicate that this term is at times expressing something of our deeper nature and at others expressing what we would mean by the term psyche. On odd occasions when the sense is obvious I have used the term psyche.

Vivian Broughton (October 2010)

1

Deep Rifts and Small Wounds

Two souls, alas! reside within my breast
Johann Wolfgang von Goethe, Faust Part One

In his tale *The Strange Case of Dr. Jekyll and Mr. Hyde*, the Scottish writer Robert Louis Stevenson (1850-1894) tells the story of a man who by day works as a reputable doctor, but by night turns into a man of pure evil. As the honourable Dr. Jekyll, he behaves like a gentleman and philanthropist of the city. As Mr. Hyde, under cover of darkness, he indulges freely in all manner of conceivable vices. Dr. Jekyll describes his psychological dilemma in terms of "... good and ill, which divide and compound man's dual nature. In this case, I was driven to reflect deeply and inveterately on that hard law of life, which lies at the root of religion and is one of the most plentiful springs of distress. Though so profound a double-dealer, I was in no sense a hypocrite; both sides of me were in dead earnest; I was not more myself when I laid aside restraint and plunged in shame, than when I laboured, in the eye of day, at the furtherance of knowledge or the relief of sorrow and suffering." (Stevenson, 1994)

Dr. Jekyll's solution is to separate the two creatures physically with the aid of a chemical concoction. His two sides should be able to live out their own lives, each with his own name and in his own time: "If each, I told myself, could but be housed in separate identities, life would be relieved of all that was unbearable; the unjust delivered from the aspirations and remorse of his more upright twin might go his way; and the just could walk steadfastly and securely on his upward path, doing the good things in which he found his pleasure, and no longer be exposed to disgrace and penitence by the hands of this extraneous evil." (ibid) Dr. Jekyll even speculates that "man will ultimately be known for a mere polity of multifarious, incongruous, and independent denizens." (ibid) Man is thus intrinsically split between good and evil, and all that can be done is to suffer patiently the associated inner agonies and contradictions or, by one means or another, to live with this split. The experiment performed by Dr. Jekyll, who attempts the latter, fails miserably. Dr. Jekyll takes his own life after Mr. Hyde commits murder.

There are many areas in which man's dual nature becomes visible. Sometimes it can be very obvious and, as in the case of celebrities in the music, film or fashion industry, is reflected by the media reports. The celebrated pop star Robbie Williams, for example, felt he needed to resort to a drug rehabilitation centre on account of his prescription drug addiction and depression. Despite his glamour, fame, and fortune of millions, he seems to be fundamentally unhappy within one part of his soul. It is also often revealed in court cases how some people possess two thoroughly different faces. In the issue of the German newspaper *Die Süddeutscher Zeitung* of 1st August, 2006, one story read: "*Stalker Hires Hitman*. In the courtroom he comes across as friendly, almost likeable. 'Hello everybody!' said Adrian J., directing a friendly nod to those around him. Behind the façade, however, there hides a different Adrian J., one that has been stalking, terrorising and threatening his ex-girlfriend for months, finally even hiring a hitman, first to castrate and then to shoot his suspected rival."

Some splits in the soul run very deep and can lead to insanity or suicide. Others, however, remain well hidden, only coming to light at times of crisis, for example, when someone, after separating from his or her partner, falls into a deep depression, or suffers panic attacks during conflicts at work.

Others' splits are not quite so obvious, but still noticeable, as when people say one thing and do another, or do things they later regret, or fail to learn from their mistakes.

The more I look for signs of this kind of inner turmoil, the more I see them. For example, a colleague at work told me, "Last week I had a successful conclusion to a family case. They all praised me for my competence, diligence and the thoroughness of my documentation. But somehow it left me feeling really sad. I still don't know why. Anyway, I've been referred a new case, and so it just carries on." While she was telling me this, I could see how it was eating away at her. She would occasionally alter her glance, her voice would sound different; she sometimes came across as attentive but went back to being inaccessible, as if behind a glass wall. She was clearly switching back and forth between different internal states.

How these splits are often subtly hidden from our consciousness, and how liberating it is when we first recognise them and accept their existence, is something I recently experienced for myself. For a number of years I have been a member of a collegiate exchange group. We mainly use the group to discuss matters related to our own work. At one session, the topic was "Understanding and Being Understood". We started by looking at mutual misunderstandings, and as we spoke of our personal experiences of not being noticed by others and the suffering this causes, the level of mutual understanding between us began to increase. During the closing discussion, everybody said they were very happy with the meeting, and, when it was my turn to speak, I also felt the need to say how good it felt to be able to speak with each other so openly.

But all of a sudden I felt a pressure on my chest and a stinging pain close to my heart. I had the courage to tell the others about the difference between my rational evaluation of the meeting and my sudden extreme physical sensations. I then fell into a strange state. My eyes were suddenly full of tears. A few minutes later the pressure on my chest began to abate. The stinging heart pain, however, had not gone away, and had even begun to increase. I realised that, while the well-meaning words of the others reached my ears – recognising and commenting on my experience – they also showed me that they didn't really understand my situation. I remained conscious of my state, although part of me thought I'd had enough – the others hadn't understood how I felt; they were of no help and the meeting was already at an end.

I kept trying to pin down this stinging pain, and eventually tears began to well up in my left eye, while the right eye remained dry. I noticed how I experienced a dividing line down the middle of my body. The left side was becoming increasingly warm and fuller, while the right side became progressively colder and emptier. My next instinct was to transfer the warmth and the feeling from the left to the right side of my body, but I realised I was too eager, and taking things too fast. Consequently, I was then able to admit that two different states were housed in my body simultaneously. I could feel them very clearly. One half of my body was in a state of emotional turmoil, the other half was unaffected. One side of me felt very intense, the other side was reflecting and engaged in deep contemplation. After a while I told the others that the experience had been enough, and I thanked them for being present throughout.

Following this experience, I not only understood rationally what it meant to be misunderstood. I could also now feel it as something very painful, a feeling I know well from my childhood. At the same time, I also saw how I was able to look the others in the eyes, even when I knew from their comments that they were not really able to understand my internal state and me. I was able to be who I was, and was able to leave them to be who they were. I was not reliant on them, but I was also not obliged to reject or judge them for their lack of empathy. I could leave them to their otherness and accept them, as they were, as friends and colleagues, and I was able to accept myself in this divided state. This resulted in a deep-seated healing process for me in the time afterwards.

Until a few years ago I had no eye for the symptoms of traumatisation. Since learning more about the phenomenon of trauma there has been a fundamental change in the way I act towards myself, and my fellow-human beings. I am now able to impart this knowledge to my students, and as a psychotherapist I am able to work in an entirely different way. Something similar recently happened to me in connection with the phenomenon of splits in the soul. Although I had read something about it, it wasn't until recently that I was fully able to grasp the idea of being consistently in contact not only with an individual, but with his many internal states simultaneously, in parallel and consecutively. After discovering, in myself and in other people, that splits in the soul were a frequently occurring phenomenon, my way of viewing the world and human beings changed fundamentally. Things became clearer, and many mysteries as to why we as humans behave in certain ways, become more solvable. To borrow an image from mathematics: where I previously tried to solve an equation containing a single unknown, I now see that the equation contains more than one, and possibly many, unknowns. There exist, therefore, other forms of approaching the problem and, consequently other forms of solution. I now see many more opportunities for understanding people better in the varied expressions of their life and, as a therapist, for helping them discover paths for healing their split soul. Splits in the soul, how they occur and the paths to healing them thus form the basis of this book.

2

The 'Soul'

I live my life in widening circles
Rainer Maria Rilke

'Soul' is a common term to all cultures, and evokes a wealth of images and associations. The Indo-Germanic (Gothic) word 'saiwala' means "that which comes from the sea": in Indo-German the sea is the repository of the unborn and the dead. Professor Hartmann from Innsbruck studied the use of concepts of the soul in the different religions and philosophies of the world in his work *Die Seele: Natur- und Kulturgeschichte von Psyche, Geist und Bewusstsein*[1] (Hinterhuber 2001). The soul is not an organ or thing in the human brain or body, but rather exists as the energy and information ('software') which keeps the human body alive. We recognise the soul from its utterances, from the perceptions, feelings, thoughts, behaviour and memories of a human being; from fears, pleasures, doubts, hopes and beliefs.

Thanks to Freud (1979) we know that consciousness and identity are not the same thing. Our psychological makeup goes far beyond what we consciously perceive, feel, think or remember. The word 'soul' comes close to the experience of human emotions, as well as the idea that there exists something we can call our own, our innermost essence. That is what I like about this word. My main approach is to use the term

[1] Not available in English.

'soul' pragmatically, and as a result the many different facets that the word reveals often surprise me. To me the 'soul' is a creative concept that, in interaction with people, raises many important questions:

- When does the human soul come into being?
- What makes a soul unique?
- With what is the human soul connected?
- To what does it open itself up; to what does it close itself?
- How many layers does it have?
- What can destroy it?

I suspect that the human soul does not start to develop merely after birth; it probably comes into being as early as the act of conception. When a man and woman love each other their relationship with their child is of a quite different quality than when a child is born as the result of rape or an 'accident'. I know from clients born as the result of rape how hard they find it to love themselves, because they themselves were not the product of love. For example, it could be that a woman does not love the father of her child, but loves another man. This confused feeling in the mother can also leave its mark on the psychological development of the child right from the very beginning.

A living being is not just a collection of chemical substances. It is solid matter, energy and information as well. The soul of a child, therefore, besides the physical substance it receives from the child's parents, probably also carries the energy and information taken from his or her parents, as well as that of their ancestors. Genes do not merely convey physical information; they also carry life experiences, concentrated and expressed through matter, of humanity in general, and the ancestors of the newly emerging human being in particular. Gerald Hüther writes: "The old and still widespread idea, that life is merely an exceptionally complicated arrangement of matter that can be described in terms of physical or chemical laws, is . . of no use in the understanding and analysis of living structures. Living systems must be seen as much more than mere forms capable of using the highly specific physical and chemical attributes of their material components in order to build or sustain a particular inner relational structure based on an internal pattern, either developed or inherited from ancestors. Therefore, what every living creature must possess, and what gives it life in the first place, is an internally laid out plan, a matrix which controls its internal organisation and governs its structuring, that is an internal image of what it should be or become." (Hüther, 2006)

Every new human soul is thus formed out of the soul of its parents, and so inherits both 'good' and 'bad' accordingly. This spiritual inheritance contains the initial 'capital' for the new life as much as the inherited 'debt' of the old. In every new life, therefore, something old must be continued, while simultaneously containing the prospect of a new beginning. Every human being, with the gifts and burdens inherited from his or her ancestors, has the spiritual potential within themselves to become something unique, hitherto nonexistent. The human soul is always unique, and must be allowed to develop within its environment of pre-existing things.

The human soul, like the body, grows through contact with others. Before birth a child takes from his mother everything he needs in order to live. Under normal conditions, the mother allows this to happen and willingly passes on to her child all she has available. For the spiritual development of a child it is also undoubtedly a blessing when the father is happy about the child's coming into being and does all he can to help the mother.

On the other hand, when a woman exhibits highly ambivalent or even hostile behaviour when pregnant (she may be frightened of the responsibility and commitment of motherhood, or may not feel sufficiently supported by the father) or perhaps decides to undergo an abortion, the exchange between mother and child is damaged at an early stage; or if whilst pregnant she eats badly or continues taking drugs: all of this will influence the child's psychological development, which will be difficult. The child will feel threatened by his own mother, and his developing soul must then fight for survival. Just the thought of abortion by the pregnant mother may prompt the child to fear for his survival. The energy for life in the making may then either persist or in some sense leave the stage at this very early juncture. Miscarriages and stillbirths could perhaps be viewed from this perspective: that the psychological burdens the child receives from his parents are too heavy for his delicate soul to tolerate, and his will to live is extinguished very early.

At birth, the child leaves the protective space of the mother and must find his own place in the human community. His nine-month-old soul now comes into contact with other humans and their own psychological needs. The first thing he encounters is his mother and her soul, which either gives him a loving welcome into the world or sees him as a burden. Accordingly, the child either receives love, attention, care, stability and generous nourishment and so can gradually take up his own position in his family, or from his first breath he is forced to experience that there is no room for him to develop his uniqueness. He senses that he is not wanted, and is rejected and neglected. The souls of children given up for adoption at birth, for example, suffer in this way. The first few years after birth give rise to further difficulties, and so the question becomes: is the soul of child able to withstand such rejection by his own parents? How can a child protect his own life and soul from threats posed by those he is most dependent on and whom he must trust the most?

Children are the means by which people fulfil their need for love and procreation, the desire to have a family and achieve happiness in their lives. Parents' unconscious and conscious desires and ideas for their child are both the motivation and the reward for the many hardships they may suffer for the good of the child. If, on a spiritual level, the mother or father tries to take more from their child than the child is able to give, or if they attempt to monopolise the child's soul for their own soul's need, to get what they lack, then there will be little space left for the development of the child's soul. What can the child do? How much of his own soul can he relinquish? What should he keep for himself in order to avoid death? How can the soul cope with the contradiction that those who love him the most can sometimes do him terrible harm?

The soul of a child is born innocent, regardless of the circumstances in which the child came into existence. For example, it is no fault of the child's if she was conceived as the result of rape. The child's soul retains its innocence so long as she gets, freely and willingly, from her parents, siblings, and, later, from many other people, that which she requires for her own development, and which she is able to repay in her own way and by her own means. If a child needs to fight to receive something, or must subdue others in order to survive, she soon loses her innocence, as a result of these conflicts. The soul of a child can then in itself become a perpetrator, taking away from others, controlling them, using and abusing them for her own needs. As a victim of her parents' actions, the child will often become the offender.

Spiritual development may therefore contain many gaps and contradictions. We can picture a normal, healthy developmental process as one in which new spiritual layers are constantly accumulating around a centre, with the old development level being enclosed by the new. Old and new are closely related and interlinked. Just as rings accumulate on a tree trunk as the tree grows in rigidity and stability, so the human soul acquires stability and strength over the years. And just as tree rings tell us everything about the growth of the tree – its development from seed to sapling, and finally to a stately, full grown tree, so the 'rings' of the soul also tell us how a human being matured from embryo to baby to small child to schoolchild, to pubescent adolescent to young adult, to adult.

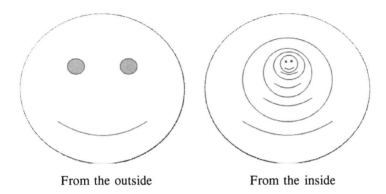

From the outside   From the inside

Figure 1: Integrated spiritual development seen from an outer
and inner perspective.

Figure 1 shows a schematic representation of the integrated development of the human soul. The first diagram as
viewed from the outside, shows only the outer layer, the oldest
personality component (the 'tree bark'). The second diagram
is a view from the inside, showing the different personality
layers, one on top of the other, from the centre. If, in this inner
perspective, we were to pull out the individual personality
layers, one by one, from inside to out, we would see each time
a new face, each corresponding to a different developmental
stage. Each of these personality components in its own way
reflects different moments in the person's spiritual development. They emerge from one another and complement each
other. Their existence is not contradictory, nor do they mutually obstruct one another.

3

The Theory and Terminology of Splits

3.1 Schizophrenic, Ambivalent, Torn, Blocked

Everyone wants to have an integrated personality. That said, contradictions and obstructions between the components of our personalities are a frequent occurrence. While many people experience inner conflict and disharmony, and may see it in others, we are still reluctant to believe that we are 'multiple beings'. From our experience of life, we are not easily able to see ourselves as being more than one person, that multiple selves inhabit us at the same time. The notion of being two or more people simultaneously, possessing different ego-states at the same time, is a shock to our sense of identity. It awakens fears of losing our psychological stability, being labelled crazy by others.

"So am I schizophrenic?" – this question invariably crops up when discussing splits. The term 'schizo' does indeed mean 'split'. Literally 'schizophrenia' translates as 'splitting of the diaphragm[2]', since in antiquity the soul was thought to reside in the diaphragm. 'Schizophrenia', however, is a very precise diagnosis of mental illness, made only when, for example,

[2] Editor's note: Phrenia originates from Greek word *phren* meaning mind and diaphragm.

someone believes he is being followed, despite there being no one wanting to do him harm, or when someone suffers from excessive feelings of guilt, despite in reality not having caused anyone harm. Schizophrenia is mainly spoken of in professional circles in relation to the existence of hallucinations and delusional ideas. Small wonder, then, that nobody wishes to be considered schizophrenic, especially as schizophrenia is still viewed by many specialists as an incurable illness. Schizophrenia is therefore not the right term to use when looking at splits in the soul in general. In my thinking the symptoms of schizophrenia are likely the consequences of far-reaching forms of splits in the soul and entanglements, resulting from specific events in a family bonding system (Ruppert, 2002). I will return to the special pattern of symptoms associated with schizophrenia in a later chapter of this book, when we deal with the topic of *bonding system trauma*.

While the term 'schizophrenic' is both too loaded and too specific for the general purposes of this book, another term, more commonly used, also fails to do justice to the notion of splits. Someone may say: 'I am torn between two things', or 'I am internally in conflict'; behind these statements there may be conflicting opinions or contradictory behaviour, the result of deep spiritual conflicts.

In fact, the everyday term 'inner conflict' comes much closer to what we will be looking at in this book. This expression creates a clearer sense of the distress felt by someone whose spiritual structure has been placed under great strain; who has suffered a deep internal fracture, or feels torn apart. The word 'block', as in 'I feel blocked about that', to my mind expresses well the idea of different tendencies cancelling each other out. We want to act, but something stops us. We want to say something, but are not able to. Blocks often express themselves in the body, for example, through muscle strain, chest pain, headaches or a physical inability to act.

A variety of feelings taken alone is not an indication of a split in the soul. Splits are present where instead of an abundance of feeling-states there exists only a limited selection of conflicting tendencies. Splits are noticeable where the many can no longer co-exist, where there is room only for one or the other.

3.2 Splitting and Dissociation

Psychoanalysis: Freud and Kernberg

In many ways psychology has already addressed the issue of the inner conflict and the split in human nature. Sigmund Freud's model of the *id* and the *superego* highlights the fundamental polarity of the human soul. The self-serving *id*, with its instinctive needs, stands in opposition to the strict and punitive *superego*, which strives to achieve a rigid adaptation of man to cultural norms and suppress his instinctual needs. Sandwiched between the demands of the *id* and the *superego*, the *ego* tries to find an endurable comprise.

To Freud, a 'split' is a psychological defence strategy, similar to repression and denial. Thus, by repressing desires within the soul (especially sexual and aggressive impulses), and denying perceptions of external reality, contradictory and irreconcilable attitudes are produced in a person. The result of this he calls 'split-egos', which to him are "imperfect attempts at detachment from reality" (Freud, 1979). With Freud, therefore, a split is the attempt to deny reality.

For a long time little attention was paid to the split as a defence mechanism in the psychoanalysis of the Freudian school. Discussion of psychological splits revived, however, when, in the 1970s, professional interest began focusing on the borderline personality disorder (BPD). More than anyone else it was Otto Kernberg who tried to explain the typical BPD states, such as denial, projection/introjection, devaluing/idealising, projective identification and fantasies of omnipotence from a psychoanalytical perspective using the concept of the split (Kernberg, Dulz und Sachsse, 2000). In this approach, all children pass through a developmental stage in which they are unable to integrate into their psychological structures the contradictory impressions they assimilate from their environment, especially in respect to their mother. For the child, the 'good' and 'bad' mother exist side by side as initially unrelated, internalised mother-images ('Object relations'). Kernberg sees it as the role of psychological maturation to overcome this primitive developmental stage, arriving at a realistic assessment that other people can be both good and bad. According to this theory, even an adult, if his psychological maturation was unsuccessful, may in crisis situations, fall back into the earlier psychological developmental stage of the split. He 'regresses' in terms of his psychology, back to the stage of the infant. (Kind, 2000)

Trauma theory: Herman, Putnam, and Huber

While psychoanalysis has its roots in the German speaking world, the newer field of trauma theory has mainly been developed in America. In part this is because, in developing his theory, Freud abandoned his concept of trauma, although he still used it initially in connection with his concept of instinct. In trauma theory, instead of a split, we tend to talk of 'dissociation'. This term originated with Pierre Janet (1859–1947), one of the first psychiatrists to recognise the importance of trauma in the formation of mental illnesses. "Unbearable emotional reactions to traumatic events produced an altered state of consciousness, which in turn induced the hysterical symptoms. Janet called this altered state of consciousness 'dissociation'." (Herman, 2003) 'Dissociation' is the division of something that belongs together. The opposite of this word is association, which describes the conflation of disassociated phenomena.

In trauma theory dissociation is primarily understood in a narrower sense, as a survival mechanism for childhood trauma. Children who have experienced massive and repeated physical and sexual abuse split their personality in order to spread out the memory-states resulting from the trauma. Most authors then, see dissociation as an ability that, in a situation of

15

helplessness and powerlessness, facilitates a way out and thus psychological survival. Frank Putnam talks of four functions dissociation can fulfil during a trauma situation or following a traumatic experience: "In particular, children often use their particular dissociative skills by purposefully entering into dissociative states in order to flee the trauma. It has been known for some time that dissociative states of consciousness can function as dissociative reactions to acute traumas, since they facilitate: 1) an escape from the restrictions of reality, 2) the exclusion of traumatic memories and affects in an area outside normal consciousness, 3) a changing of or disengagement from the self (such that someone else or a depersonalised self experiences the trauma), and 4) a neutralising of the sensation of pain." (Putnam, 2003)

In a broad sense, dissociation is generally recognised as the ability of the human psyche to adapt to particularly difficult and stressful situations in life. Ludwig (1983) defines dissociation as follows: "Dissociation is the fundamental psycho-biological mechanism that forms the basis of a variety of forms of changed consciousness, including conversion hysteria, the hypnotic trance, the medium trance, the multiple personality, the fugue state, possession by spirits and the motorway trance. This mechanism is of immense value to the survival of the individual and the species. Under certain conditions it fulfils seven important functions. It enables: 1) the automation of behaviour patterns; 2) effective and efficient use of energy; 3) the resolution of seemingly unsolvable conflicts; 4) escape from the constraints of reality; 5) the isolation of catastrophe experiences; 6) the cathartic abreaction of certain feelings; and 7) the strengthening of the herd instinct (for example, renouncing the individual 'I' within the group identity, a higher degree of suggestibility, etc.)." (Ludwig in Putnam, 2003)

The trauma expert Michaela Huber also sees more in dissociation than the connection with trauma. For her, dissociating means the ability, in everyday life, to shut off and avoid burdening the human psyche with sensory overload. (Huber, 2003)

Autobiographies of dissociative identity: Schreiber, Chase, Casey, Fröhlich

In the literature on trauma, the most extreme form of dissociation is unanimously agreed to be Dissociative Identity Disorder (DID). This term has essentially replaced Multiple Personality Disorder. With dissociative identity disorder there no longer exists a distinct 'I' or self: multiple ego-states now exist side by side within the psyche of the traumatised person. The more intense and long-lasting the traumatic experiences, the more partial identities this model accumulates, each leading its own separate life in the psyche of the affected person. This leads to the development of alter-personalities, that is, personality states that exist in parallel with one another. These, in the same human body, have different characters, different ages, different sexes and often even their own names.

The topic of multiple personalities or Dissociative Identity Disorders was popularised through a range of autobiographical publications such as *Sybil* (Schreiber, 1994), *Aufschrei* (Chase, 2002), *The Flock* (Casey, 1997) and *Vater unser in der Hölle* (Fröhlich, 1996). These reports sparked much controversial debate, mainly in the United States, about the potential and scale of a split personality. Having myself worked as a therapist with many clients who fit the diagnoses 'dissociative identify disorder' and 'multiple identity', I know that such extreme splits in the personality, in which there remains scarcely any stable core identity, is very possible, and that above all it occurs when young children repeatedly suffer the extreme trauma of sadistic and sexualised violence.

3.3 Theoretical Approaches to the 'multiple person'

The idea that we as humans do not have an integrated soul, but are instead composed of many different part identities is increasingly finding support among psychotherapists the world over who deal with these kinds of serious problems. The American professor of psychiatry Richard C. Schwartz provides an overview in his book, *Internal Family Therapy Systems* (1995), of the various authors who became convinced of the 'multiplicity' of the human psyche. Among others, he mentions:

- C. G. Jung and his concept of the archetype; that is the division of individual and collective consciousness;
- Roberto Assagioli and his views on split personalities;
- The Object Relations Theorists (Melanie Klein, Otto Kernberg, Donald Winnicott): the assumption that a child partially adopts the identity of his or her parents;
- The self psychology of Heinz Kohut, which differentiates between an ideal ego and the real ego;
- The Transactional Analysis of Eric Berne with its different ego-states (parent, adult, child);
- Milton Erickson's hypnotherapy, which works therapeutically with the different states of consciousness of a person; and
- The Ego-state Therapy developed by John Watkins and Helen Watkins.

To this I would add the concept of the 'inner voice' developed by Hal and Sidra Stone for the Voice Dialogue Method (Stone and Stone, 2000). This has also gained a foothold in Germany, where it has been implemented creatively in the differentiation between primary voices and suppressed voices, and their various energetic qualities and positions within someone's overall psychic structure (Wittemann, 2006). I would also mention the model of the 'inner child' developed by various authors and used in therapy and counselling (Bradshaw, 2000; Chopich und Paul, 2005; Wolinksky, 1995).

Given the diversity of opinion, Richard Schwarz concludes that, "Regardless of the theorised source of inner entities (learning, trauma, introjections, the collective unconscious, or the mind's natural state), some of these theorists, more than others, view them as complete personalities. They share a belief that these internal entities are more than clusters of thoughts or feelings, or mere states of mind." (Schwartz, 1995)

In my work I choose to speak about personality components, ego-components or split personalities. I see the main reason for the emergence of these parts of the personality as being traumatic experiences. Parts of the personality exist not only temporarily in the wake of a traumatic experience; they also have an enduring presence in the human soul. Splits caused by trauma will persist if their action is not undone through a process of inner healing.

4
Trauma and Splitting

4.1 Dissociation in Difficult Life Situations

It is easy to observe dissociative psychological processes in ourselves. When a situation becomes emotionally too difficult, we become less sensitive or withdraw within ourselves. For example, if we see too many images of poverty and misery on the television, we must withhold our feelings of compassion so that we don't fall into despair ourselves.

People working in certain professions are required to sideline, suppress or suspend their feelings. A doctor would be incapable of doing his job if he felt the same pain suffered by his patient. A butcher would be unable to slaughter animals if he felt sorry for them. If they are to perform their duties correctly, police, paramedics and firemen need to control their fear, their compassion for victims and their spontaneous and rapidly surfacing feelings of anger towards the perpetrators. If they fail to save someone's life, they must not feel personally responsible.

4.2 Dissociation and Stress

Some dissociations are only temporary. When the difficult situation has passed, we are able to release our suppressed feelings again. The longer a difficult situation and the associated emotional strain last or grow in intensity, the harder it will be to feel the emotions again that were temporarily pushed to one side. In this situation, if we are to feel psychologically integrated again, we must achieve a greater distance from the stress-inducing situation. I find it helpful when discussing dissociation and splits of the soul to distinguish between difficult life situations, stress situations and trauma situations. While difficult life situations usually lead to short-term dissociation between feeling and thinking, stress situations lead to longer-lasting dissociation and emotional blocks, which after the stress situation recedes, are gradually able to reintegrate. Deep splits leading to lasting divisions between body, feelings and thinking are, in my opinion, essentially the result of traumatic experiences. I therefore use the term "split" predominantly with this meaning.

4.3 Traumatic Emergency Reactions

Our understanding of traumatisation has grown considerably over recent years (van der Kolk, McFarlane and Weisaeth, 2000). An increasing number of specialist journals devote their pages to the latest developments and research in trauma theory (examples in Germany include *Trauma und Gewalt, Zeitschrift für Psychotraumatologie and Psychologische Medizin*). Traumata are the life-threatening and mentally overpowering experiences each of us may suffer at some time during our lives. In their textbook of psycho-traumatology, Gottfried Fischer and Peter Riedesser define a traumatic experience as "... a vital experience of the discrepancy between threatening situational factors and individual ways of coping, involving feelings of helplessness and defenceless surrender and therefore a lasting shaking of our self-image and understanding of the world." (Fischer und Riedesser, 1999) Trauma therefore predominantly means the experience of helplessness and powerlessness.

    People have been having these experiences since time

immemorial. What is more, animals are also repeatedly exposed to traumatic situations. It is not surprising then to realise that nature has developed its own solution to such a universal phenomenon. The instinctual method of coping with traumatic experiences revolves around sacrificing everything for survival. To preserve life then, when it is necessary, we will neglect all the qualities that enrich life, that make it pleasurable and beautiful.

This principle is valid on the personal/individual and group levels. So how does this work in reality? Let us first have a look at a very stressful situation, for example, the case of someone who has been involved in a car accident. One of my clients described the following scene to me: she lost control of her car, which veered off the road, rolled over and caught fire. She had her young child with her in the car. Despite being seriously injured herself and trapped between the driver's seat and the steering wheel, she was still able to release the safety belt of the child seat and rescue her child from the burning car: she threw the child out the broken car window onto the wet grass and afterwards also managed to free herself and get out of the car.

What had happened? Although this woman was in a pretty hopeless situation, she suddenly found the extraordinary strength and energy required to free both her child and then herself. In this extreme situation, she no longer felt pain in her body. She acted intuitively in the right way to save her child and herself. Only when there was nothing left to be done did she collapse into unconsciousness.

The mobilisation of exceptional strength and the suppression of feelings of pain are the characteristic behavioural traits of people in trauma situations. As long as there is still a chance of saving your own or someone else's life, the body goes into overdrive (stress reaction) and suppresses the attendant pain. Perhaps all acts of bravery are a result of this mechanism; in any case, the more desperate the situation, the greater the mobilisation of these survival energies.

Another kind of emergency mechanism comes into play in

situations where it has become pointless to act and it is more dangerous to take action than to do nothing. Within a split second, a process of paralysis is initiated that causes a complete shutdown of the body's muscular system and hence its movement. The body goes into a state of shock. An animal's feigning death is its last attempt at tricking a predator that reacts mainly to movement, into overlooking it. Even where the predator inflicts a bite, at least the animal will have felt no pain: the shock reaction sent it into a state of narcosis.

Stress reactions therefore mobilise all of the body's powers, whereas a trauma reaction demobilises them. Within a very short space of time, these entirely opposite processes give rise to enormous tension within the human body and the soul.

4.4 Split Up and Split Off

Stress situations do not have to result in a trauma situation, but all trauma situations start off as stress situations. So what happens *after* a trauma situation, assuming it has been survived? Is the previously suppressed pain then experienced to its full extent? Is a complete memory of the trauma and all its details preserved? Clearly not. Some people can remember something and others remember almost nothing. Are the pain and memories forgotten? This is also clearly not the case, for it would contradict the principle of memory if such intense and significant experiences were not recorded. Learning to avoid repeating a dangerous situation requires that we create a record of the experience in our memories. So what form does this compromise between the life-saving process of forgetting and the remembering of past life-and-death situations in the future take?

This is where the mechanism of splitting comes into play. If we assume there has been no previous trauma experience, then we can say that the pre-trauma integrated soul now undergoes a split. One part of the soul is shielded as far as possible from the traumatic situation; in what follows we will call this the *healthy* part of the soul. The other part, which holds the record of the experience of the trauma, we will call the *trauma* part of the soul. A further part, a mirror-image of the trauma part and solely concerned with overcoming the traumatic experience, is also created which we will call the *surviving* part of the soul. Thus there are three different components of the soul. These are actively kept apart through dissociative processes and henceforth develop independently of each other (Figure 2).

One of the main goals of the splitting process is to keep the traumatised part of the soul away from conscious perception, feeling, thought and action as far as possible. This is the main task of the survival component, and to this end it enjoys unlimited access to the conscious and unconscious psychological processes when the trauma part makes its presence felt. The

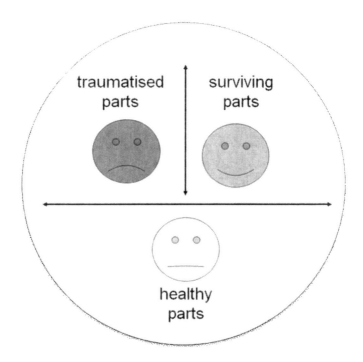

Figure 2: The splits in personality structure after experiencing a trauma situation

healthy part of the soul must make room for the survival part whenever the survival part deems it necessary. Thus, while the structure of the soul is split *up*, the part carrying the memory of the trauma is split *off*.

Depending on the type and severity of the trauma, a trauma-induced splitting of the human soul may occur immediately. However, it can also take weeks, months or even years before the survival part fully gains the upper hand over the trauma part in the personality structure – and in particular in conscious experience – and a reasonably stable post-trauma daily existence becomes possible. It takes a certain amount of time for the survival part to force the trauma part out of the conscious mind.

4.5 Healthy Parts

What are healthy personality structures? According to Freud, the reality principle supersedes the pleasure principle among mature and psychologically healthy people. While with the pleasure principle it is feelings that are in charge, the reality principle is determined by a person's intellect. It is open to debate, however, as to whether this opposition between feelings and intellect really defines the difference between mentally ill and healthy people. Intellectuality is not healthy *per se*, nor is emotionality in itself synonymous with mental ill health. To my mind it is indicative of mental health when the individual psychological functions, such as perception, feelings, imagination, thought, memory and action, develop well and interact well together. Someone with a healthy personality structure is able, in any given developmental phase, to enter into positive contact and creative exchange with his or her natural or social environment.

Consequently, I see healthy personality structures as being defined by qualities such as openness to perception, an ability to deal with feelings, creative power of imagination, clarity of thought, retentiveness, an ability for self-reflection, empathy, the ability to handle conflicts and a readiness to take responsibility. There is such a thing as healthy fear, for example, which warns of real dangers. There is also healthy anger, which helps you articulate your concerns and establish boundaries vis-à-vis other human beings. Similarly, healthy love is attentive, but not possessive. Healthy grief is able to express acute pain, where necessary. A healthy sense of shame keeps social or sexual behaviour within limits acceptable to others. Healthy pride in respect of personal achievements builds confidence. Healthy feelings of guilt lead to appropriate social equality and compensatory action. Healthy personality components are authentic, real, harmonious, true, honest, centred, modest and respectful. Unhealthy feelings are exaggerated, eccentric, artificial, unreal, driven, withdrawn and shameless. It is a sign of mental ill health when feelings are completely absent in situations in which we would normally expect emotional reactions, that is, where feelings of fear, anger, love, guilt, pride and shame are entirely absent.

In the model described above, the healthy part of the soul represents everything that had been able to develop prior to the occurrence of the traumatic experience and was not then destroyed by it. It comprises the well-integrated personality structures the individual was able to develop by the time of the traumatisation and is able to develop further after – and in spite of – the traumatisation.

Resilience

Traumatisation does not affect everyone in the same way and not everybody develops the symptoms of 'post-traumatic stress disorder' (PTSD). Emmy Werner (2000) and Michael Rutter (2000) spent over 40 years observing the development of 700 children on a Hawaiian island. They found that a third of those children who grew up in difficult circumstances – in chronic poverty and with parents suffering from mental disorders – nonetheless developed into adults well equipped to cope with life's challenges. As common characteristics among these children they identified that they actively searched for solutions, had a winning attitude and found people outside their families that acted as role models for them. Since then, under the heading of 'resilience', research has focussed on identifying the factors that might determine exceptional resistance to setbacks in life, such as illness, unemployment or the loss of loved ones. This research named the following factors in resilient people as being responsible for ensuring their survival of difficult life situations:

* Resilient people accept their fate, do not close their eyes to it nor try to run away.
* Resilient people rely on social contact; they do not solve their problems alone.
* Resilient people don't see themselves as victims.
* Resilient people remain optimistic and believe that things will improve one day.

Coherence

The resilience research reaches similar conclusions to those already drawn by the 'salutogenesis' research (Antonovsky, 1997; Margraf, Siegrist and Neumer, 1998). According to the concept developed by Aaron Antonovsky (1923–1994), mental and physical health derive from a 'sense of coherence', something that remains intact even while undergoing traumatic experiences, in so far as these experiences are viewed as *comprehensible*, *manageable* and *meaningful*. People do not therefore see themselves as the objects of other people or adverse circumstances. Vis-à-vis their own fate, they remain their own subjects, with their own thoughts, feelings and actions.

An answer as to how this sense of coherence comes about, how it originally develops, is given by attachment theory. According to John Bowlby (2006), it is a secure maternal attachment that prepares the ground for stable emotional foundations within the first three years of life, and then helps the individual to cope with crisis situations that occur in later life.

Henry Krystal, who has studied the traumatisation of

Holocaust survivors, assumes the existence of an originally inherited, optimistic infantile state oriented towards positive nurturing: "Adults are almost totally unaware of the depth of emotional reserves of the soul; that these exist can be seen in a pronounced optimism, particular vitality and desire for discovery in social and professional encounters, which give the unshakeable impression of being liked and worthy of love. The basis for this is an inherited infantile magic state, which is 'programmed', so to speak, to receive positive nurturing and to thrive. If the infant has established a functioning self-awareness and discovered the 'external', good object, the mother, she, if she is sensitive, translates the needs of the child into her affective reactions. She immediately tries to meet his needs and re-establish a state of wellbeing. Through her behaviour she gives the infant a sense of being loveable and complete. This consolidates a feeling of omnipotence that can be seen later in the belief in the magical power of our own desires." (Krystal, 2000.)

According to Krystal, people with a healthy surplus of this infantile narcissism are able to preserve their optimism in psychological stress situations and retain the initiative, even if they limit themselves to thinking and fantasies. In severe psychological stress situations, they are still able to recognise the chances of their condition improving. In the event of a positive outcome to the risk situation, their most prized memories are primarily those relating to their own actions, which preserved their lives and self-confidence.

4.6 Trauma Parts

Traumatisation can affect a child's soul during or even before birth, and can also occur throughout one's entire life. The earlier the traumatisation takes place, the greater the effect it has on that person's development. It hinders the creation of healthy personality structures.

The trauma part is the soul's repository for the unpleasant feelings induced by the trauma: anxiety attacks, powerlessness, hopelessness, unbearable pain, impotent fury, endless shame, gnawing feelings of guilt, etc. The effects of traumatisation are tangible and real. They cannot be undone. All that can be done is, where possible, to shield the conscious self from their full impact.

While the survival part grows older, the traumatised part of the soul stays the same age it was at the time of the traumatic experience, because it is unable to have any new experiences after the split happens. Its access to further life experiences and conscious existence is cut off by the automatically and unconsciously activated trauma control mechanisms, and then denied by the conscious strategies of the survival part. It is unable to learn anything new and thus remains for its entire life in the same developmental state it was in at the time the trauma occurred. It remains enclosed in its own world with no prospect for change, solely concerned with enduring the memory of the trauma. Acting alone, it plagues itself with questions about how to escape the trauma situation; questions, however, that will never lead to a suitable outcome. It is only concerned with the history of the trauma as its only handle on reality.

Sometimes the trauma part is sent into a state of alarm by images, voices, smells or moments of physical contact that resemble the original traumatic experience. In trauma theory these events are known as the triggers that bring the trauma part into action. In such moments the trauma part is wrenched out of its withdrawn state, where it becomes disconcerted and starts to panic. There is the danger that the splitting-off of the traumatic experience into the unconscious is no longer working and the survival part will lose control over the conscious.

When such retraumatisation occurs, depending on the original trauma situation, the individual in question may change dramatically, and all of the trauma-related reaction patterns become visible. When we look more precisely at individual types of trauma we will see how and which correlations with the symptomatic profiles of psychiatric illnesses then become visible (e.g. panic attacks or depressive disorder). Essentially, every retraumatisation induces some form of psychotic state. The affected individual now no longer experiences him or herself in the present, but rather thinks, feels and acts as if living in the past when the trauma occurred.

For a long time I viewed the content of the split-off trauma part only in a negative light; that was until I came to realise that within it the original healthy part had also been preserved. Depending on the type of traumatisation, the original pain, fear or anger is still there in the trauma part. It stores the fundamental relational emotions within it: love and sorrow, with all their different degrees and intermediate forms. These are then locked away as if being sent to jail; and in this jail they are deprived of life, although at the same time they are protected and preserved. In every traumatic splitting something is retained that is of great value to the healthy parts of the soul.

4.7 Survival Parts

The survival part sits on the trauma part as if atop a lighted kitchen hob: it is always seeking to increase the distance between itself and the oppressive heat coming from the traumatised part. Logically, therefore, it cannot act independently of the traumatised part and is in fact defined and ruled by it in all its forms of existence.

The survival part has access to all the soul's available resources, which it needs to cope with life after the trauma. It can think, feel and act. It possesses all the experiences and memories of a human being except for those pertaining to the various traumatisations this person has lived through. It is even possible for the survival part to have a partial memory of these traumatisations, although this will lack the essential component of an inner emotional connection to the situation; it has none of the corresponding feelings. A purely mental, 'cognitive' memory of the trauma, viewed in this light, also means nothing to it. That is the whole point of the split: part of the person is supposed to become and remain free of the body's overexcitement, the mortal fear, endless feelings of abandonment and loneliness, feelings of being overwhelmed, sensations of powerlessness, complete lack of hope and perspective, unbearable pain, endless fury, deep shame and tortuous feelings of disgust or guilt which, depending on the type of trauma, have taken hold of the human soul.

The suppression of these feelings initially only refers to the trauma situation. Contact with these feelings can nonetheless present a general difficulty for the survival part, for there is always the risk that overly powerful feelings will trigger the memory of the trauma, creating an affect bridge and activating the traumatised part of the soul.

The survival part is thus the guardian of the split. It must focus all its energy into ensuring that the traumatic memory and conscious experience do not come into contact again. On the one hand, splitting is an automatic and unconsciously activated survival mechanism which is at our disposal without our conscious involvement, and which regulates our brain metabolism accordingly (e.g. through morphine, the body's anaesthetic, and the blocking of nerve connections). On the other hand, splitting is also a consciously maintained process that is kept going by the will to survive and suppress bad experiences, i.e. via the survival part of the soul. The survival part does its utmost to ensure that the trauma part never regains control over the conscious experience and action. It forces the trauma part out of the conscious and keeps the lid tightly shut on it.

The survival part is fundamentally afraid that perceptions and feelings would reopen the floodgates to the emotions stored in the trauma part. It is afraid of being swept away by these feelings and losing control again. From my observations, the survival part has developed five main strategies of maintaining the split between itself and the traumatised part of the soul:

- Avoidance: the survival part evades all situations that resemble the initial trauma. It avoids watching images that might trigger memories of the trauma; it even avoids listening to or pronouncing single words that might refer to the trauma. It evades all feelings that might stir something up within it. The survival part divides its environment between emotional danger zones and security zones. As avoidance always results in new avoidance behaviour, the emotional safety zones in a person's life may become increasingly smaller and the danger zones ever larger. An individual's entire life may thus become one single avoidance and detour strategy. The blocking of feelings becomes the essential feature of the survival part. The survival part sometimes takes on duties and tasks to the point of complete exhaustion in order not to experience the traumatic feelings. It is grateful for every detour that prevents the person from resting, for rest is dangerous and feelings may begin to surface uncontrollably. Faced with uncomfortable questions, i.e. any questions that relate to the traumatic experience, the survival part avoids interpersonal contact and resorts to forgetting ("I don't remember.")

- Control: the survival part tries to bring under its control any critical situations that, despite all the precautions taken, it has been unable to avoid. On the one hand, this strategy is internal: the person's own feelings are rigorously pushed aside. On the other, it is external: other people's behaviour is controlled. Others are secretly manipulated or openly censured as to what they can and cannot say and do so that the individual's memory of the trauma is not recalled. By means of subtle hints or heavy threats, the survival part defines forbidden areas as out of bounds. Diverting itself or others onto harmless topics and concerning itself with non-essential matters when forbidden feelings and memories arise is a well-practised control strategy of the survival part. A controlling survival part can become a dictator within its environment in that it deliberately demands the dependence of other people on it and tries to subject all interpersonal relationships to the power of its control so that threat-

ening topics are avoided. In its control and power strategies the survival part also exceeds the limits of its own
abilities and is often only brought to a stop by a total
physical breakdown

- Compensation: because avoidance and control make life
  arduous and austere, because the flavour of life, the satisfying emotional connection to the environment is lacking,
  and because the natural means of satisfying its needs are
  no longer available to it, the survival part seeks compensation elsewhere. It searches for a substitute for that
  which it is no longer able to enjoy naturally due to its
  avoidance and control strategies. Faux happiness,
  clownish behaviour and hysterical laughter become the
  masks behind which it hides itself. Excessive eating and
  drinking become substitutes for those pleasures that can
  arise out of interpersonal contact. Everyday drugs, like
  coffee and nicotine, or even stronger drugs, are expected
  to provide artificially induced, or alleviating and satisfying experiences when the situation for the survival part
  becomes unbearable. Other people are also used by the
  surviving part as a means of compensation: children are
  expected to replace partnerships, clients, friends and
  work colleagues, family relationships, etc. In its extreme,
  the survival part becomes an artist of the artificial.
- Illusions: for the survival part illusions are an important
  source of survival aid. Because the reality of the trauma
  is so unbearable, the flight into illusion represents a
  possible means of avoiding vulnerability. How were
  people in war situations able to hold out without having a
  belief in a better future? How, in the wake of a natural
  disaster, could people begin rebuilding without believing
  the disaster wouldn't strike again immediately? How can
  someone who was raped as a child ever again be in a
  normal relationship without thinking that the man or
  woman he or she is now with won't turn violent? Not
  every hope for a better world is in itself illusory, however.
  Illusions should not be confused with necessary

confidence or healthy optimism. Confidence and optimism are characteristics developed predominantly by securely bonded children. Their experience with their parents tells them they can rely on them and trust them. They can therefore build self-confidence and expect to be able to cope with difficult situations in the future. Illusions, on the other hand, create a pleasing appearance. They are idealised and false images of reality. Illusions put a gloss on reality and resemble delusional ideas. They are a means by which to fool oneself and others. Illusions are the fantasies of the survival part. It clings to the ideal of a beautiful and salubrious world: the ideal man, the dream woman, a healthy family, great professional success, a unique career, the miracle doctor, the charismatic evangelist, eternal life, undying love, reincarnation, etc. The people in real life onto which these illusions are then projected are not really perceived as themselves. They are not experienced as the men, women, children, politicians or doctors that they really are. Even if these idealised people recognise these projected illusory fantasies and fight against them, the survival part does not give up and protects itself against a collapse of its mental house of cards. After every collapse it builds new houses of cards and then clings even tighter to its images of a healthy world. Relinquishing these illusions means recognising the trauma, truly feeling the inner void and endless anxieties, and being forced to feel the intense pain again.

- Further splitting: if all the aforementioned strategies fail, the survival part can always resort to further splitting: the part it can no longer bear to live with is pushed into the unconscious, while the remaining part feels relieved, even though it has lost yet another chunk of its connection to reality.

The survival part does its best to ensure that the person in question is able to go on living after suffering a traumatic life experience. It is fundamentally unwilling and incapable of connecting the problems that appear in the person's life to the split in the soul it acts to maintain. It is also incapable of imagining performing a reversal of the split. It wouldn't know how. It views the split as the solution and not the problem. Consequently, in all the life problems that inevitably arise as a result of such extreme coping strategies, it also doesn't see the connection with the traumatisation, the burden of which is carried by the other part of the person's soul. The survival part thus assumes superficial causes to personal and professional crises. Because the traumatic experience must remain hidden from consciousness, the survival part's theories of life and its difficulties remain superficial, confused or arbitrary. A prisoner of the present, it sticks to its own speculations as to why its problems are there. The fewer the theories it hears from others concerning the truth about its traumatic past, the more attached it becomes to its assumptions. The survival part is therefore no friend of trauma theory. It is unable and unwilling to recognise the psychological reality of the trauma. We will see more precisely with the individual types of trauma how the avoidance, control, compensation and illusion strategies of the survival part manifest themselves and take effect.

Because of the loss of its connection to reality as a consequence of the splitting processes, the surviving part continues to create situations that will lead to further traumatisations: the more extreme the strategies of the survival self, the greater the likelihood of new traumatisations happening.

In the terminology of psychoanalysis, the strategies of the survival self would be known as *resistance* to change, *defence mechanisms* or *character deformations*. In terms of Gottfried Fischer's psychotraumatology, they can be attributed to the 'trauma compensatory schema' (Fisher, 2000). According to Hal and Sidra Stone's model of 'inner voices', the strategies of the survival part correspond to the voices of the 'protector', the 'inner critic' and the 'controller'. Comparing the theory of van der Hart, Nijenhuis and Steel there is a parallel between my concept of the survival parts and their term of the 'apparently normal part' (ANP), and between my trauma part and their 'emotional part' (EP). (van der Hart, Nijenhuis and Steel, 2006).

4.8 Multiple Splits

Different traumas or repeated traumas of the same kind lead to multiple splits. With every trauma, one part of the individual's soul becomes the trauma part, another the survival part. If the individual experiences a further trauma situation, his or her soul must again undergo a split, and an additional survival part is created together with a new trauma part (Figure 3).

Every new traumatisation breaks the individual into further separate pieces. The more traumatisations suffered, the more pieces of the soul will be created and the more complex the personality structure becomes – and so the greater the conflicts between the different parts that develop. With multiple splits it

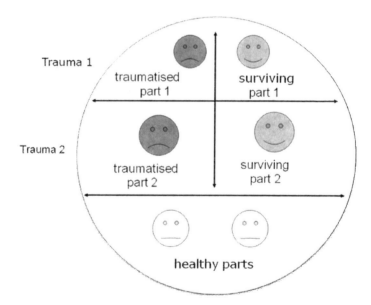

Figure 3: Splits in the soul after a second trauma experience.

becomes increasingly difficult for the different parts to find a reasonably stable inner balance. A multiply traumatised person sinks further and further into his inner chaos. The healthy part of his soul becomes less and less able to maintain an orderly-looking façade; it has an ever-diminishing quantity of psychological resources available with which to cope with life's problems.

The personality structure of a repeatedly traumatised person is inevitably 'multiple'. The individual split-up and split-off parts can, in extreme cases, become completely independent personalities with different names, that battle for their own individual survival, struggling for primacy within the affected person, spying on and fighting against each other, and, where possible, striking compromises and forging alliances amongst themselves. Behind a facade of normality, which one of the survival parts endeavours to maintain towards the outside world, a battle rages among the various split personalities for supremacy over the conscious mind and behaviour (see Michaela Huber, 1998).

4.9 Extreme Polarisations

The trauma and survival parts are mirror images. The more intense the experience of trauma, the more far-reaching the withdrawal of the trauma part of the soul, and the more expansive and more radical the survival parts must then become. The survival part is the counterforce to the experience of powerlessness encountered in the trauma situation:

- The extreme weakness of the trauma part is compensated for by the survival part by means of excessive strength and dominance.
- A trauma part, reduced to its basic vital functions, can be confronted by a manic survival part that is thirsty for vitality, and at times lives its life in an unrestrained manner, without regard to anything else.
- A child whose traumatisation consists of not having

received any attention at all from its parents often develops a survival self that becomes enormous and overblown in order to make sure it is seen. The narcissistic urge of this kind of survival part possesses sufficient energy to become a great artist, a well-known politician or famous scientist.

- A child with an extremely damaged trauma part may have an excessively angry and aggressive survival part that stops at nothing in order to avoid being hurt again.
- To an extremely anxious trauma part seeking desperately to gain a foothold, the survival part can act as an opposite reaction, making itself fully independent and not wanting to become attached to anyone.
- To a trauma part that must keep silent about something, a frantically wandering mind in the survival part, which talks and talks and searches everywhere for something but never really lays hands on anything concrete, can provide a solution.
- Out of the extreme trauma of shame and guilt feelings, a highly moral survival part can develop as a mirror image.

Which traumatisations lead to which types of survival part will be looked at more closely in later chapters, but perhaps it is already possible to see that with the extreme types of survival parts we are already looking at severe personality disorders (borderline, narcissistic, antisocial or hysterical personalities) and schizophrenia (paranoia, manic disorder, schizoaffective disorder).

4.10 Stability and Balance

A psychological system requires rebalancing in the wake of a trauma experience. There is a short film ('The Balance') that demonstrates this clearly[3]. In the film a number of people are standing on a small platform suspended high above the earth.

[3] You can see this film at http://www.clipfish.de/video/983501.

Each time a person moves, the platform tilts to one side. To avoid the platform overturning and someone falling into the abyss, any time someone moves, another person must perform a counter movement. Consequently, there is always someone moving on the platform, with everyone becoming tense when it is their turn to perform a balancing movement.

We can view the relational system of healthy, trauma and survival parts in a similar manner. When one part moves, the others must react. Although, due to the split, they view themselves as being independent of each other, they are not. In fact they remain dependent on each other; if the trauma part unconsciously begins to act, the survival part comes under enormous stress; if the trauma part becomes more active, this cannot in the long term be ignored by the healthy part; if the reaction of the survival part becomes stronger, this also affects the healthy part. So, for as long as the trauma is only dealt with through these splits, the level of psychological unrest will, at best, only become less intense sporadically and there can be no real inner stability. There is always the danger that the traumatised part will suddenly move into the foreground in an uncontrolled way and the whole system will come crashing down.

4.11 Physical Foundations for Splits

The healthy part of the soul is the most likely to be capable of recognising the splits in its structure as a reality. Seeing oneself as split, however, always requires great effort and a readiness to confront oneself. As already mentioned, the survival part is highly reluctant to acknowledge the reality of a split in the soul, and also the trauma part hides itself and is silent for most of the time. That most people are not consciously aware of these splits in their souls, or only see them as extreme possibilities, tells us little about the actual presence of these splits. Our consciousness represents an attempt at a psychological adaptation to our given life situation. It in no way comprehends reality as it is, but rather interprets and explains it from the perspective of the necessities of life and its existential needs.

Perhaps this also explains why it is that we human beings only slowly become accustomed to splits of personality. Maybe we have to familiarise ourselves with them gradually if we wish to discover real solutions to our psychological problems, and not just illusory evasion strategies. The older we become, the more we are confronted with the question as to whether we are just chasing shadows or whether we are in fact capable, with our entire psychological reality, to shape our own lives.

Brain and body

One thing that makes humans special is our brain. It is the body's central organ. It is where all the individual components of the body are represented, creating the necessary connections between the various parts of the body. Every cell of our bodies is infused with our souls, and our psyches; souls and minds are all deeply anchored in our bodies. Body, soul and mind are the different manifestations of a living entity.

Imaging procedures used in brain research are unearthing new findings on a daily basis (Spitzer, 2005, 2008). In contrast to the traditional view, according to which the brain's structure is established at an early stage, we now know that:

- Throughout the course of human life, depending on the stage of life, the brain undergoes powerful structural, biochemical and functional changes and it is not genetically determined (Bauer, 2002).
- That imprinting through relationship experiences in early childhood has significant consequences for the development of brain structures (Hüther, 2005).
- That the female and male brains differ from one another in many fundamental aspects (Brizendine, 2007; Hüther, 2009).

From the anatomy of the brain we can see that it comprises different strata:

- An older brain area (brain stem) which regulates the base functions of the body, such as the beating of the heart, breathing, sleep and waking patterns and sexual functions;
- A midbrain area (limbic system), which mainly processes feelings and memories; and
- An area of the brain that is relatively young in evolutionary terms (neocortex) and which provides the neuronal substructures for the intellectual faculties such as thinking, speaking and imagination.

The brain must also coordinate the different aged areas of the brain and their different tasks. It must meaningfully correlate perception of internal physical states with the perception of the outside world afforded by sight, hearing, smell, taste and tactile sensation. The senses must be linked to the subjective interpretation of what has been perceived, i.e. with our 'feelings'. Our feelings must be coordinated with the thoughts that then guide our actions.

Body awareness, feelings and the mind

Body awareness forms the foundation of our soul. It is out of this body awareness that feelings grow, which, as Antonio Damasio describes it, always have a 'somatic marker', i.e. they are grounded in our bodies (Damasio, 2005, 2006). These feelings relay an impression of whether what we sense is good or bad for us, whether it will bring us pleasure or not. Our feelings have our thoughts on a leash, even if our minds might claim the opposite. As a brain researcher, Damasio holds a clear position here in favour of the primacy of body awareness and sensations over the purely intellectual and cognitive: "I see feelings as having a truly privileged status. They are represented at many neural levels, including the neocortical, where they are the neuroanatomical and neurophysiological equals of whatever is appreciated by other sensory channels. But because of their inextricable ties to the body, they come first in development, and retain a primacy that subtly pervades our mental life. Because the brain is the body's captive audience, feelings are winners among equals. And since what comes first constitutes a frame of reference for what comes after, feelings have a say on how the rest of the brain and cognition go about their business. Their influence is immense." (Damasio, 2006)

This means, therefore, that the unconscious governs the conscious more than we humans would like. Our early experiences, especially our infantile experiences, form the foundations for what as adults we perceive, feel and therefore also think.

Conscious reasoning seems likely to have been a late addition of evolution. When malaise, sensations of pain and fear inform us that something in our body or social existence is not running smoothly, a mental search process is initiated to find the quickest possible remedy to the problem. This thought process creates a certain amount of breathing space in which we need not react immediately. If we don't hit upon something quickly that could bring relief from the problem, we begin to confront its possible causes through thought. We humans are therefore essentially better everyday pragmatists than we are researchers of what it actually is that causes our problems. As long as something works reasonably well, we adapt to the given circumstances without much thought, or we legitimise what our feelings induce us to continue doing with poor reasoning.

What we think to ourselves need bear no relation to reality so long as we always have practical solutions with which to avoid our problems. This is why the human intellectual world is so full of abstruse notions, absurd ideas and half-truths. Our thinking is not geared towards 'objectively' obtaining a theoretical image of our reality. Rather, it serves the individual person or group of people to which it feels it belongs. Only in exceptional cases do we humans take the time to search for causes, e.g. in the event of serious personal crises or social catastrophes. Indeed, it is often only in emergency situations that we are forced to look more closely at the roots of our unhappiness. In moments such as these, our mind can soar to unimaginable heights and bring to the fore deep insights and truths about human beings and the world. Thus, in my experience, traumatised people who have the courage to take a closer look at themselves are often the best connoisseurs of their soul. It is the experience of trauma and mental disorders that most forces us to rethink and expand our understanding of our inner selves.

Predetermined breaking points

Every human being possesses natural, predetermined breaking points, so to speak, in terms of the splitting of the soul. In situations where we are supposed to unite and coordinate things by our own cognitive efforts, matters may sometimes be left in an incoherent or incomplete state. In such situations the connections are easiest to dismantle; this mainly concerns the interface through which physical sensations, feelings and thoughts interact.

Medicine makes use of this fact, for example to bring about a numbing of pain. Using chemical substances, the anaesthetist interrupts the transmission of pain from the body's 'periphery' to the brain. Splits in the soul also involve a numbing process in our nervous system: the transmission of pain is interrupted; the arrival of the signal anxiety in the cerebral cortex is blocked. Certain sections of the nervous system can be denied access to the conscious mind by inhibiting the stimulus conduction. In a similar way to a medical anaesthetic, it is likely that the effects of the numbing agents in trauma-induced splits of the soul also wear off over time, so producing the disruption to the flow of information, particularly the pain within the nervous system. The anaesthetist must continue injecting the anaesthetic, and the brain must synthesise the body's own anaesthetic anew. Therefore, trauma-induced dissociation is not a one-off event, but rather a metabolic process aided and maintained by the psychological mechanisms already mentioned. I suspect, among other reasons, that this is why traumatised people are so quick to become tired: they are using so much additional energy to maintain the splits in their souls.

Figure 4 indicates different possibilities of a horizontal split in body awareness: the signals from the brain to the vocal chords can be interrupted, and a person will be unable to speak about something. Someone may be carrying a heavy weight on his shoulders without understanding why. The chest and heart region are able to sense an isolated application of pressure and pain, without any more information reaching the consciousness. There can be a thick lump in the stomach unrelated to everything else. Sexual desire can be blocked,

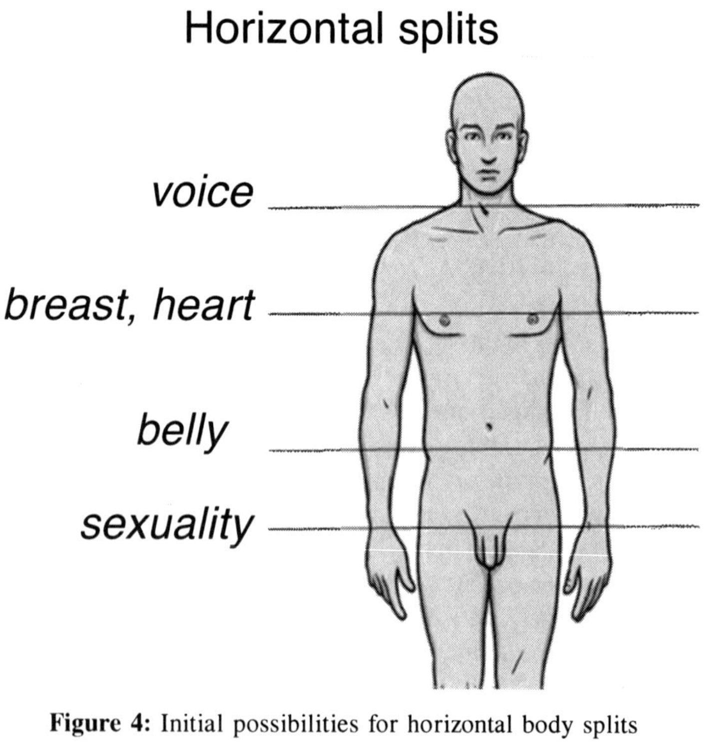

Horizontal splits

voice

breast, heart

belly

sexuality

Figure 4: Initial possibilities for horizontal body splits

although we would very much like to be able to feel it. Arms, hands, legs and feet can have isolated sensations (pins and needles, numbness, agitation).

The clot

One of my clients went to the doctor for treatment after feeling a pressure in his stomach. For a couple of days after the treatment he felt no further symptoms. However, the problem resurfaced again. His voice became hoarse and he could hardly speak anymore. Over the course of his psychotherapy, the correlations began to become clear: he had split off the traumas of war suffered by his mother that he had unconsciously soaked up, which resulted in the feelings of loneliness that had developed in him during his childhood. These extreme anxieties had created the feelings of tension in his stomach. During his treatment session he first visualised these as a hideous, slimy clot. The medical treatment had freed the upward path, but the process stalled at the next breaking point in the transmission of his pain to his conscious. The client was not yet able to speak about his childhood experiences and also felt unable to cry; previously he couldn't breathe sufficiently to do so. During a therapy session, while he continued to experience the same physical sensation and surfacing images, suddenly and spontaneously all trauma energies that had been stored up in his body, his pain and fear were all discharged. He spent a number of minutes crying heavily, then he fell quiet and felt relaxed and comfortable in his body. The physical blockage, which until now had separated his traumatised childhood self and his adult survival self, had been diffused.

Similarly, the two halves of the cerebrum with their different duties also represent a kind of predetermined breaking point, which can be used for splitting. While the older half of the cerebrum in evolutionary terms processes the more emotional experiences, the younger half deals more with the analytical/logical processes. Thus a separation of emotions and thoughts can occur when there is a block of the information exchange between right and left halves of the cerebrum. The left half of the cerebrum is thought in particular to have the function of recording the mental activity of a human being from a meta-position, of commenting and generally creating self-awareness and self-confidence. If, as a result, the cooperation between the right and left hand sides of the brain is blocked, a large part of this experience is pushed into the unconscious, with the remaining part representing the residual consciousness, which, though it can still be used for intellectualisation, can no longer be clearly felt.

Figure 5 demonstrates the vertical form of a split. We can, for example, recognise these forms of splitting in someone who feels divided down the middle, having two entirely different sides to his or her face or body or has certain health complaints that appear in only one half of the body.

When we come to understand these correlations, it

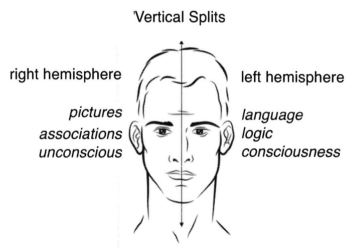

Figure 5: Starting points for vertical splits

becomes clearer why early traumatisation can have so many
different negative effects on the development of a human
being. Early traumas disrupt the necessary integration
processes in the body and the personality structure from the
very beginning. If a split is active in the background for a long
time, the risk of physical illness increases because the body
becomes increasingly incapable of reconciling and balancing
out the contradictory impulses it receives from the survival
part and trauma part of the soul. Trauma makes the body the
servant of two masters, like a horse with two riders on its
back. One of them applies the spurs, the other pulls at the
reins. Small wonder then, that under these conditions the body
one day has a partial or complete breakdown, because in principle it is being expected to be both active and passive at the
same time. Autoimmune deficiencies seem to me particularly
to represent cases of illnesses caused by splits in the soul;
these are illnesses in which the immune system attacks its own
body, rather than protecting it.

Throwing yourself against barbed wire

One of my clients grew up in a family dominated by an
atmosphere of extreme aggression. His parents were
always arguing and the children were often physically hit.
On the other hand, he was also the confidante of his
extremely nervous and deeply split mother. He felt he
was her prince, whose job it was to protect her from the
violent father. He later married a woman about whom he
said that trying to get close to her was like throwing
himself against barbed wire. It was during this marriage
that he first started to suffer from rheumatic muscle and
limb pain, which increasingly affected his physical
mobility. His doctors diagnosed a rare autoimmune defi-
ciency and he was treated mainly with cortisone. During
his psychotherapy, however, the more he began to recognise the splits in his soul, and the more he was able to

free himself from the contradiction between his extreme fear of his violent parents and his eternal longing for love from them, the more his physical condition – to the astonishment of his doctors – improved.

The activation of splits

We human beings store up our experiences. This is a positive attribute, for it makes us capable of learning. The storing of extremely negative experiences, however, comes with pitfalls and disadvantages. It raises our sensitivity towards harmful sensations; the more negative experiences we have, the more sensitive we become. For someone who has lived through extreme stressful experiences, a normal life event easily becomes a stress situation. For someone who has been forced to undergo a traumatic experience, a common stress situation can bring the traumatised self, with all its anxiety and help-lessness reactions, into play. If we have already had traumatic experiences, then normal life events are experienced as stress situations, and stress situations as trauma situations. This explains why we may often overreact in harmless situations: behind this behaviour lies the activation of a split off experi-ence.

Self-awareness as an added component

Consciousness is just one of the qualities of our physical and psychological existence. It is not a permanent state. It can be there one moment, but partially or completely disappear the next, for example when fainting or sleeping. Perhaps consciousness is similar to what a computer loads into its virtual memory in the form of programs and files. It allows us to deal with the life tasks we are faced with at any given moment; all other programs are not conscious at that moment.

'Identity', 'I' and 'self' are not psychological values that were there from the outset. Their existence is in itself a product of psychological development. Frank Putnam advanced the view "that the consolidation of our self and our identity over and beyond the behavioural states and the modulation of transitions between different behavioural states belong to the many development tasks that we achieve during the course of our growth period" (Putnam, 2003). Presumably it was only the development of the other half of the cerebrum that enabled this far-reaching stride in human development through which man became aware of himself and developed self-awareness (Ivanov, 1983).

Parallel processes

Many different states exist simultaneously and in parallel within us, which our nervous system records, coordinates, influences and is itself influenced and guided by. Our brain is a highly networked structure that processes large amounts of information simultaneously and can also mirror itself. This means that more than one identity state can be created within us. As we will see in a later chapter, there are special kinds of nerve cells called 'mirror neurons', which it is thought allow us to simulate the mind-states of other people within ourselves. The multitude of different possible physical-soul-mind states gives rise to the question of which of the many available states in the end becomes the identity state we experience as our 'real' self. Seemingly we can only conceive of one identity state as being our self-awareness that calls the shots in the present moment. In the meantime, the other candidates for the dominating 'I' must remain unconsciously in the background, where they await their opportunity to move into the centre of the conscious mind.

Psychological states that have had the most recent contact with the outside world are normally correlated with the conscious self. If there are splits in the soul, however, it is possible for the self undergoing the current life experience to be so strongly influenced by the traumatised parts of the soul that it projects past traumatic experiences onto the real world more readily than it can take in new information from the environment. However, the affected person is unaware of what is happening. Someone who has experienced extreme violence, for example, may catch a glimpse of the abuser by whom he feels threatened in an entirely innocent person.

5

Types of Trauma

In my books *Confused Souls*[4] (*Verwirrte Seelen*, Ruppert, 2002) and *Trauma, Bonding and Family Constellations* (Ruppert, 2008) I make a distinction between four different types of trauma:

- Existential trauma,
- Trauma of loss,
- Bonding trauma, and
- Bonding system trauma.

Trauma and emotional bonding should be understood in combination. This is one of the main findings to come out of my psychotherapeutic work with many seriously traumatised people. A traumatic experience almost always influences a person's emotional bonding for the following reasons:

- because a traumatic event also affects other people (e.g. in cases of existential trauma it affects loved ones and helpers)
- because the loss of another person is only felt as a traumatic loss if an emotional bond to this person already existed.
- because a traumatic experience directly affects a person's

[4] Not available in English translation.

51

bonding system and the capacity to bond is to a large extent impaired.

• because a traumatic event in human bonding systems – especially within a family – has such devastating consequences that it can destroy relationships over many generations.

• and because the ability to cope with traumatic experience depends on how well bonded the person in question is and which relationships he or she can fall back on in terms of reliable resources (Gasch, 2007).

I fully agree with Anngwyn St. Just, who spoke out against the limitation of the term trauma to isolated shock events (St. Just, 2005). Trauma is in most cases a social phenomenon. Trauma and bonding processes are inseparably interwoven in the human soul.

5.1 Existential Trauma

Existential traumas are a matter of life and death. They are purely matters of survival (for example, natural disasters, traffic accidents, war situations, etc.). The main emotion of existential trauma is fear of death. In most cases, the affected person freezes at the end of the trauma situation. The following example shows clearly how the survival self and the trauma self behave following an experience of existential trauma. After the war in Croatia (1991–1995), one of my students, Josip Stricevic, conducted a study about how veterans of the war were currently living (Stricevic, 2002). The following case study is an extract from his diploma thesis, which I have shortened and edited.

"I was ready to give myself up"

"Mr L is 55 years old, married and has four children. He was involved in the war, he told me, for four years, five months and three days. He and his family were driven out of the village in which they had worked for generations as farmers. Before the war, he had a beautiful house, many fields and machines to work them. The village was then occupied by Serbian guerrilla troops and completely destroyed, including Mr L's house. The Serbs plundered all the houses and then set them on fire.

"Like many others, Mr L started out in the army as a simple soldier sitting in a military dugout. After his village was occupied, he could no longer sit and wait in the trenches. Alone, he would repeatedly sneak behind Serbian lines and check if everything in the village had been destroyed. During one of these trips he was spotted by three Serbian Tschetniks. They chased him through shoulder-height bushes, where he could hide himself. 'But suddenly they were standing right above me. I lay curled up under the small, sparse bushes, but they didn't see me. I couldn't understand it. My fear had become too much. I was ready to give myself up. But just as I was about to stand up, something within me said I should stay still just a little longer. That was what saved me. They moved on.'

"While Mr L retold these events, I was able to identify the first signs of a re-traumatisation: his voice became shaky and low, he couldn't keep his hands still, and in no time at all he was dripping in sweat. I kept repeating that he was here now, where he was safe. This calmed him down, he took a deep breath, fell silent for a short while and then continued: 'When they were out of sight, I started running again, but they heard me. They started firing grenades at me. At this point I was running past a spot where there were some corpses of Croatian soldiers lying on the ground. I ran towards them and used them to cover myself. The smell was unbearable, but these boys saved my life, for I noticed how the shrapnel from the grenades penetrated their bodies and protected me like a bulletproof vest. After a while, the Serbian soldiers ceased firing, and some of them came towards me. When they saw the corpses, they were amused and said, 'Now the pig is lying next to his brothers, where he belongs.' They stamped on a few bodies with their boots and then walked off, having assumed they were all dead. I lay in that position for a number of hours until I summoned the courage to get up and return to my unit.'

"His fellow soldiers noticed a deep change in him. They told him he was becoming increasingly withdrawn, would talk to himself and could sometimes be unresponsive. They advised him to see a psychologist. He felt insulted by their advice, saying he wasn't crazy and didn't need to see a psychiatrist. He wasn't a mental case, he was just tired, he said.

"Despite this experience, he couldn't stop himself from returning to his village time and again, until one day he was caught. He spent many months in captivity, but was able to escape with the help of a young soldier in the Yugoslav People's Army. After marching for days on end, he returned to his unit. From there he was ordered home but refused to leave his post until one day he had a breakdown and woke up days later to find himself in hospital. He was completely disorientated when he woke up. He was suffering from partial amnesia and was unable to recall the time of his breakdown. He was diagnosed with post traumatic stress disorder (PTSD) and personality change, and as a result was no longer allowed to take part in the war.

"Today, he is again living with his family in his village. He suffers from nightmares, panic attacks, social anxiety and suicidal thoughts. He has isolated himself from his surroundings. He spends most of his time going for walks, as this is what seems to calm him the most. This also being the place where he was caught, he is always drawn towards the places where he was beaten and where he covered himself with the dead soldiers. When he reaches these spots, he always has the feeling he is being followed by Tschetniks, or that they are lying in wait for him in the bushes. To counter these feelings, he has to take 14 tablets a day. He receives psychotherapy once a year for two weeks.

"His pension situation is clear: he receives a basic pension, which barely meets his living costs. His family works in the fields, and he tries as best he can to help. But there are days when he is too afraid to go to the fields. He often suffers panic attacks when in the fields and runs away. His neighbours won't have much to do with him, as his family works and he spends the whole time going for walks. Although he fought for the village, he and some of his fellow soldiers are a minority. They are often accused of themselves being to blame for having insisted on playing the heroes. At first, when he heard these things he would often hit the person in question. Today, however, he avoids public places, being afraid of losing control."

We can easily trace the origins and consequences of existential trauma in this story. The trauma situation itself consists of Mr L as a soldier coming face to face with the possibility of his own death. He proceeds to act in a rational and intuitively correct way. Seeing no escape from the situation, he ceases all activity and surrenders to his fate. Fearing for his life, he is completely at the mercy of his enemies. It is a matter of pure luck that he is able to survive. Petrified, he remains lying there for a number of hours.

When he finally gets back to his feet, the split in his personality has already taken place. He now has a survival self, which returns to his body and carries on living as if nothing had happened, and a trauma self, which out of fear shuts itself off from other people and is unapproachable. In this state of shock it is as if he is frozen. Mr L's survival self is incapable of speaking about the trauma situation. He is unable to tell the others about what he has just experienced. As a consequence, the other soldiers are unable to understand his behaviour, though they sense he is no longer the same person they knew.

Mr L's survival self rejects the observations of his fellow

soldiers that something is wrong with him. He looks for a plausible explanation for the change in him, something familiar and normal and therefore unrelated to the trauma he has just experienced. He believes it's all just a matter of being 'tired'.

His survival self continues to act as if the trauma had not happened and so he revisits the same dangerous places. Again it is by luck that he avoids capture and imprisonment. But the survival self is still none the wiser. It behaves as if everything had not happened. This demonstrates the principle of polarisation: the extreme powerlessness of the traumatised part of his soul corresponds in the survival part with a blind heroism that views itself as invulnerable. Through the renewed trips to the village, the survival self again exposes the trauma self to the triggers of the fear of death, so much so that the entire psychological system ceases to function. Finally, the emergency mechanism of a blackout causes a closing down of his entire conscious state. The loss of memory suffered after he awakes from the blackout indicates that Mr L was in his trauma self immediately before the blackout occurred.

After the war, the survival part of Mr L's soul mostly retains the upper hand. Repeatedly, however, the trauma part is triggered causing frequent re-traumatisations, especially as Mr L keeps on returning to the very same places where he felt the fear of death, as if seeking to understand or resolve something rendered incomprehensible to him through the dissociation of his experience.

The telling sign of existential trauma is panic attacks, i.e. phases during which the trauma part becomes the dominating conscious self and the body undergoes a number of minutes of tremors, sweating and respiratory arrest.

In nightmares, the trauma part is also able to break through the perception threshold, when during sleep the soul tries to deal with conflicts through dreams. However, a trauma cannot be dealt with by dreams. Dreams always lead us back to the same moment of blacking out and helplessness from which we are only able to escape by waking up and switching to the survival part.

Mr L's social phobias, i.e. his general fear of other people, can similarly be explained by his trauma part. The trauma part has an extreme fear of other people and is no longer able to distinguish between friend and foe. Mr L's trauma self is still at war. Mr L has become fundamentally untrusting of people and is unable to speak about it.

Why also are there thoughts of suicide in cases of existential trauma? Presumably because the survival part desires salvation from all its problems through death. If someone has a gun held to his head for long enough, he begins to see pulling the trigger as deliverance from his fear.

The example of Mr L also shows how a social milieu often reacts to someone who has suffered an existential trauma. There is widespread ignorance in understanding his unusual manner. Nobody recognises the split in his personality caused by the trauma in his behaviour. The issuing of medication only sought to influence his brain metabolism. The psychological problem was thus reduced to a physical one. The use of drugs to block the body's ability to feel reduces the trauma part's capacity for expression, but only as long as the medication continues to work and, since the brain gets used to the intake of drugs and develops strategies to cancel out their effect, in ever-increasing doses. So Mr L becomes addicted to the medication. The medication also takes away from his healthy personality components any remaining emotional connection to the environment, which leads to further withdrawn behaviour and, for this part of his personality, the loss of the ability to relate.

The yearly two-week psychotherapy treatment offered to Mr L could be a starting point for improving his mental state, however it appears not to be a trauma-specific type of therapy and, at any rate, two weeks would not be sufficient to deal with the trauma-induced splits in Mr L's soul.

The longer Mr L's personality changes persist, the less patience his social milieu shows towards him. He becomes increasingly shut out and morally judged. His incapacity is interpreted as his not wanting to change, and this only leads him to yet further social withdrawal. He feels misunderstood and unfairly treated. He is barely able to control his anger, and thus becomes a danger to others because he believes he has to defend himself.

In Croatia there are stories of war veterans who, from desperation and a lack of prospects, run amok. From the other interviews conducted by Josip Stricevic with Croatian war veterans, it becomes clear how many take refuge in alcohol; if the trauma component of the soul inundates the conscious self with its fears and anxieties, the survival part seeks to quell these fears with beer and spirits. Given that this fear becomes a dominant feeling for soldiers, existential trauma situations, which they experience cumulatively, produce deep splits in their souls, which they are no longer able to overcome. This gives rise to a spiralling into fear of death and violence. The fear of death felt in their own souls then becomes a mortal danger for others. The war takes place both within and without the person, and thus inevitably continues in peacetime within the families and communities to which the soldiers return after the war.

Since fear is such a dominating feeling, in existential trauma the healthy parts of the soul are often suppressed once the avalanche of fear in the nervous systems has been triggered. Fear is probably the greatest impediment to reversing a split in the soul. Figure 6 contains a summarised schematic depiction of the basic split that occurs in existential trauma.

Trauma of Existential Threat

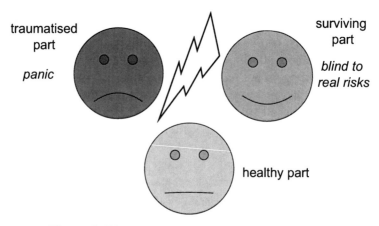

Figure 6: The split that occurs in existential trauma

5.2 Trauma of Loss

Trauma of loss involves the loss of an important bond by a lasting absence or death of another person. A trauma of loss situation can arise, for example, when a baby has been separated from her mother for too long a time, when the mother of a child dies while young, or when a child's parents divorce early or a child is given up for adoption or into permanent care. Separation anxiety, anger, pain and grief are the lasting feelings of trauma of loss. Depression is its long-term consequence.

The consequences of separation during early childhood

The bonding process between parents and their children, and especially between a mother and her child, is extremely delicate and easily disturbed. I took the following example from the book 'Loss' (2006b, Bowlby, p. 405) because it convincingly shows how a split in a child's soul comes into existence and lasts. It is about John, a boy of one year and five months who spent nine days in a children's home because his mother was having another baby. The children's home where John was brought was recognised and approved because of the training of its nurses, but there was no one nurse responsible for John's care.

> "The mother went into labour during the night, and on the way to the hospital she left John behind at the children's home. When Mary, a young, smiling nurse, greeted him the next morning, his reaction was friendly and he cooperated while being dressed. He was also friendly to the other young nurses who came and went. In the evening Mary took him to bed, but she didn't stay with him and John was upset and cried in protest. The second day also began quite well. John spent a large proportion of the time playing in a corner, away from the other children, and occasionally he would look for a nurse to feed him; his overtures were easily overlooked, however, and he was often pushed aside by other children. For most of the day he remained quiet and didn't complain." (ibid. p. 405)

John thus initially tries to deal with his sudden separation from his mother by waiting. He hopes his mother will return soon. At first, still full of trust, he turns to the nurses at the home and seeks their comfort. For two days he endures this inner tension and the anxiety of being separated from his parents. He waits quietly until the first big disappointment comes: his father reappears but doesn't take him back home with him.

> "When the father made to go home, John began to cry and fought to be taken with him. Nurse Mary was able to comfort him, but when she also had to leave, John again began to cry. From the third day onwards, John became increasingly distressed, at times standing forlornly at one end of the room or crying for a long time. Although he continued to try and get closer to one or other of the nurses, he now more often played in a corner or would crawl under a table, where he would cry alone." (ibid., p. 406)

John's suppressed pain of separation now bursts out, and the nurses are no longer able to console him. He experiences the fact that his father doesn't take him with him as a cause of great disappointment and rejection. As a result he becomes increasingly withdrawn and no longer allows the nurses to approach him. The splitting of his soul has begun.

> "By the fifth day his overtures to the nurses had become less frequent, and even when a nurse tried to comfort him, he barely reacted. Afterwards he turned instead towards a giant teddy bear, which he hugged. He also cried a lot in silent despair, sometimes rolling around and wringing his hands at the same time. Occasionally he would cry out furiously, though not aimed at anyone in particular, and during one brief visit he hit Nurse Mary in the face." (ibid., p. 406)

John no longer lets others comfort him, seeking instead comfort in a teddy bear. He can cling to the teddy bear. It is always there. It can't leave him. Like many children in his situation, he transfers his need for bonding to something no one can take away from him, something he alone has access to. He is distressed that his mother and father are not there for him, and his powerlessness makes him unresponsive, angry and aggressive.

"When his father visited him again on the sixth day, after two days' absence, John bit and hit him. Then suddenly his face lit up and he went to get his outdoor shoes and started walking towards the door full of hope; but then came the disappointment, as his father set off without him. John went over to Nurse Mary and looked back at his father with a pained look. Then he also turned away from Mary and sat down to one side while taking his blanket in his arm. During the following days John was a picture of despair. He didn't play, didn't eat and wanted nothing, and at best he reacted for only a few seconds to the fleeting attempts of the young nurses to cheer him up. When one of the other children tried to push him out of the lap of one of the nurses, his voice took on an angry tone. Otherwise he just lay on the floor for long periods in apathetic silence, his face nuzzled into the head of the giant teddy bear." (ibid., p. 406)

It is as if something is dying inside him, which is also why he stops eating. All of this places him in a critical and life-threatening situation. He has given up hope that his parents will come and collect him. When his father comes to visit again on the sixth day, John once more begins to have hope. He again clearly indicates his need to be taken home to his mother. His repeated disappointment at his father's departing without him, leaving him at the children's home, only heightens his despair. In giving up any hope with respect to his parents, he also gives up himself. He sinks into hopelessness. The splitting of his soul has become even deeper. A part of him slides further and further into depressive thoughts, the other part separates itself from this traumatised part and therefore increasingly from his parents, too. This all becomes visible when his father returns again on the eighth day. John no longer actively goes over to him and shows him his need to be taken with him. His passive behaviour is a way of protecting himself from the rising pain he feels at the prospect of once again being disappointed and left behind. His unresponsive withdrawal shows the survival part of his soul is now trying to become accustomed to being alone. He must come to terms with it.

"When on the eighth day his father came at tea time, John cried convulsively and was neither able to eat nor drink. At the end of the visit he was in a state of total despair, and no one could comfort him. He crawled down from Nurse Mary's knee, crept into his corner and lay crying beside the teddy bear, without reacting to the efforts of the confused nurses." (ibid., p. 406)

This is also why his so desperately longed-for mother, when she eventually comes on the ninth day to collect him, is unable to reach him. He is surprised at her sudden reappearance. The two affected parts of his soul are now in conflict with each other. While one part again gathers hope and naturally wants to go straight to the mother, the other part no longer trusts her. John's running to another person and then to his father, is a kind of compromise solution to this dilemma. The long and hard look directed towards his mother comes from that part of his soul which, out of disappointment, has already separated itself from her, whom he sees as the source of his emotional suffering. John's look says: "You caused me to despair, I am deeply wounded and I am very angry." On the morning of the ninth day, John's state was unchanged. When his mother came to the children's home to collect him, he was clinging desperate and motionless to the lap of one of the nurses.

"On seeing his mother, he began writhing around and crying loudly. He looked furtively towards his mother on repeated occasions, but each time he turned away again with a loud cry and agitated expression. After a few minutes the mother tried to take him onto her knee, but he resisted and cried out, rearing himself up and running away crying towards Joyce Robertson (who was present as an observer). Joyce Robertson comforted him and after a short while gave him back to his mother. John now lay still in his mother's lap but did not look at her once." (ibid., p. 407)

The situation changed when his father arrived shortly afterwards. John now pulled himself away from his mother and went to his father. In the arms of his father, he stopped crying and for the first time he looked directly at his mother.

"'It was a long, hard look,' said the mother. 'He's never looked at me in that way before.'" (ibid., p. 407)

During John's first week back home with his parents, the split in his soul continues to affect him. Although now, viewed from the outside, everything ought to have been normal and the parents again bonding with their child, it is not easy for John to reverse the split that has occurred within him. He is at its mercy. His life is more often dominated by his past experience of separation than by the presence of his parents. During the first week back home again, John cried a lot; if he sensed the slightest delay of attention towards him he would lose his patience and have tantrums. Then he rejected his parents on all levels.

> ". . . he accepted neither attention nor comfort, didn't want to play with them, and retreated physically by going into his room and closing the door. In the second week he was calmer; in the third week, however, he came across as being unhappier than ever before. His tantrums returned; he refused to eat, began to lose weight and was sleeping badly; however, he had now become clingy. His parents, in shock at his state, gave him their maximum attention and did what they could to rebuild his trust. Their efforts met with a certain amount of success, and the relationship with the mother improved significantly." (ibid., p. 407)

This improvement however was fragile and four weeks after John's return home, he again stopped eating for a few days and rejected the attention of his parents. Three weeks later John was for five days extremely disturbed and for the first time openly hostile towards his mother. The nine days of separation in the children's home had the effect that John had lost his fundamental trust in his parents. He took refuge with a part of his soul in a state of reclusion and remained imprisoned in this part of the soul. It was exceedingly difficult for him to renounce this fallback position and again be able to trust his parents. "You could leave me again from one day to the next!" is what his survival-self fears. "So I must brace myself and avoid entering such painful separation situations again which leave me so powerless. It is therefore better either to reject the offers of comfort or to punish the person who caused me this pain." Like every traumatised person, he remains hypersensitive to the original trauma and checks carefully for signs as to whether his mother will leave him again. Situations in which he does not know where his mother is reactivate the experience of his traumatic over-excitation, his spiritual pain and the acting out of this pain through accusations and anger directed at his parents. His disappointment at having been abandoned makes him continually angry. He continues to punish his parents for deserting him for nine days. He covers up his pain with aggression. The traumatised part of his soul shows itself over and over again in his listlessness and despair, his giving up and refusal to feed himself and, when he becomes more active, his anxious clinging on. Even where experience shows that his parents are not going to abandon him again, John still doesn't fully overcome the split he endured. His traumatised part remains active. Even three years later, when John was four and half years old, he showed different sides of his split personality. Often he was an active and lively boy, but still had abnormal fears of losing his mother and was always upset when she wasn't where he expected her to be. So he could become hostile towards her, sometimes without reason.

So, if a separation of only nine days can leave such deep scars in a child's soul, how much more must month-long stays in the isolation of children's hospitals or homes overwhelm a child's psychological strength and cause live long lasting splits in his soul.

Early loss of the mother

The greatest loss-related trauma is suffered by children who lose their mothers at an early age, either due to the mother's death or because they have been separated from the mother permanently, for example by adoption or long term placement with a foster family or in a children's home. No child, from my observations, is able to survive this situation without undergoing a split in his soul. This fact is often not sufficiently heeded by those who are working with these children, nor is its full extent recognised by those affected themselves. Consequently, the early death of the mother, adoption or a stay at a hospital are, in my experience, only rarely granted the importance that they actually have for the overall psychological development of a child, i.e. that they lead to splitting within the bonding system. A part of the child records the traumatic experience within.

The survival part of the child wants to hear nothing of the loss. He has adapted himself, as far as was possible, to the new situation. He even reacts angrily when asked to attend to the small, helpless and lonesome child in his soul. There is great resistance here to this insight that the early loss of the mother is always a traumatic experience. There is great fear that the split will no longer function and the survival part will be dragged down as well into the abyss by the feelings of fear, abandonment and despair of the traumatised part.

The traumatised part, on the other hand, continues to hope that the mother is not gone forever and will still return. It is disappointed, angry, desperate and full of pain. It neither fully gives up hope of the mother's return, nor openly displays its pain or grief for the irretrievable loss. It has no more contact with its environment and, with its feelings and thoughts cut off from the present moment, turns in circles. This state is a typical symptom of depression.

In order to highlight the aspects of the trauma of loss caused by death, I have again chosen a case study from a degree thesis written by one of my students, Christian Probst (Probst, 2004). In his thesis he was talking with the parents of a child who died in an accident 20 years previously. I have abridged and edited the case study.

Death of one's own child

Bernd T died at the age of 18 after suffering a broken neck in a self-caused car accident. He had been given the car by his parents only a few hours before. Mr and Mrs T described their feelings on being informed of his death. Mrs T: "It felt as if someone was trying to rip my heart out of my body. My whole body was burning from the inside out. All I actually remember today is that at the time I was totally at a loss. I was completely beside myself; to an extent it felt as if I was witnessing the whole event, not as someone involved, but as an outsider."

Mr T: "Because the police officer was matter-of-fact and direct, I adopted exactly the same reaction. I also remained matter-of-fact. I only wanted to know when, how and where it had happened. Straight afterwards I gave our two other children the news in a similar manner as the police had done to us. It really affected my daughter, even today; I still don't think she's fully got over it."

The trauma situation for the parents consists of the realisation of a permanent loss, the death of their own son. When death is blatantly clear, one's powerlessness to do anything about the loss is very real. The greatest shock caused by a trauma of loss is when the loss is not announced gradually, as it would be in the case of a chronic illness, but occurs suddenly and unexpectedly.

Mrs T's reaction is a typical trauma of loss experience. A deep pain coming from her heart suddenly overwhelms her. The heart is perceived as the human body's centre of love, affection and warmth. It is a picture that basically says everything: in trauma of loss the person one loves is ripped out of the heart. This must be followed by a dissociation from this reality, so that the pain does not lead to a total collapse. It is in this moment that the split in Mrs T begins to occur between the trauma and the survival part of her soul. During this process she feels like someone observing herself from the outside.

Mr T, on the other hand, remains apparently emotionally unaffected while hearing the news of the death from the police. There is an immediate shutting down of his emotions. He remains in control by asking questions and passing on the news to his other children, thus avoiding an outwardly visibly traumatic breakdown.

These two different ways of dealing with a trauma of loss are also found in the reactions of the dead child's siblings.

Mrs T: "Our then 22-year-old daughter was always a delicate soul. Ever since the night of the accident she became significantly more sensitive and empathetic. Unlike her brother, she's far more open about her feelings, and she's not ashamed to show them. That's why she was so appalled that my husband was so cool and announced the news of his death so unemotionally. Ever since he was young, our son Manfred was very close to his brother Bernd. Even today he still refuses any attempt to discuss the subject. If anyone starts talking about it, he leaves the room or disappears one way or another. There was and still is no way of getting close to him on this matter."

The different reactions to the trauma of loss and how it is dealt with also appear to be gender-specific. While women show their feelings more quickly and easily, men often try to block out their feelings and avoid any emotionally induced loss of control. The reasons for this presumably lie in the different basic mental and physical constitutions of the two sexes as well as the different role expectations of men and women in a society. On a cultural level it is expected of men to be tall, strong, independent and ready to act in crisis situations, and they therefore perceive feelings like fear, pain and grief as admissions of weakness, as unmanly and effeminate. Experiencing the death of his son as an emotional reality is therefore a problem for Mr T. In the interview he said:

"The biggest joke was the behaviour of the cemetery employee. It was not wanted that I be allowed to see my boy one more time before the burial. I only asked him to take the lid off briefly one more time before the funeral ceremony began. He told me there were rules and he was supposed to respect them. Then I threatened I would wait 10 minutes outside the funeral chapel, and if no one opened the door for me, I would break it in. At the time I was in no way concerned about the rules and regulations. You can be sure I would have kicked in the door, whatever the cost. When you're desperate, you do many things you maybe wouldn't understand in a normal situation. At the time, the only thing I wanted was to make sure my boy was really inside the coffin, that there had been no mistake or mix-up, and that we weren't being handed an empty coffin, something we'd heard of happening at that time. I'd probably have dug my son up another 50 times had I not been able to see him just one more time."

So long as Mr T's feelings of pain are blocked out and he consciously pushes them away and tries to keep them under control, he is able to remain at least superficially in control, even though as a result he does not reach a state of accepting his loss emotionally. His survival part covers for his de facto helplessness by means of an exaggerated outward behaviour and anger towards others. As becomes clear in a later passage of the interview, in arguments with his wife, he always returns to his son's grave. He says:

"I simply didn't want to waste time on the trivial matters that take up a large part of your daily routine. For me this daily routine no longer existed."

While this enables him to avoid being overwhelmed with feelings of pain and grief, it leaves him stranded with the traumatised part of his soul in a state that leads neither to a coming to terms with the past nor a new perspective on the future. He steps out of the present, without knowing how to deal with the past. His son's grave remains his external fixed point; internally stagnation rules.

The split in Mrs T's soul becomes clearly visible through the following statement:

"It struck me how, pretty soon after the death of our son, I was scarcely still able to keep track of things over longer periods of time. It began with my missing appointments, buying things we still had enough of at home, or failing to buy other items. At first it wasn't much of problem, but after a while I started wondering whether I would ever regain what was originally a good memory."

Lapses of concentration and loss of memory are just a few of the many symptoms that occur after a trauma of loss experience. In my opinion, these can be explained by the fact that from time to time the traumatised part of the soul gains the upper hand over the survival part. The present is of absolutely no importance to it, for it lives in the past. It is preoccupied with something quite different: the loss of the dead person.

Further frequently encountered symptoms stemming from the survival self include: feelings of futility, bleakness, irregular sleep and poor appetite. Suicidal tendencies can also be present if the trauma self seeks reunion with the lost person in death, as a way of not accepting the loss. Altogether these are all symptoms that correspond to a case of depression.

Following a trauma of loss experience, the survival part becomes preoccupied with various issues to which it seeks an answer:

- The question of guilt – to which Mrs T says: "I've always heavily reproached myself for giving Bernd the keys to the car. If I hadn't done that, he wouldn't have been able to drive the car."
- The question of the meaning of life – Mrs T: "I'm still firmly convinced that Bernd's time was simply up. He was only meant to live a short life. That's presumably why he lived life so fast and intensely, while other people suffer for over 80 years, want to die but can't. There's no explaining fate, so there's nothing you can do but accept it."
- The question as to whether life comes to an end with death or whether there is a life after death – Mrs T: "I don't know how I could ever have accepted his death had I not held the same belief, one I still hold today, that my son, in the place he has gone to before us and where we also hope to go, is doing well."

A trauma of loss for the survival part of the soul is a source of perpetual questions about life, for which it provides various possible answers. Religious answers and beliefs that promise life after death, or the possibility of a reunion with the dead, have a strong appeal in such a situation. They bring consolation and feed the hope of a reunion with the person who died young. The harder the death is to cope with, the greater the need of the survival self to cling to the idea of eternal life.

Abortions

An abortion is also a traumatic event in terms of bonding. The bonding process between mother and child that begins with conception is brought to a sudden end with an abortion. After having an abortion most women feel the pain of losing their child. If the pain is cut off, the women feel empty inside with no drive, have feelings of guilt and no hope for the future. They often display the typical symptoms of depression.

An abortion can also produce affect bridges to existing splits; traumatisations from the past are thus able to re-enter current experience:

The black cloud

A young woman came to me because after having had an abortion she began suffering from panic attacks and feelings of guilt and was close to checking in voluntarily to a psychiatric ward. She had become pregnant after her first sexual contact with her new partner. Both decided immediately on a termination. After the abortion she began showing the expected symptoms of depression. She became tired, weak and felt strong feelings of guilt towards the aborted child. In this mental state her panic attacks were mixed with heavy back pain, which she was unable to explain. She felt as if a black cloud was threatening her from behind and covering her.

Through the therapy it became clearer that her symptoms of depression were directly related to the abortion. But the panic attacks and the back pain turned out to be trauma-related feelings inherited from her bonding with her mother. Her grandmother was five months pregnant with the client's mother when her husband (the grandfather) died. This black cloud therefore came from the time when her grandmother was pregnant with her mother, an emotional symbol for the pain of loss felt by the grandmother over the death of her husband. The woman epitomises the grandmother's fear and feeling of being overwhelmed at the prospect of bringing another child into the world with no husband there to support her. In therapeutic practice, back pain often turns out to be a symptom of dissociated fear, suppressed grief and feeling overburdened.

In Figure 7 I have provided a graphic summary of the basic pattern of a trauma of loss situation. The healthy self is able to function properly in all situations that have nothing to do with death. Nonetheless, the survival self registers everything to do with life and death with its eyes wide open. The healthy self thus finds it hard to rediscover its normal vitality. Vitality is tied up with the fear of losing again that which one loves the most.

Trauma of Loss

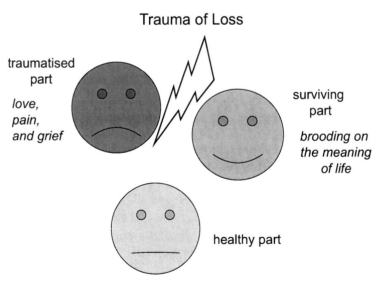

traumatised
part

*love,
pain,
and grief*

surviving
part

*brooding on
the meaning
of life*

healthy part

Figure 7: Splitting in a trauma of loss situation

5.3 Bonding Trauma

In psychological trauma, the split is both a life-saving process and the cause of the many negative, long term consequences already described here. Psychological bonding on the one hand has a life-supporting function: it ensures that we belong to people and groups of people; on the other hand, it harbours the potential that not only positive things are exchanged between people and passed down from one generation to the next, but destructive things as well, together with all the unsolved psychological conflicts, in particular those resulting from traumatisation.

These two fundamental psychological processes – trauma and bonding – are now able to work together in a particular way. I have chosen the expression 'bonding trauma' to describe this. Bonding trauma means that a child's basic need for emotional bonding with her parents becomes traumatised. The child feels overwhelmed and powerless to bond with her mother or father; she is unable to influence the bonding process herself, and is unable within the frame of reference of the family to feel a sense of belonging without it being accompanied by fear. When a child's basic need for bonding becomes traumatised, this has profound consequences for her entire personality development.

The basic need for bonding with the mother

The phenomenon of a child's need for bonding was not discussed for a long time in the field of psychology. This omission was first redressed through the work of John Bowlby (1907-1990) and his research team. Bowlby presented his findings systematically in his trilogy of studies *Attachment*, *Separation* and *Loss*. (Bowlby, 2006) These were a revelation for me, and I now see that events pertaining to the mother-child bond are the foundation of all later psychological and soul development. In my opinion, therefore, it is possible to gain a good understanding of mental health on a theoretical level, and to treat mental illness well in practice, all from the perspective of the mother-child bond.

From the beginning of its life, a child has a symbiotic link to his mother. Even while still in the womb, a child senses his mother's moods and emotional states, and bonds with them, for it is these that constitute his environment. He bonds with both the positive and negative emotional states of the mother. How could a child, during this early stage of life, be able to distinguish between what is good and what is bad regarding his further individual development? Bonding is necessary for the child and so always happens. To paraphrase Paul Watzlawick's axiom that "One cannot *not* communicate" (Watzlawick, Beavin und Jackson, 1972), we can say that "a child cannot *not* bond".

Coming after some nine months of intense togetherness in the womb, and the prenatal imprinting with the mother, the birth process represents a further important developmental and highly sensitive phase of the bonding process, especially for the mother. Mother and child are now physically separated from each other. As the child is completely dependent and unable to protect and feed himself, he is entirely dependent on the mother. It is therefore of primary importance to his survival that he is accepted and loved by his mother and that the inner connection between mother and child remains intact after birth. The mother must see it as her task to provide her child with strength, to take full responsibility for the child's further development and to be ready to accept the personal hardships that this entails. She can only do this properly if she holds positive feelings towards the child; if she loves her child with her whole heart.

Oxytocin

In its own way, nature ensures that the biological link created between a child and his mother before birth is continued through a psychological process: that of emotional bonding and bonding behaviour. The process of birth stimulates hormones in the mother that strongly increase her readiness to accept the child emotionally. Among other things, oxytocin is released into the mother's body in reaction to the stretching of the opening to the uterus. Oxytocin is essentially what we can call the bonding hormone. During the final, particularly painful stage of birth, large quantities of endorphins are also released into the mother's body. Endorphins act as opiates to relieve pain, reducing fear and making the act of birth easier for the mother.

Regrettably, the process of giving birth in modern societies has increasingly become the subject of more practical and rational considerations and so reflects a split between heart and mind. It seems sensible to spare the person giving birth the pain associated with the delivery process as much as possible; any threat to the child must be avoided at all costs. Caesarean sections, a method in fact only meant for emergency cases, are now used as a precautionary measure in up to a third of all births. In terms of bonding, the medical reasons for intervention act as an obstacle to the psychological need to initiate as intense an emotional bond as possible between mother and child throughout the birth process. Cutting out the birth pain with anaesthetics and medication also numbs the nerve tracts required in the intense feelings of love and happiness. Happiness and pain are two sides of the same coin. It is only in her head that a mother does not love her child; in her body she will. Providing the mother with pre-natal support has been shown to help make the birth process an intensely rewarding experience for both mother and child (Kennell, 2007).

Immediately after giving birth, the mother's extremely high endorphin levels represent the physical prerequisite for a feeling of elation when she holds her newborn baby in her arms, thereby fostering her love for the child. An extra dose of oxytocin flows through the mother's body the first time the child suckles on her nipple. For both mother and child, this moment can be one of the utmost bliss. The child does not yet need his mother's milk for this. The feeling of physical intimacy and eye contact with the mother is enough. The impressive series of images in a book by Marshall and Phyllis Klaus (2003) shows how a child, as soon as it is born and with its own strength, never fails to find its way up from tummy to nipple. The photographs make it clear how intensely the child seeks eye contact with the mother. It wants to see its mother and to be seen by her.

Mirror neurons

Even at this early stage of life, eye contact is already responsible for an intense exchange of feelings. It is likely that a large part of what can be called 'mirroring', i.e. an intense recording of the movements, sensations and feelings of another human being (Bauer, 2005), occurs through the eyes. In terms of mirror neurons, we might therefore say that immediately after birth both mother and child begin mirroring each other intensively. They create emotional representations of each other within their respective souls. Eye contact remains a lifelong gauge of the quality of the bonding between them. The eyes are indeed the windows to the soul.

The symbiotic component of the soul

The structure of the soul, which is formed from birth onwards through bonding processes, is so fundamental and such a great influence on the child's later development, that it seems only sensible to me to speak here of a "symbiotic component of the soul" that every human being possesses. This component of the soul is created together with the growing human organism and remains active until the end of life.

From experience I would say that we deal with these symbiotic parts of the soul in every psychotherapy session. This is particularly true when the person's original symbiotic needs were not fulfilled satisfactorily and as a consequence his or her bonding-oriented psychological structures are insufficiently able to organise and stabilise themselves. People with defective psychological bonding structures find it hard to interact with others, and are often at the same time unable to keep their distance.

A mother's ability to bond

A healthy child is fundamentally in need of bonding, and willing and able to bond. This, however, is not something we can always assume of mothers. The very act of reproduction and conception of a child can be experienced by the mother either as the most beautiful experience of her life or, at the other extreme, as rape, debasement, and humiliation.

One woman wrote this to me: "I have a very dear husband and daughter, a truly loveable and harmonious family, and also no financial problems to speak of. Only personally I don't have any inner peace. Though I'm always searching for it, I just can't seem to find my peace. I find it very hard getting to sleep, and sleeping through the night when I do get to sleep. And then I realised I've been having these fears and insomnia since childhood. I'm the fifth child. My next youngest sister is eight years older than me. My mother always used to tell me she didn't want to have me and that my father is to blame that I'm here. He apparently forced himself on her while drunk. My mother never protected me. Whenever there was a row at home, it was 'Because you're still here, we can't change our situation'. My mother never caressed me, and I always had to do what I was told."

How can we expect a woman who has been raped to look forward to having the child in her belly? Understandably also a pregnant woman's anticipated joy at having a child is dampened if, during pregnancy, the father of the child leaves her for another woman.

There are many reasons why a woman's willingness to bond with her child may be absent or only partially present, and over-shadowed by feelings of stress. In this sense, maternal love, i.e. a mother's love for her child, starts with the woman's love for a man, the father of the child. It begins with the acknowledgment of the sexual union of a woman and a man and the possible consequences. On the other hand, the creation of a new life itself does not depend on the love between a man and woman. The sexual act can exist without the presence of love – indeed it happens millions of times every day. Sexuality and love are able to exist entirely independently in the human soul.

A bonding trauma situation therefore arises if the mother is incapable of creating an emotional bond with her bonding-needy child. This is primarily the case where the mother herself is traumatised and has a split in her soul. This leaves her unable to react to her child through her healthy self, because any intense feelings generated through contact with the child will immediately send her into the state occupied by her survival self, which aims to suppress and ward off all such feelings. In the right circumstances, she is still able to feed, wash, change and dress the child. However, all intense physical contact brings with it the risk of retraumatisation. Breastfeeding is no longer pleasurable and in fact becomes more of a torture, with the mother either refusing to do it or switching to bottle-feeding as soon as possible. The mother is incapable of allowing any warm, stress-free physical contact to take place between herself and the child. When she touches her child, it can feel to her as if she is holding a doll in her arms, because her survival self has sprung into action.

All contact initiated by the survival self tends to be mechanical. Since an intensive emotional exchange can also take place through the eyes, a traumatised mother will avoid eye contact with her child. It is now known that mirror neurons, which provide the neuronal basis for empathic responses to other people, no longer function properly under stress conditions. A traumatised mother suffers substantial difficulties when trying to mirror correctly her child in herself. This also means she is incapable of correctly interpreting her child's needs (Brisch, 1999). The mother's survival self ignores, fails to appreciate or misinterprets her child's emotional needs. Instead it focuses more on its own needs and moods rather than those of the child. To the survival self of a traumatised mother, the child represents a permanent threat, which it needs to keep under control.

The newborn child then perceives his mother – traumatised and functioning in survival mode only – as a mechanically-operated body and doesn't feel her warmth and love. He is held tight, but feels no stability. The tone of his mother's voice is not soft and warm, but cold and impersonal. The child senses that his mother is avoiding all emotional advances. The more the child seeks emotional intimacy, the greater the inner distance and the thicker the protective wall the mother erects between herself and the child.

The child therefore receives no feeling of safety from his mother. He finds no emotional refuge in her. He always fears being abandoned. If he protests more vocally, by crying and screaming, in order finally to win the attention of his mother, this only leads to further rejection by the mother's survival self, which feels itself under too much pressure and incapable of an adequate response. The mother may, for example, give the child food even though what he really needs is warmth and safe physical contact. Consequently, the child becomes increasingly distressed at his fruitless efforts to enjoy the emotional support of his mother.

The more the child cries and makes demands, the more likely it is that the mother's trauma part will be triggered. If the mother finally ends up in a retraumatised state, her trauma part will relive through the child its own emotional pain and its own impotence and powerlessness. Depending on the type of traumatisation suffered, the trauma part either

- clings to the child, in order to find some comfort for its own desolation,
- flees from the child, or
- becomes aggressive towards the child, whom it sees as the original culprit, and therefore, through confrontation with the child, tries to fight against the impotence it experienced itself as a child. In such cases the child is in great danger of being beaten, mistreated and seriously injured by his own mother.
- In some cases, mothers in a retraumatised state may

suffocate or even kill their own children. What they themselves suffered as children in terms of rejection, neglect and violence they do also to their own children. The victim becomes the perpetrator.

In all these cases, the child is deluged by the mother's various trauma feelings in the form of panic attacks, aggression and rage, despair, or confused sexual feelings and shame, depending on the particular type of trauma suffered. He is made to fear for his life by the actions of the mother's traumatised self; he is almost suffocated by her symbiotic embrace, his trust is shaken to the core by her feelings of hate or he suffers a profound sense of worthlessness as a result of her shame.

What does this bonding trauma situation do to the structure of the child's soul? What are the consequences of his traumatic bonding experiences with his mother? How does this affect the bonding with the father? Generally speaking, bonding trauma mostly gives rise to a complex structure of splits in the human soul.

Splits in the child's soul related to the mother

The first level of the split consists of the child's decision, despite the neglect, and often even rejection, of the mother, to go on living and face up to the existential threat posed by not being wanted by his own mother. From the outset, the child is aware of the fear of being left alone and abandoned. The original splitting of the soul is a result of the fact that he still somehow needs to conserve and protect his will to survive and the core of his vitality. One patient described his childhood feelings as follows: "It was a matter of great need. Nobody heard me, nobody understood me correctly, and I nearly died as a result. I feared for my life. It was if I had an apple stuck in my throat, I made a wheezing sound, and everyone only looked on and did nothing or didn't even look at all." In retrospect, the patient experienced his refusal to give up and die while in such a situation as a conscious decision: "The motivation to die was there and it was strong, for it was precisely this fear, which I'd being feeling so strongly recently, connected with the feeling of being isolated and abandoned in a state of great distress, or being consciously ignored or treated as unimportant, immaterial, annoying: a burden. There was something that happened really early on, and it was so bad I again decided to go; that is, to die. It feels like an entirely conscious decision, although I was actually far too young for that. It was as if I had thought, I can't stay there, I can't survive that. This surely explains more my basic fear, my feeling of not being understood everywhere I am, of being incapable of trust and having to get through it on my own." This part of the child's soul perceives others as being fundamentally untrustworthy and threatening. It is desperately stuck in his fear: "That's why I just lie in bed and sleep and hope I wake up sometime and it will all be over; but it doesn't work, and the fear is always there, day in, day out. I'm running through the world all alone simply trying to survive each individual day. And every morning when I wake up there's the hope that the nightmare is over. But the fear only gets worse."

Consequently, from the beginning of his life, the child is forced to devise a survival plan to be used against this fear. First and foremost he achieves this through the feeling of unconditional love every child shows towards its own mother, whatever she does to it. The child's love for his mother is always there and is in fact indestructible. Love is the willingness to see another human being in an overall positive light, to see the good things in someone, rather than the bad. Love is the approach that expects positive things from another person. Love is idealistic, in the sense that the reality of the negative, 'evil' sides of other people are overlooked or concealed. Through love, the possibility of the other person showing more of his or her good rather than negative side in the relationship is increased. If I smile at someone, it is very likely he will smile back. This is why nature makes little babies look as lovable as possible appearing 'sweet', 'cuddly' and 'cute', and why, when they see them, adults tend to 'melt'. Children are born with a repertoire of expressions and behaviours designed to steal the hearts of adults and, in particular, their parents. They smile, look at you with those big wondering eyes, nestle up against you, smell nice and are emotionally sensitive, etc.

So, if her mother does not accept a child in a bonding trauma situation, the child doesn't cease his solicitations of his mother's love, but instead redoubles his efforts. The less love the mother shows towards the child, the more he strives to elicit that love. With the increasing duration of these frustrating experiences, the idealistic view of the 'loving mother' becomes an illusory position. While the withdrawn part of the child's soul is forced to experience extreme anxieties as a result of the severe lack of love coming from his mother, the survival part takes refuge in the illusion of an all-encompassing, all-powerful and everlasting maternal love. The experience of absolute good in the child's soul competes with that of absolute evil as part of a survival strategy. The child tries to create and maintain the ideal of the good, loving mother. He remembers every occasion that the mother behaved in a loving manner and exaggerates them. "My mother was a very good cook," one patient told me. On closer questioning, however, it turns out that the mother only ever cooked for him on three occasions.

Part of the role of the loving side of the survival part in the child's soul is to make himself useful to the mother. In his willingness to love his mother, the child also senses his mother's worries and suffering and tries his best to help. In doing so, however, he allows the mother to offload all her anxieties, anger, despair and physical pain onto the child. This is in fact precisely what makes the child feel valuable, for now the mother needs the child insofar as he is able to make her feel a little better. In this way, the child's survival self is able to combat his fear that his mother may no longer need him, is going to abandon him or disappear forever. The child lives under the illusion that if he places himself fully at the disposal of his mother, this will help her and she will then be able to love the child and she will not leave. Some children are able to sense that their mothers are suicidal and they use all their love to try to ensure they don't die. Because a child loves his mother, his willingness in this process, despite being overburdened, is almost limitless. He places all his energies at the service of the mother. He sees no alternative – in the wild he would have virtually no alternative. One of my patients said the following about this: "I lay in my little bed at night and listened to how my mother was feeling. I wanted to send her all my energy, to keep her there. I would think: I have so much." Precisely because he senses how weak his mother is, the child's loving survival self tries, with all his strength and self-sacrifice, to rescue the mother from her devastation and despair and keep her alive.

Besides fear and love, there are other basic emotions present during every bonding event, namely: anger, pain and grief. Anger normally occurs when the child's fear of abandonment becomes overwhelming. Through his protests, the child attempts to win his mother back again. This explains a child's natural recourse to crying and screaming. In a bonding trauma situation, however, children quickly realise that their anger and protest is achieving very little – on the contrary, their anger only provokes more rejection and often, even violence from the mother. As a result, they are unable to integrate their anger as a healthy capacity of their souls. As with other bonding emotions, the anger takes on a life of its own. It builds up but fails to dissipate afterwards because the mother fails to respond to it and reduce the anxiety it caused. In extreme cases, it can even escalate to hate and fantasies of murder towards the mother. As this cannot be expressed openly, however, this potential anger among children with bonding trauma is often offloaded onto other people, e.g. siblings or a toy or other objects. Hyperactivity is a syndrome that matches this kind of childhood behavioural disorder.

Also split off within the soul of a child suffering from bonding trauma are his feelings of pain and grief. Such children often express their pain, which they are unable to process emotionally, through physical sickness: e.g. neuro-dermatitis, asthma, colds, sore throats, ear infections, etc. It is also very confusing for the child if the mother, immediately after a display of anger and rejection, suddenly becomes extremely friendly towards a stranger, leaving this person with the impression that the mother is like this with everyone.

Children suffering from bonding trauma are also equally overwhelmed by distress and grief. They are unable to show this to their mother because it will either make her angry or she herself will become depressed. Left completely to their own devices, they split off their feelings of grief, cry secretly in bed at night and at times have depressive moods.

The childhood survival self, which maintains the symbiotic bonding to the mother despite all the negative experiences, focuses, from a position of dependence, its entire attention on the question of how to influence and mollify the fundamentally uncontrollable mother. Not only is this split-off grief open to emotional blackmail if the mother threatens the child with rejection, abandonment or violence, he is also immediately seduced if the mother tells him how much she loves him and how grateful he should be to have his mother there with him. Consequently, the child must do everything she asks, and love her dearly. In extreme cases, this can include the mother having the child sleep in the same bed with her when she so desires and sexually abusing him or her. Sexually abused mothers not infrequently repeat the abuse they themselves suffered with their own child. This also distorts the child's sense of shame, for the mother tells the child that what she's doing is perfectly normal. This can go so far that the child is apportioned all the blame for what is being done to him. "You are bad, so now mummy must do this with you!" a child might be told. This also unsettles and confuses the notions of responsibility and guilt. The child feels guilty for what others do to him and consequently also fails to learn what it means to take responsibility for what he might do to others.

If the mother is distressed and unhappy, the symbiotic part of the child will continue to feel guilty and responsible. However, he fails to understand that he is not being noticed at all by the mother's suffering parts. The mother sees in the child either her own mother, from whom she would like to receive love and recognition, or her father, of whom she is afraid. The child cannot comprehend these transference processes and continues to take things personally in his traumatic entanglement with his mother.

As he or she grows older this symbiotic childhood survival self will consist of an accumulation of strategies for adapting to the mother's moods, her suffering and, ultimately, the various facets of her split soul. Naturally, this does not lead to the development of an autonomous self in the child, able to address her own needs and interests. The child's adapted self is unable to differentiate between what she wants and feels, and what she is expected to do, think and feel. The demands the mother makes of her become her own needs. For this part of the child's soul, what is asked of her – how to behave so her mother "can love her", "need have no trouble with her", "need not blame her", "need not punish her" – represent the entire substance of her existence. Since her mother is not able to establish a healthy boundary between herself and the child, the child's internal and external boundaries are also blurred. If the mother switches into her trauma state, the symbiotic component of the child also adopts these maternal trauma feelings in her own soul, as if they were her own. The symbiotic survival component of the child thus largely consists of, on the one hand, limitless love seeking, and, on the other hand, excessively hostile, aggressive or violent "introjects" of her mother. These become part of her own psychological structure – her false self. A part in the child rejects, devalues and punishes herself.

Given her dependence and desire to be accepted and belong to the family as a child, she is unable to separate herself internally from the criticism, reproaches and violence of her parents, siblings or other relatives. She absorbs everything. Consequently, those people who harm her paradoxically also become part of her. This explains why the insults, disparagement and absurd accusations remain in the child's soul when the people behind her are no longer actually present.

Given her need to be recognised and loved by precisely those people that hurt her the most, a dependent child finds no means of resistance within her soul with which to separate herself from her torturers.

To conclude, a child suffering from bonding trauma is unable to develop the basic emotions of bonding – fear, anger, grief, love, guilt and shame – in a healthy manner and allow him or her to grow within himself or herself to form an emotional whole. The child's basic feelings remain in an underdeveloped raw state. To ensure survival, he must split off all his bonding emotions into isolated psychological structures. His fear, love, anger, pain, grief, shame and guilt all lead individual lives within him and, as he grows older, become more extreme and unrealistic rather than adaptable and flexible. This primary stage of the split in a child who is suffering from bonding trauma in relation to his mother is summarised in Figure 8. As the diagram shows, the child's adapted survival

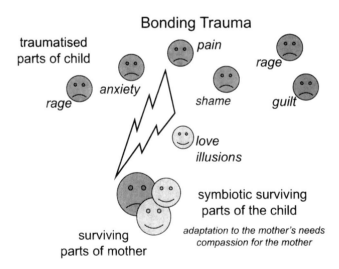

Figure 8: The split in a child in relation to the mother in a bonding trauma situation

self, which maintains the symbiosis with the mother in all circumstances so as to ensure his survival, is not separated from the split components of the mother.

Splits in relation to the father

Since the traumatised child finds no stability from her mother, she is significantly more open to other offers of bonding elsewhere. She is in a sense easily seduced. If a father is available, the child focuses her bonding endeavours with increased vigour on him. As traumatised mothers mostly seek partners who are also traumatised and deeply split themselves, as a rule the child is in great danger of becoming entangled in the father's splits. Her symbiotically needy survival self is now additionally saddled with her father's unresolved trauma parts (for more on this, see the example "Grit your teeth" in Chapter 6).

Experience shows that it is highly likely that the child's search for physical contact and warmth – emotional intimacy – will be sexualised by the father and the child will be forced to suffer sexual approaches from him. Such instances give rise to a further level of psychological splitting in the child. As with the mother, a part of the child also idealises the father. The more she empathises and mirrors the father's soul, the clearer she senses his helpless traumatised part and notices that the father is not happy. She sympathises with him and wants to help. If the father exploits the child's offer of sympathy and becomes sexually intrusive, the child is again forced to undergo an internal split. One part of the child continues to idealise the 'nice daddy' and sympathise with him; the other must suffer the pain, the feelings of disgust, shame and contamination related to the father's sexual attacks. The part that idealises the father to a certain extent behaves as if insane. It acts as if the contact with the father were merely a game, laughing, for example, in an exaggerated manner, exposing her body, showing her genitals, using verbal sexual expressions – in short, behaving shamelessly, because her own sense of shame has been violated by the father and she is no longer able

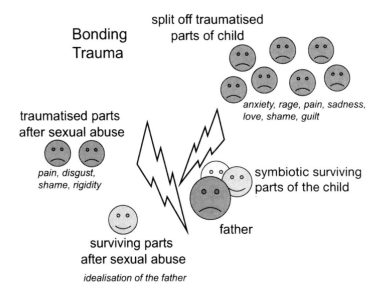

Figure 9: The splitting in a child in a bonding trauma situation after sexual abuse by the father.

to differentiate herself from him. Stomach pains and sexual desire, fear and joviality, impotent rage and cuteness, the feeling of being a princess and of being worthless alternate within the child, depending which part is in ascendance at the time.

Figure 9 depicts these different levels of splitting. The part traumatised by sexual abuse remains stuck in the confusing feelings evoked by the abuse. The survival component that has split off from this has no memory at all of the abuse. When asked, it always answers that it knows nothing about it and could never imagine the father having done such a thing.

Like a god

During a constellation facilitated by someone else when I was in the role of a representative, I had an extremely interesting experience as to how an incestuous father-daughter relationship can come about. I was placed in the constellation as the father of a client. I felt physically very ill, and from time to time I would lose all the energy in my legs; I really felt I was about to collapse. It felt as if I had a kind of iron ring around by chest that was squeezing me but also giving me some stability. When the representative for the daughter suddenly started approaching me with her back towards me, what I really wanted to do was to turn my back on her so she wouldn't come into contact with me and my suffering. I told her I was feeling a strong pressure around my chest. To this the representative of the part of the daughter answered: "Yes, strong, that's what I'm looking for: something strong; powerful!" At first I was puzzled at her response, which didn't seem to make sense, but then I suddenly started to enjoy the idea that this child admired me and was clearly looking to me for stability. I slowly began to feel strong inside. And the more this child fed me the illusion that I was strong, the more powerful I felt in the role.

As the constellation continued I gradually began to think that everything around me was mine and that I should follow my own will. The more I believed in these fantasies, the more the representative for the daughter admired me. In the end she was fully worshipping of me as the father. I could say anything I wanted and she would only give me applause and admiration. Increasingly I began to believe she would do anything I asked of her. Eroticism, esotericism, sexuality, trance, and drugs – it all mixed together in me to create an intoxicating state that got more and more intense and no longer knew any limits. In the constellation I, as the representative for the father, and the representative for the daughter, moved our bodies back and forth rhythmically and in time. I understood that there was nobody in the world that could stop us indulging in these fantasies.

After this constellation it was clear to me how the adult seducer and the seduced child both needed each other, were helping each other escape from their psychological pain, and together were moving further and further into a delusional state. Without the child, the father in his miserable state would sooner or later have succumbed to severe psychological difficulties. The admiration and worship of the child seduced him into embracing delusions of omnipotence. The part of the child that needed to bond with someone having found no stability in the depressed mother, surrendered to the father, clearly seeing a form of support in the fantasised strength of him.

The constellation also contained the traumatised part of the child. This part lay on the floor feeling wretched, dirty and unclean. This was the part that experienced the sexual abuse and also felt that what the father was doing with her was not right. This part recognised the unfolding madness between the father and the other, symbiotically dependent part, but felt completely powerless to do anything about it or to rescue this part from its deluded world. This part also held no hope of anyone being able to help it.

If the traumatised child has no natural father available to him, he can also direct his need for male love and stability towards older brothers, grandfathers, stepfathers, uncles, neighbours, etc. Abusers have a particularly good sense for children who are weak and in need of love, and are therefore easily seducible.

Young boys, whose mothers are incapable of bonding, are also open to seduction by their fathers or other men. They then also develop a similar split. One part sympathises with the abuser, the other feels afraid and disgusted by him. The sexual abuse of young boys is seen socially as an even greater taboo than the abuse of young girls, and is now being discussed more in public. The sexual abuse of sons and daughters by their mothers, however, is still largely kept silent. (Homes, 2004).

Saints and whores

The issue of abuse becomes particularly confusing when the child – and here I refer predominantly to the cases of girls – also feels pleasure in the abuse. The child feels complicitous and perverted, and her conscious and healthy parts feel ashamed. In order to avoid these confusing feelings, she disso- ciates during sexual contact later in life, leaving her body, always running away from intimate relationships or doing crazy things in her relationships with men and in her sexuality. In these dissociated states, she is incapable of taking herself or other people seriously. She indulges in illusions, dreaming of a fairytale prince who promises undying love and comes to her rescue. She is magically attracted to similarly confused, foundering and struggling men, and rushes into outlandish and extremely sexualised relationships with them. She continues to re-enact the abuse experienced in childhood as an adult woman.

If a girl is abused by her father, it leaves its mark on her later experiences of sexual pleasure. How should a girl, who is gradually becoming a woman, deal with her sexual desire? The following relationship patterns frequently occur: as an adult she tries to re-enact the original situation with her father. What was forbidden, reprehensible and shameful in the father-daughter relationship now seems more fitting as an adult. So she therefore seeks men with similar characteristics to her father (age, appearance, smell etc.). When a man appears who fits with this father pattern, her sexual desire is awakened in one part of her and she is seemingly able to enjoy life. The man senses nothing of the original scenario into which he is being drawn. But when reality comes back into play, and the other parts of the woman realise that something is not right and that this man is not, in fact, the right partner for her (e.g. he is already married or is an alcoholic like her father), the illusory bubble bursts and the newly roused desire for the father remains unsatisfied. The pendulum now shoots back in the other direction, and it seems totally impossible for her to satisfy her 'true' desire. Sexual abstinence or frustration in relationship with a 'normal' man, who cannot arouse this desire in her, appears to be the only possible alternative to the delusional love dance with her father. It may then occur that an adult woman who was abused by her father as a young girl will oscillate back and forth between the extremes of the promiscuous sinner and the abstinent saint.

Pure violence

Sons can be placed in extreme situations by violent fathers. If they witness their father's violent behaviour towards their mother, for example, their only form of defence is to undergo a split so that they can forget the experience. One of my clients suddenly discovered one such split-off, traumatised part of his soul while at work:

> "When this part of me is active, I become a complete scatter-brain. I can't remember where I parked my car; I can't commit names to memory or recall names I already know. I forget appointments, have no overview of things and as a result I feel totally overwhelmed. I can clearly see this part of me in my current work. I can't remember the names of people I work with, not even my colleagues, even though I once knew them all. And although I consider myself to be intelligent, it now feels limited. I'm slow on the uptake when it comes to meaningful connections, consequences and logical ways of proceeding. I'm completely wrapped in cotton wool and can get so angry because I know I should be capable of these things. I'm not living in the real world at all and see everything through a kind of frosted glass. So I'm also prone to completely twisted ideas, because I don't understand, don't see it. So you can tell me anything and do anything with me."

Ambitious survival parts

Some sons who were unable to establish a bond with either their traumatised mother or father, develop an extremely ambitious survival part. The aim of this part is to prove to the father that his son deserves his recognition and attention by dint of that fact that he has won the admiration of many other people. Using professional achievements he tries to impress his unreachable father and show him that he really is someone. Daughters may also develop this ambitious part, in order to prove to their mothers that they deserve their love. However, none of these efforts ever prove successful; however much they achieve during their lives, it is never sufficient for them to establish a warm and loving relationship with their traumatised mothers or fathers.

Perpetrator-victim splits

So a bonding trauma is connected with neglect, excessive demands, violence, and often also sexual abuse. The child is clearly the victim of this situation, of his traumatised parents. As the innocent victim, he must also try and stop his parents' negative energy from gaining access to his soul. He partially identifies with this negative energy in the hope that this will help him protect himself better, but it develops his own feelings of anger and hate towards the perpetrators, his parents. He is then filled with an abundance of perpetrator energy himself. But what should he do with this perpetrator energy? The child uses it either in the form of aggression towards people weaker than himself or turns it against himself in self-destructive actions.

By resorting to aggression and destruction, he loses the ability to distinguish between right and wrong. He no longer knows the difference between good and evil and completely loses his orientation in his muddling up of good and bad feelings. In the end he becomes indifferent to everything. This emotional chaos is the breeding ground for suicidal thoughts and acts.

A perpetrator-victim split may give rise both to sadistic (as the perpetrator, taking pleasure in inflicting pain on others) and masochistic behaviour (as the victim, taking pleasure in inflicting pain on him or herself), depending on which internal component happens to force its way into the foreground at the time. The following example, in which the perpetrator-victim split is already visible in a very small child, serves to illustrate these confusing incidents in the soul of someone suffering from bonding trauma.

Sexual intercourse with dolls

Two-and-a-half year old Samira was taken into care by the youth welfare office after a teacher at her nursery school spotted signs of choking on the little girl's neck. A bite mark was also discovered in the girl's genital area. The following came from a social worker's report:

"In the beginning Samira gave strong indications of problems while she was with the foster family. The foster mother reported how in various situations and different places Samira would approach unknown people and raise her hands to be lifted up. In the first few days after her being put with the foster family, Samira continually pointed to her lower abdomen saying, 'Ouch mama.' Furthermore, she would hold her hands to her throat, as if wanting to strangle herself. She often displayed signs of anxiety. As soon as the foster father tried to hold her, she began crying, screaming and hitting out at him. When in the presence of the foster family's son, Samira would no longer react and did not respond when spoken to.

"In the nursery Samira would grab the other children between their legs, and would continually undress herself in front of them, or lay herself on top of them. She also grabbed her foster parents in the crotch and acted out sexual intercourse with her dolls. In addition, she would stretch the legs of her dolls so far apart that they broke. During the first visit from her biological mother, Samira looked very tense, sat upright and stiff in her lap, saying nothing."

Samira displays the same attachment behaviour of sexually traumatised children who outsiders erroneously see as being 'sweet' or 'overly friendly'. Here the symbiotic survival part of the bonding traumatised child is in action: the behaviour attracts the attention of the mother ('Ouch mama') to the cause of its suffering (pointing towards its abdomen), i.e. the sexual abuse. In contact with the foster father and the foster parents' son, the child's traumatised part, which is full of anxiety and sometimes rigid, becomes visible. In contact with the other children, a different part of Samira's soul comes to the fore. In grabbing her playmates' genitals, undressing herself and acting out sexual intercourse between her dolls, she is displaying the typical signs of a perpetrator-victim split. She imitates the perpetrator and the sexual acts he performs on her. Her grabbing of her neck, as if she wanted to strangle herself, can be seen as the mirror image of an act the perpetrator did to her.

When, some weeks later, Samira displayed what seemed to be normal behaviour towards her mother, the inspector recommended giving the child back to her mother. In her symbiotic survival part in relation to her mother, Samira had clearly learned to normalise her contact with adults to such an extent that even an inspector could be fooled. While in the care of social services, her traumatised part was temporarily able to remain in the background. But it is still there. When Samira is again placed back in the trauma situation (her family of origin), the violence against this child does not come to an end. The development of a serious personality disorder in Samira is therefore clearly foreseeable. How could she ever develop trust in other people if her mother and all other adults ignore the signals of her sexual traumatisation? In her despair at not being properly noticed by anyone, what else will she have to live through in her life? What will her perpetrator parts do to others later in her life?

For boys who become the victims of sexual abuse there arises the additional difficulty of confusion as to their sexual identity. Boys are extremely ashamed of the abuse they suffer and may no longer feel like real men. By developing a perpetrator part within themselves, they try to prove their masculinity.

Becoming a perpetrator seems more acceptable to them than being a victim, because it corresponds better to male gender stereotypes.

The consequences of divorce

A deepening of the splitting process is observed in children whose parents are going through an acrimonious separation and divorce, in which the custody of the child is at stake. For example, if the mother tries, through an extreme splitting of her soul, to win the child over to her side in her conflict with her husband, by portraying the father as bad and evil to the child, the child will often adapt his or her symbiotic survival part to the mother in an exaggerated manner, lavishing her with declarations of love and imitating her behaviour and arguments (ten Hövel, 2003). In custody cases, therefore, inspectors may receive an entirely spurious impression if they only see this side of the child, a side that feels totally dependent on the mother and therefore idealises her. This causes even more confusion if the inspectors fail to realise the enormous pressure the child is under, and how far the splits in his soul have advanced. Inspection reports in which the dissociative phenomena and splits in adults, as well as children, are not noted and clearly highlighted are essentially worthless. The inspectors will then be misled by the appearance of normality the parents and children generate through their adapted survival parts during the inspections of the care and custody proceedings.

Anger, aggression and ignorance

Children who have suffered bonding trauma do not carry just their own anxiety, anger and despair within them: they are also burdened with the unresolved feelings of anxiety, anger, shame or powerlessness of their traumatised parents. This can make them hyperactive or depressed as young children. They are unable to control the feelings that arise within them since these feelings are only partially their own. They will react inappropriately to the mildest of stress situations, as they constantly feel overwhelmed, being quick to oppose their parents or teachers. At the same time they remain strongly tied to their parents and, through displays of dependence and attachment, try to stay close to the parents, in particular the mother.

When these children reach adolescence and have to become more independent they start to feel increasingly overwhelmed, particularly by the demands of their schools. They are not really able to make the most of their growing freedom and options, and transform their defiance and anger towards their parents, who also feel overwhelmed and powerless, into the notion that they no longer need to follow rules, and can do whatever they want. They abuse their freedom by arbitrarily breaking parental and societal rules.

The destructive strategies and behaviours of bonding-traumatised children are well known to all those involved with them:

- Expressing their anger aimlessly towards other people or objects; when others defend themselves from their aggressive acts, this results in an escalatory spiral of aggression, and the others are always blamed.
- Directing their aggression towards themselves (e.g. pulling out their hair, cutting, scratching or piercing) and increasingly neglecting themselves.
- Indulging in self-destructive behaviour e.g. through drug abuse.
- Seeking distraction through sexual promiscuity.
- Stimulating themselves with aggressive music and lyrics; they are susceptible to political ideas that provide them with hate figures (e.g. 'migrants', 'foreigners', 'capitalists', 'the bourgeoisie') against which they can vent their aggression.
- Hanging around the parental home expecting their parents to fulfil all their needs without taking any responsibility for jobs to be done; they moan and complain, sometimes

have emotional breakdowns involving sobbing and tears alternated with making strong declarations of love towards their mother or father.

If we observe young people who have remained entangled in emotional chaos by having been emotionally overwhelmed by their traumatised parents, we notice how much their chaotic feelings also restrict their thinking. Although these young people are capable of amazing feats that can be indicators of high intelligence (e.g. breaking into and hotwiring cars within seconds), they are unable to use their cognitive potential constructively, abusing it in the pursuit of increasingly radical survival strategies and entering further into conflict with their social environment, which they understandably view as being increasingly hostile the more counter-aggression they provoke through their inconsiderate behaviour. They become violent not only towards their own parents, but also fight with the police and act as if above legal punishments. Even imprisonment cannot change their negative attitude towards the adults who try to stop them from acting out their (self) destructive feelings. The survival self of the bonding traumatised youth makes him gradually immune to the well-intentioned educational influence of parents, teachers, social service workers and even the police and judiciary.

These young people do not recognise the negative consequences of their aggressive behaviour for themselves or others, and their survival self refuses to use common sense in properly understanding the consequences of their actions. They display a lack of seriousness. They fool around, trying to outdo each other with 'cool' and sexist expressions; they are attracted as if by magic to others who, like them, live in emotional chaos. Since their emotional wounds, as well as those of their parents that they carry, run so deep, their survival self searches for an escape in extreme superficiality.

As a consequence, urban and rural sub-cultures of bonding-traumatised youths gradually lead to the creation of adult environments in which violence, drug use and unemotional sexual experiences are seen by all involved as being normal. All standards of decent behaviour between people are gradually lost. Feelings are no longer respected – neither one's own nor those of others. Serious professional goals are given up because they are 'uncool', with the only remaining goal being getting money, something acquired through prostitution, drug dealing, human trafficking, weapons dealing or other ruthless criminal schemes.

This is also why these people are unconcerned when their thinking becomes increasingly cloudy or their brain is slowly destroyed through drug abuse. The result is a gradual mental degradation accompanied by a false sense of pride in their questionable achievements: consuming as many drugs as possible, having as many sexual partners as possible, the ability to fight, and not being affected by the emotional responses of others.

An example of such a subculture of highly emotionally and psychologically disturbed young men (mostly), are groups of hooligans. They come together under the pretext of being football fans, and their main purpose is to drink as much alcohol as possible and find extreme forms of excitement in fighting with other hooligans, people of other nationalities, or the police. The author Bill Buford lived for some years with such young men, and described the craziness of these youngsters pretty well (Buford 2010).

Bonding-traumatised mothers and their children

In order to illustrate more clearly the subject of bonding trauma we will now take a look at another case study from a thesis by one of my students, Simon Holz (Holz, 2005). I have abridged the original text for the purposes of presentation in this book.

The dream man and the problem child

Mrs M came to the advice centre to talk about her problems at home. She has been married to her husband for four years and has a five-year-old daughter called Susanne. The couple have been living together since the birth of their child. The husband has a top position within a large company. Mrs M is a housewife and looks after the daughter. She came to ask for advice, as she was no longer able to cope with her daughter.

Mrs M has been in therapy since the birth of her daughter. Her therapist diagnosed her with 'borderline personality disorder'. She began therapy following a serious marital crisis after the birth of her daughter. In fact she had wanted to have therapy long before her relationship with her husband, but she was so happy with him that she thought her problems had been solved by meeting her 'dream man'.

When only eleven years old, Mrs M had already been admitted to the adolescent psychiatric ward after intentionally drinking washing-up liquid in an attempt to take her life. She spent four weeks there before finally coming home, after which she received no further care or support. She described her life before meeting her husband as chaotic. She would constantly be having affairs and between bust-ups would live alternatively with different men for weeks at a time, all so as she didn't have to return home. She was often out partying, taking cocaine combined with alcohol and amphetamines. She paid for this lifestyle with money earned through part-time prostitution. As a result, she was often picked up by the police and taken home. Her mother would always be waiting for her and would beat her using a poker as a punishment. She had received frequent beatings during her childhood and was often locked in her room for days on end. She thinks other things may also have happened to her, but for the moment she can't remember because any memories have been too deeply suppressed. Her mother was never willing to talk and would either start to cry or beat her whenever she asked about her past.

Mrs M describes herself when she gave birth to her daughter and during the following years as an unthinking, chaotic and stubborn person. She is now afraid she might have treated unfairly or even mistreated her daughter. She admits to having hit her in situations where she didn't know what else to do. From what she knows and understands today, she thinks she may have placed her daughter in the same situations she herself was put in as a child. This is something she finds hard to admit. In recent months she tried to talk about this with her daughter and explain to her why she behaved this way. However, she finds herself unable to get close to Susanne emotionally. Susanne is very uncommunicative, withdrawn, too grown up and diplomatic for her age. She's also very moody. Although she sees her mother as someone she can trust when feeling really down, as soon she's feeling better again she pushes her away and accuses her of abandoning her. These affectionate and depressed phases were followed by bouts of accusation, which Mrs M was unable to cope with. Although Susanne enthusiastically began a course of painting therapy, she refused to continue after the fourth session.

Mrs M blames herself entirely and wonders desperately how she can develop a good relationship with her daughter. For some time now her husband has also been levelling similar accusations at her. He has already threatened to move out together with the daughter if nothing in her relationship with her daughter changes in the near future. Her husband rejects Mrs M's ideas of initiating a joint discussion between them, since he is convinced the problem has nothing to do with him. He doesn't want to sacrifice his time needlessly on such things. Susanne also rejects the idea of a joint discussion with the therapist.

Mrs M's story displays the typical signs of a bonding trauma. Her mother is unable to provide her with warmth and stability. Most likely traumatised herself, she can only survive conflict situations by responding with aggression, striking out blindly and mistreating her child. Her referral to the child and youth psychiatric ward on account of her suicidal behaviour shows how helpless and desperate Mrs M must have felt as a child; she saw death as the only means to escape from her internal turmoil. It is likely that sexual abuse in her childhood also contributed to her experience of rejection and violence at the hands of her mother, but she is unable to recall this at present, as it would be too threatening for her. Her chaotic pre-marriage lifestyle, when she was involved with many different men and worked as a prostitute, is suggestive of sexual abuse.

The use of drugs in the case of a bonding trauma is usually as indiscriminate as it is excessive. The survival part takes whatever it can get to try and prevent the feelings of the unbearable external and internal reality: cocaine, alcohol, medication, heroin – anything as long as it works as quickly as possible. The survival part longs to feel good and seeks the fastest possible means of numbing any bad feelings. In the short term, this is achieved most effectively through the use of hard drugs.

Typical of bonding traumatised children is the constant search for someone to provide them with the stability that they so desperately desire to fill their inner void and neutralise their deep-seated fear of abandonment. Mrs M clearly found someone in her husband who understood how to keep himself separate from her and not be drawn completely into her emotional chaos. He is powerless, however, to do anything about the increasing conflict between his wife and their daughter. He threatens separation but this instils fear and horror in Mrs M's symbiotic part. However, under this pressure, she visits the advice centre.

Her daughter Susanne clearly displays the two sides of her bonding trauma. When she is in her symbiotically needy state, she is affectionate, depressive or full of accusations about being abandoned. When in her survival part, she pretends to be independent, does not want to hear anything about her mother and behaves in a calculated and manipulative way in order to get what she wants. She might suddenly become enthusiastic about something, but then rapidly returns to a state of lethargy and rejection, and refuses contact. Here the child has adopted the split in her mother's soul as the basis of her own personality structure. She is as connected with her mother's over-developed survival part as she is with her helpless traumatised part. As the mother keeps switching back and forth between the two, the child finds herself unable to rely on any stability in her mother and a battle ensues designed to test her mother's reliability. There was no basic trust established between mother and child in the beginning, and there is certainly no way for trust to develop now when the survival parts of the mother and child are engaged in mutual blaming. Where survival parts come into conflict with each other, the result is often war. The more the child demands real feelings from her mother, the more the mother's survival self starts to fear contact with her traumatised part, leading her to resort to counterattacks.

The mother's therapy may to an extent be able to counteract this, so that the splits already present in the daughter are not consolidated and deepened. They have, however, already been deeply enough entrenched in the child's soul as means of adapting to her bonding trauma. One day Susanne will herself need to turn to therapy if she wants to escape these splits, for she also is on the way to developing a personality disorder.

While daughters often spend their whole lives entangled with their traumatised mothers and are scarcely able to get away from them, sons are more inclined to break away from their mothers. However, a part of their souls will still remain bound up with their mother, as the following example makes clear.

I must be stronger!

Thomas' mother had what in psychiatry would be called a hysterical personality disorder. She was overly anxious, suffered sudden mood swings, was high-spirited and charming when meeting people from outside the family, and watched her son at every turn. Thomas tried to get rid of the torture and humiliation of his mother's overly anxious behaviour by devising ever more daring games and tests of courage for himself. Later in life he would continue to seek adventure and conflict. On the other hand, he would immediately consult a doctor over the smallest of things. He was plagued by numerous physical complaints, and he consulted countless specialists. Until he began therapy, his only way of escaping from his mother's overprotective stranglehold was to bolster his survival part, turning himself into a fearless knight and warhorse. His survival self would panic when any symptoms of physical sickness became noticeable, for to him this represented weakness and only increased his fear of being dragged down with his mother. The background to his mother's trauma was that she had a late abortion before he was born, for which she felt guilty her whole life.

Dependence, lack of responsibility and power

If men are dominated by their traumatised anger component, they lose the ability to show consideration to others and will kick the victimised child in their soul aside, so that their survival self becomes so highly aggressive that they no longer show any mercy in their conflict with others. In their relationships with women, their deluded ability to love, which is complemented by the equally illusory love ability in the women they are likely to choose, will occasionally come to the fore. But given the slightest problem, however, the aggressive survival part will resurface, and they may then beat or rape the woman to whom only a moment before they had promised the entire world. In violence against woman, the pent-up hate for one's own mother, which cannot be shown directly to her, finds a release. In this sense a pimp, for example, may well claim to love the wife he sends out to work as a prostitute on the street. Unfortunately, in a crazy way, this may actually be true.

The splitting off of the bonding emotions due to traumatic experiences of violence also leads to an inability to enter into a mature partnership with a man for women. A woman's fear component seeks stability from a 'strong man', primarily this is seen as someone who, as described above, has developed a cold, aggressive survival self. When the traumatised childhood parts of both people momentarily come into contact, something akin to a mutual understanding of each other's psychological needs is able to exist for a short time. This explains why male-female relationships can be maintained over a long period of time despite the day-to-day existence becoming saturated in persistent stress and extreme violence when the survival self of both parties is activated.

A survival self that results from traumatisation through violence can no longer take responsibility for itself or other people, even their own partner and children; nor does it respect social rules and conventions. That part of the person discards everything that stands in the way of its blinded manifestations. The aggressive survival self is incorporated into its unconscious attempts to come to terms with its own painful traumatic experiences. In dealing with his own trauma, the person traumatises others: through them he tries to get power, to make them dependant on him, to possess them like an object and to manipulate them at will.

What may come of children born of such violent relationships is shown in the following example:

Family terror

Veronika's story, which she told during a seminar, would have been enough for five lifetimes. Her mother tried to abort her using a knitting needle; as a baby she was passed around among immediate family and relatives to be sexually abused. Twice her father held a gun to her head and cocked the trigger. Her mother hit her frequently, and even as an adult, her brother still tried to rape her. During the Second World War her father had executed some partisans; her mother adored her father and, despite his violent excesses, wouldn't leave him. From a constellation with Veronika it became clear that even her mother's mother had not been able to differentiate between love and violence. On account of previous violent traumatisations, violence had been reframed as a form of attention among the female line of the family many generations before.

In a later constellation Veronika looked at her father's family line and here it was also possible to see how the spiral of power, powerlessness and violence had placed everyone in the family under its spell and how none of the people involved knew any way out other than to act violently towards each other.

Veronika was the only person in her family to take a different route and to deal with her past through therapy. Though her family on both her mother's and father's side would despise her for it, she was determined to find her own way out of the violent chaos.

The following example also spotlights a deluded attempt to combine family intimacy, insensitivity and violence.

"The weak are not to be pitied!"

As her daughter had been behaving extremely aggressively towards her for some years, a patient at one of my seminars made a constellation based on her family. The representative for her grandmother stood in the constellation like a rock in the storm. It became clear that, besides the many children she had had, she had apparently also aborted an equal number or let them die after birth. About this she said only that it had been necessary: the strongest children would prevail and survive; the weak were not to be pitied, for they only hinder the raising of the others. She was entirely convinced on this point. There was no place whatsoever for emotions with her – i.e. in her unfeeling survival self. To her, feelings were weaknesses that were to be thoroughly despised. This behaviour could also be found in her daughters, her granddaughter and eventually also her great-granddaughter (my patient's daughter). Since her birth this child had been extraordinarily unsettled. She cried continuously and, in later years, began to attack her mother both verbally and physically at every opportunity. The relationship between mother and child had become a battlefield. When this splitting off of feelings of love towards children that had persisted for generations became clear during the constellation, the patient became more relaxed and was able to accept her childhood pain and grief, and then the representative for the child also became calmer.

After the constellation the parents reported that the child, who had not been present during the constellation seminar, had also to a large extent ceased fighting against her mother.

Personality disorders

Bonding trauma in the end leads to the different forms of personality disorder well known in psychiatric and clinical literature as borderline, antisocial, hysterical and narcissistic personality disorders (Saß, Wittchen und Zaudig, 1998; Kreisman und Straus, 2002). Rarely do people with such psychological splits have much of a healthy self on which they can rely. In their close inter-personal relationships their traumatised parts will panic and call into action their more extreme survival strategies, alternately showing their clinging, aggressive, self-destructive and/or other excessive behavioural patterns, developing extreme strategies to counter the rising inner trauma feelings. Their internal chaos is continually repeated through the chaos they create in their lives on the outside. This causes traumatised children to become their own most dangerous opponents to personal development. As adults they humiliate, punish, torment and harm themselves, even when they no longer have contact with their traumatised parents. They become the next generation of parents who will traumatise their own children.

5.4 Bonding System Trauma

I use the term bonding system trauma to express the idea that it is not just a single person that can be affected by trauma, but also an entire system of interpersonal bonds. A bonding system trauma produces some special symptoms of psychological disorders.

The incidents that bonding system trauma situations lead to are often the logical consequence of a bonding trauma situation. If men and women coexist with their splits such that they alternate between fighting and clinging addictively to one another, and only continue to function through their survival strategies, it becomes inevitable that they will do things that are no longer considered normal, not even in an emotionally insensitive social setting. The worst situations are:

- Incest between parents and children, sexual relationships with other relatives or between siblings

- Having many abortions, especially during late pregnancy
- Killing children after birth, killing older children by apparent accidents
- Giving children born out of incestuous relationships away to children's homes or for adoption

Splits in the core identity of the soul

Bonding system traumas occur when things happen within a bonding system that go against the basic purpose of bonding: namely, holding something together that belongs together with love. If, for example, a mother kills her own child or causes it to die through neglect, this generates a fundamental contradiction in her soul and in the souls of all those connected to her. A mother who commits this act can therefore only go on living if she undergoes a split in the core identity of her soul. To survive such a situation she must split into one component that acts as if nothing has happened and another component that stores somewhere deep within her the horror and pain of what she has done, and the feelings of guilt and shame that come with it.

In my seminars I often work with people who come from families in which some of the events described above have taken place. In these cases, it can be observed quite well during the constellations process how the different parts of the soul that are encumbered with the heavy burden of guilt behave. They lose their inner compass after such deeds. One moment the traumatised part is able to feel horror at what has happened, cry out about what he has done, the next he will suddenly burst out laughing. This part of the person can be very kind, and then suddenly completely evil. The person can sit disinterestedly, and then suddenly jump up and run around. The feelings become unpredictable even to the person himself. This part of the person is continually going round in circles, if not externally, then in their mind. The person may talk to himself because he can no longer make himself understood due to his fear of contempt and punishment. He is ashamed of what he has done which can in no way be undone.

The survival part of his soul seals off the traumatised part from the environment. It tries to give an outward appearance of calm and dispel all suspicion that any injustice has been done, that it was impossible that the person could have done such a thing, or could have actively supported such a criminal act. The survival part conceals from others the split-off fear and pain. In an abstract way – since the connection to the actual deed committed has been erased from the person's consciousness – the survival part is always afraid of being discovered and found guilty or judged morally. He sees everyone as attempting to find him guilty of something and trying to get the truth out of him. This part keeps silent as far as is possible. If it tries to dispel any suspicions, would that not leave him looking all the more suspicious? The survival part is overcautious, exceptionally untrusting and increasingly paranoid. The extreme denial of guilt exists alongside a permanently guilty conscience in an abstract form. Therefore, this survival part, which will feel guilty at the slightest excuse, then goes on the offensive should someone get too close or become too inquisitive. Where necessary, the relationship of the parent with his or her children will be sacrificed if the children start to look too closely into their lives and family history. The creation of diversions and acting as if everything were normal become the main preoccupations of a survival self that holds a traumatised guilt/shame component that is responsible for crazy actions. The conscience of a perpetrator no longer functions properly, because all the feelings required have been split off. The survival self no longer has available any of the basic emotions required for a realistic evaluation of what is right and what is not.

Figure 10 gives a schematic view of this kind of splitting. A healthy self, if this existed before the deed was committed, scarcely is present in a bonding system trauma, because essentially anything at all will wake the memory of the deed that is being kept secret. The survival self controls everything.

Bonding System Trauma

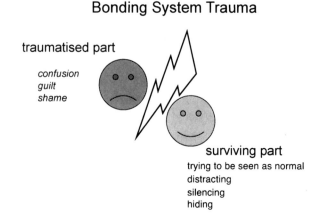

traduced part

confusion
guilt
shame

surviving part
trying to be seen as normal
distracting
silencing
hiding

Figure 10: The splitting that occurs in bonding system trauma.

Fear, hate, emotional coldness, feelings of guilt and shame are the dominant feelings arising from this type of trauma situation, and are felt by the entire family. Everyone is in a state of total confusion and near insanity, and they are thus no longer able to take proper responsibility for their actions.

The confusion of children

All bonding relationships with a traumatised person, especially a mother carrying such heavy burden of guilt, are unconsciously over-shadowed by the deed.

Children born into a bonding system in which things have been done that affect this nucleus of their parent's identity, sense that something is amiss. What their parents say is one thing, what they communicate emotionally, however, is something else entirely. Their parents' eyes, gestures, facial expressions and vocal intonation all say something different from their words. Even where the parents are silent, it is precisely this silence that shouts that they cannot speak about something. On the other hand, when they speak a lot about something, it is clear to the children that they are trying to hide something else. A patient of mine with manic-depressive symptoms once told me that his father would almost never talk about his family, but instead would talk extensively about his coin collection. Distraction is one of the main survival strategies to avoid going crazy.

These children, of course, receive no affirmation from their parents for their experience of discrepancy. Everything is perfectly normal! The children are dismissed as sick, oversensitive or even crazy when they talk about what they feel and insist that something is not right. In such situations the children, as with all children in relation to their parents, will be acting for two reasons:

- They are looking for emotional stability for themselves, and
- They hope to be able to help their parents find this stability.

Children who grow up in such confused families tend to show symptoms through their behaviour because they are not able to say verbally what is wrong. Through crazy behaviour, they are expressing the fact that there is something crazy about their family.

Crazy child?

In a seminar a female participant explained that when she was about two years old she took a chair, placed it next to the stove, climbed up on the chair and placed her right hand onto the hot burner. Shortly after she had received medical treatment for the burn, and her hand was in a bandage, she went back to the stove and this time placed her other hand onto the burner. Within her family there was a war between the men and the women, there was incest, child abuse, murder and suicide.

The child's illusion of being able to heal the split

The position for children in these families is very difficult. While bonding with their parents they become entangled in their parents' split-off trauma emotions. Through the bonding process they are drawn into their parents' own traumas, and the parents themselves may already be holding the traumas of *their* parents. From my observations, the emotional effects of murder and incest on the mother's side of the family can be felt for three to four generations, among the children, grandchildren or great-grandchildren. If the children in this situation try to withdraw, they feel abandoned and lonely. Some do indeed opt for the lonely route in order not to be constantly subjected to their parents' oscillating emotions. Others, however, are unable to separate themselves from their parents, and remain symbiotically entangled, empathising with their parents' confusion, and so moving closer to the family secret. Although they can clearly sense the emotional atmosphere, they don't really understand the full context of what happened; they only partially sense the emotions, images and thoughts from their parents' soul.

One man wrote of his psychosis: "While in a state of psychosis, I hid an Iron Cross from the Second World War. It took me the whole day. It was all very real to me. I can't understand how it could all have been a hallucination. First of all, I ran around the graveyard all night and looked at every grave. I was looking for something there, though I can't remember what. At that time I had a particular interest in the Second World War. Maybe it had something to do with the fact that my father had been in the Second World War. After his death I found his pay book from the Waffen SS. He'd never spoken about it. While in this psychotic state, I also began looking for my father, who had disappeared after the war. I think I'm equally entangled in my father's history as I am with my mother's. This makes it particularly hard for me to keep things separate. I've been looking for peace all my life but never found it. Actually I feel confused all day long."

Asking the parents what all this means is hopeless. Instead the children persist in trying to find a solution to the emotional puzzle of their parents and grandparents – which the parents and grandparents do not want solved, because that would have meant facing up to what had been done and admitting knowledge of their wrongdoing. The attempts to find some clarity serves only to confuse those children further who are searching for something tangible, and they will then turn to fantasies of adventurous journeys into the past. They dissect everything in their minds and then reassemble what they have, sometimes in the most absurd ways in the hope of finding some traces of an underlying truth. They seek solutions that try to combine things that do not go together properly: guilt and innocence, love for the perpetrator and love for the victim, good and evil, heaven and hell, love and death. In their fantasies these children often take refuge in religious ideas where such contradictions seem to be reconciled. They hope that if they sacrifice themselves for the salvation of the world, or develop an ideal attitude in themselves, some order will be instilled in the souls of their parents. This would enable them to have the intimacy with their parents that they on the one hand have missed so much and, on the other have come to fear. In principle, this means that if they take on the madness themselves, attempting to combine these impossible contradictions in their own souls, then the others in the family will be healed, and can give them the love and stability that they need. From my observations, a bonding system trauma in this way can be a cause of schizophrenia and psychosis among the children and grandchildren of parents who are emotionally entangled in this way. The less normal the original event that happened in the family, the more determinedly the schizophrenic survival self will try to go beyond reality in search of an ideal world.

To illustrate this I have chosen here as a case study a letter sent to me by a woman in a psychiatric clinic after having read my book 'Confused Souls'[5]. It was in this book that I first published my theory that schizophrenia and psychosis were the result of family secrets. Secrets in families lead to confusion and a loss of a sense of reality and, predominantly among children and grandchildren, are expressed through psychotic and schizophrenic symptoms.

"My mission in the family"

"I keep having schizophrenic episodes. The distortion of reality occurs at the same time every year – you could almost set your watch by it. No drugs have helped. At first, when the strongest chemical concoctions were being used on me, from a conventional medical perspective, I enjoyed four years of peace. The drugs were designed to cancel out the signals my soul was receiving. I was in high spirits and had a zest for life. Unfortunately, this came to an end recently, and at times I wanted to die. Because I see my mission in the family as having failed. I was a happy, easy child and as such was expected to cure the trauma my parents had suffered during the war. My mother is as hard as stone. She married without being in love. I grew up without love. I'm unable to speak to my mother or my father. My mother won't speak and my father is like a mute. My mother sticks to shallow subjects like fashion and appearances. My father makes sure he never has any time left over. He's a workaholic. As soon as there's a break of more than half a minute, he starts hounding everyone. In addition, he always was, and still is, not really there. Although I have a fantastic brother, we were never able to stand each other, as we only reflected our parents' relationship. I have many reasons to believe I have another sibling. This paralyses me emotionally and triggers feelings of anger and contempt in me. My mother tells lies half the time. She can no longer distinguish between lies and truth. It takes a really big lie for her to be able to do that. The true events in your book sometimes cause me to wake up full of anger towards those involved. Your book enabled me to find several

---

[5] Not available in English translation.

pieces of the puzzle. This overwhelms me but also gives me energy and confirms that what my parents tell me isn't true: i.e. that there's no explanation for my illness. All the therapists played along. I'd never had psychotherapy, although I have been going to a doctor for nine years every one to three months to collect pills. The treatment is like coffee and a chat, nothing more."

The concealing of such traumatic events that is essential to the bonding system, and the suppression of the truth, require a cooperative environment. This mainly refers to the spouses. In my experience, people from traumatised family systems will seek partners who, like them, are carrying a similar kind of secret from their own family. Each shields the other with an unspoken agreement not to enquire about the other's past.

Psychotherapists and psychiatrists have an opportunity when they see children with symptoms of psychosis and schizophrenia in their practice to encourage the shedding of light on the darker side of the family. Due to the assumption that schizophrenia is a genetically determined metabolic disorder, however, parents who bring their schizophrenic children to doctors, psychiatrists or psychotherapists are not required to look into their own souls. Needless to say, this does not help them or their children in the long run. The confused children become a lifelong burden for the parents, causing them shame by their failed lives or by their suicide. The only means that I can see of escaping from schizophrenic illnesses is for the person to have the courage to confront the darker side of the family history. I have met many parents with schizophrenic children who have chosen this path, even though it is not easy. This is beneficial to them and their children.

The legacy of rape in war

In order to understand how these bonding system traumas were able to occur on a large scale in, for example, German families, we can take the events that occurred at the end of the

Second World War. As the Russian army invaded eastern Germany at the end of the war, moving towards Berlin, rape occurred on a massive scale. "According to Reichling, 1.9 million German women and girls were raped during the advance on Berlin, by men from the Red Army, of which 1.4 million were in the former German eastern territories during flight and expulsions, and 500,000 in the subsequently Soviet occupied area... We can't say how many children were born as a consequence of these rapes. Dr. Reichling estimates some 292,000... The documents that exist for Berlin allow us to make the justified claim that approx. 20% of women became pregnant and of these 92% had an abortion... We don't know how the women dealt with what happened, whether and how many children were aborted, died after birth or were killed." (Sander und Johr, 2005)

Most of the women to whom this happened have remained silent throughout their lives. Their husbands have rarely asked them about it, one reason for this being that it was also a source of shame and humiliation for the men, for it showed that they were unable to protect their women and children from the mass rape. The subject was also a taboo for the post-war society, which was incapable of dealing with it, either on a social or political level. The children born of these rapes were co-opted into these dark unspoken secrets and so were forced to undergo a kind of psychological endurance test until their tender souls split into pieces and they lost all their trust in other people.

The Russian boy

A patient, who had endured lifelong suffering, involving many psychotic episodes, wrote this to me: "When I was about eight years old I lay down on my back on the living room table and began to complain of stomach pains. My brothers, who were five and eleven years older than me, laughed and said: he's faking again. Laughing, my eldest brother then explained that I wasn't born into this family,

I was really a young Russian boy and they had found me in the black pit, a place in their Silesian native village. My mother laughed too. I began to cry and, in my state of mental anguish my inner self tore in two pieces in a way that I could feel physically. I started crying so hard that my mother began to try and comfort me and tell me none of it was true, but the split could no longer be repaired. The way my mother had laughed had shattered my basic trust in her. Should I believe what I hear or what I feel?"

During his therapy he finally came to the conclusion that he was a child born of a relationship between his mother and a Russian man.

6
Splits and Entanglements

The permanent linking of smaller and larger emotional entities within an individual and between different people forms the basic principle of emotional bonding. The principle of a split is the separating of emotional links within a person's general structure or within a human bonding system. Given that bonding and trauma are directly connected, any splits in the soul will inevitably have an effect on interpersonal relationships. Splits hinder the development of healthy, stable partnerships, making loving parent-child relationships impossible, setting siblings against each other, tearing apart friendships and sowing disagreements at work. Families, work groups and entire societies can be drawn into heavily polarised conflicts by people with splits in their souls, and these can escalate continually according to certain patterns (Glasl, 1999). The survival parts of the people and groups involved are fighting each other. Adolf Hitler is a prime example of how someone who feared for his life as a child, and lived out his entire life in a megalomaniac survival mode, was transferring his illusionary maternal love onto an entire nation, only to drag it down with him into the abyss of his illusions. Hitler was a human being who externalised the deep feelings of shame he adopted via his maternal bonding to such an extent that in his paranoia he identified an intrinsic inferiority in other people (above all Jews) and developed the delusional idea that they needed to be destroyed for him to feel better.

I define entanglements here as relationship patterns in which two or more people are connected emotionally through their surviving selves, unconsciously projecting their traumatisations onto one another and, despite continuing relationship conflicts that bring nothing but suffering and hardship, are unable to separate themselves from one another.

6.1 Unhealthy Symbiosis

Symbiosis means the 'living together of two living creatures for mutual benefit'. The term is used in psychology to describe the state of the unity between a child and his mother in the early stages after birth (Mahler 1972). During this stage of life, the child is incredibly dependant on his mother both physically and psychologically. For her part, the mother needs to feel that this is her child, whom she loves more than anything else and whose life she must protect as she would her own. When love flows between mother and child in this way, it confirms to the child his right to exist, nurtures his basic trust in his existence, confirms his self-worth, and cultivates his love of life and growing independence. The mother also receives affirmation through the positive exchange of feelings with her child. We can call this process a beneficial symbiosis. For as long as these symbiotic processes are restricted to the mother-child relationship, they have a purpose. However, if the relationship between a mother and her child remains symbiotic as the child grows, then something is not right and will disrupt the further development of both.

In an unhealthy symbiosis, instead of love and happiness, negative feelings such as fear, anger and despair are exchanged between mother and child. In such cases the mother does not recognise the real needs of her child, projecting her own needs onto him, and the child then finds it difficult to distinguish his own needs from those of his mother.

Mother-child entanglements mostly occur because the

mother herself has a needy childlike component, which failed to receive the appropriate symbiotic care from her mother that she would have needed to develop a healthy independence. This childlike needy part of the mother expects to find the needed love and acceptance from her own child, so that the child is seen to be treated symbiotically in the way that this part of the mother would have liked for herself. But of course this means that the child's real needs are not taken into consideration. The child becomes an object for satisfying the needs of the symbiotically unsatisfied part of the mother, and a tool in her survival strategy of ensuring through contact with the child that she is no longer alone. The survival self of the mother therefore turns the child into the object of her need for love and the child is not loved for his own sake.

The child, on the other hand, can sense the symbiotic need in his mother, and would like to help her, hoping that in this way he will be seen as an individual and have his own symbiotic needs met. He gains his own sense of a right to exist through the symbiotic care of his mother. Such entangled symbiotic bonding relationships make it difficult for those involved to distinguish between 'I' and 'you' throughout their lives; which feelings belong to which person, and who acts and who reacts, can no longer be determined.

I need you to be my protective shield!

During Josef's constellation, his unhealthy symbiosis became clear through the fact that the representative for the traumatised part of his mother stood hiding behind his back, not wanting to be seen. Josef could only see the representative for his mother's emotionally inaccessible survival part, which he could sense was in need of help. He couldn't touch the part of his mother that concealed itself behind him out of shame. For the mother, who had been traumatised through severe sexual attacks in her childhood, the child was the protective shield that she used to present herself to the outside world as an ostensibly normal woman. In having the courage to recognise that his mother was trying to hide her trauma behind him, Josef was able in this constellation to step out from his unhealthy symbiosis with her. He later wrote to me: "That my mother probably suffered sexual abuse, rape and torture in her childhood makes me very sad. I now understand the megalomaniacal fantasies I had of being able to change anything I wanted to. But it was like Don Quixote's battle with the windmills. There's nothing I can change, neither in my mother nor my girlfriends." Up until this point he had always been strongly attracted to women who resembled his mother in that they didn't want to recognise and deal with their experiences of violence, but whose emotional needs, however, he could feel very clearly.

6.2 Child Dependency Patterns

Children are dependent on their parents in a broad sense:

- for material things (food, clothing, home, money), and
- for emotional support, comfort, attention, parental love and recognition.

They therefore show a basic childhood need to place themselves in a position of dependence vis-à-vis their parents. It is only during puberty that children first become aware that it is possible for them not to be dependent on their parents for the rest of their lives. The task of a child's psychological development during puberty is to become independent from parents. Against the resistance her parents put up, the child must test out her ability to become responsible for herself. Parents who themselves were able to become independent from their parents in a positive way, are able to allow their child an increasing amount of freedom. However, parents who are still symbiotically entangled with their own parents will try to retain their children in a state of dependency.

The 'hero' and the 'black sheep'

Children whose parents have splits in their souls and so try to preserve their child's dependence on them in order to fulfil their own psychological survival deal differently with this situation. Some children adopt an understanding stance towards their parents, taking on household chores and trying to improve their career opportunities by obtaining good marks at school so they can become financially independent of their parents or contribute to the family upkeep as soon as possible. These children help their parents avoid having to acknowledge their traumatisations and continue concealing the splits in their souls. They will suppress their anger, because anger achieves nothing for them with their parents, whom they perceive as weak. These children always leave their own needs to last. They also remain conformist and ambitious in their later professional lives. They like to take responsibility for things that are essentially too much for them or don't actually meet their own needs. They may work themselves to death although they would much rather do nothing or play. These 'heroes' are 'perfect' children, they become 'perfect' wives, 'perfect' sons-in-law, 'perfect' bosses – but in the symbiotically needy part of their souls, they spend their whole lives with a deep sense of loneliness.

The 'black sheep', on the other hand, adopts the reverse strategy. He behaves as if he is always more needy than his parents. This child does everything to seem irresponsible and as dependent as possible. His parents must constantly worry about what the child will destroy next. There are constant conflicts with teachers and other pupils, drug use, early sexual relationships – the range of possibilities is vast in which the child can instil fear and terror in his parents in order to gain their attention and prevent them from drifting away from him. In order to discover what it is his parents are hiding in their soul, these children take on the role of the 'enfant terrible'. They try to surface all the splits in their parents' soul. Through acts of defiance, they try to force their parents to take responsibility. They are always demanding and make no preparations whatsoever to look after themselves. They get used to their position of dependence and show little interest in escaping from it. They fail to develop their talents, so as not to become autonomous and independent. The parents are unable to bring up these children to be independent and responsible for themselves as long as they themselves are trapped by the splits in their own souls and are still functioning in a survival mode.

6.3 Carrying the Parental Splits

So children are able to sense the traumatisations in their parents' soul. They fear them and yet must assimilate their parents' split-off trauma parts into their own psychological structures. They carry their parent's trauma with them in their souls.

Grit your teeth!

Konstanze clenches her jaws together strongly and consequently displays tension all over her face. During her constellation she picks a man to represent this symptom and, on seeing the stooped posture the representative adopts, she immediately makes a connection: "Like my father!" In the course of the constellation, Konstanze explains that her father was in the SS and a soldier on the Russian front. He was flown home after being injured and so escaped the Siege of Stalingrad. Konstanze was the one to whom he told stories about the war. As a child she had a lot of sympathy for him and could feel that he was always reminded of his dead comrades. So she endured the horror of what he described and conveyed through his sudden fits of violence, fearing he might do something to her. In order to cope with the enormous tension between her and her father, Konstanze had to undergo a split. One part of her was overloaded with the burden of her father's trauma. Another part of her seemed to know nothing about what the father was doing to her by telling her his stories. This part was close to the father, gave him warmth and felt a certain amount of warmth coming from him. The entanglement with the father was encouraged by the fact that Konstanze's mother was emotionally inaccessible to her, having been abandoned emotionally by her own mother.

Through the constellation Konstanze was able to recognise clearly the split inside her and in the end adopt a conciliatory position between the two parts. In the final discussion, she said: "I now have the exciting feeling of how the left and right sides of my brain are able to reconnect."

The pattern of dependency and entanglement people learn during childhood leaves its mark for the rest of their lives. It develops unconsciously, and for as long as it is not addressed, it continues to influence the person's feelings, thinking and actions. Even in situations where there is no longer any need for dependency, people stick with the old emotional patterns that ensured their survival in childhood. They still fear not being able to survive without them.

From the perspective of the split we see that one personality component has grown up and become independent, while the other part continues to feel dependent like a baby and continues fighting with the person on which it was originally dependent. This original person is later replaced by friends, partners, children or work colleagues. These are experienced and treated like the original people, i.e. the mother or father. They are loved, taken care of, feared, hated and fought against in the very same way.

A mother's negative experience of sexuality and the splits that this give rise to will also influence the behaviour of her son towards his girlfriends and female partners. A son finds himself attracted to the traumatised part of his mother in his partners, for it is there that he senses a connection with her feelings. The survival part of the female partner, however, keeps him at a distance and lets him starve emotionally, as is illustrated by the following example.

Trapped!

At a constellation seminar a participant named Rüdiger was looking for a solution to his relationship difficulties with women, which took the following form: with one woman, whom he described as his ideal woman and who was interested in him, he couldn't bring himself to commit to the relationship, with the result that after awhile she turned to another man; another woman he was interested in put a clear stop to their relationship, but he could not let go of her. In his constellation, the relationship-seeking part of Rüdiger's soul seemed symbiotically tied to his mother. He seemed to be moving back and forth in a narrow space between the two parts of his mother. He could only scurry from side to side: as soon as he came close to the traumatised part of his mother, he stopped because he could sense her grief; and when he approached the mother's survival part, it blocked Rüdiger's attempt to come closer. The survival part of his mother demanded that he be well behaved. So Rüdiger was trapped. He couldn't move closer to any aspect of his mother, because she would either be angry and reproachful or sad and unstable. He also couldn't escape her, because he didn't know where else to turn.

6.4 Entangled Relationships in Couples

The female as mother replacement

Children who are abandoned at birth, given up for adoption or placed in homes and foster families, or those whose mothers die young are unable to survive without clinging to illusory images and fantasies of their mother. It therefore comes as no surprise that people who had such a tough childhood tend to act as if the sun is constantly shining, always laughing and being sociable, and never seeming to have any problems. These people lend a sympathetic ear to other people's troubles. They are very helpful, worry about others, help them solve their problems and experience themselves as saviours. Behind all this there often lies a tragic history.

Mr Sunshine

Both privately and professionally, Christian was always on the move and very popular among his large circle of friends. He was involved in many projects. While he was on a foreign holiday, he met a local woman, took her back with him to Germany, married her and they had a daughter together. He looked after his wife and daughter devotedly, even buying his wife an apartment in her home country so she would have somewhere to stay whenever she wanted to visit her parents and relatives there. Gradually, however, his wife became more and more 'difficult'. She became increasingly demanding, accused him of things and would sometimes be very depressed, then suddenly turning aggressive again. She turned their daughter against him. From Christian's description, his wife seemed to display the typical behaviour of a child who had suffered bonding trauma. We can assume that as her daughter grew up, split-off traumatised parts had been re-awoken in her reminding her of her own childhood and probably also of sexual abuse. Christian admitted in conversation that he had met his wife in a red light district.

Christian's world suddenly collapsed like a house of cards; his wife was refusing him any meaningful interaction. Eventually, she also denied him contact with their daughter. The conflict escalated in the usual way: lawyers, police, judges and child welfare officers were all involved in trying to control the steadily escalating conflict.

It was only at this stage that Christian sought personal help. It emerged in his first psychotherapy session that he had been abandoned by his mother when only two years old and had never seen her again. He grew up with his father, who made sure he never came into contact with his mother again. To the father, Christian's mother was a source of pure provocation and to be blamed for everything.

During Christian's therapy, the deeply sad, frightened and distressed child that had been abandoned by his mother gradually came out from behind the 'sunshine part'. Only when Christian was ready to recognise and lovingly accept this part of himself was he able to find a solution to the conflict with his wife that was satisfactory to him. He set about questioning his entire life up to then, including his never ending willingness to help, and the exploitative circle of friends he had collected around him in his role as 'Mr Sunshine'. He became more realistic in terms of what he could really do for others and what he needed for himself. Previously he had always looked after the others in the hope it would make them love him and stop them abandoning him as his mother had done.

The male as mother replacement

Choosing partners is usually made by unconscious criteria. If two partners have splits in their souls, then each discovers in the other a part from which he or she hopes to gain a degree of stability in his or her emotional equilibrium. When partners reveal the different parts of their souls in a constellation, it becomes clear how these parts relate to one another and why this couple sought each other out in the first place, but are not really able to achieve a stable partnership.

Don't desert me!

Monika persuaded Paul to go with her to a constellations seminar. Neither had any hope left for a solution to the continually escalating conflict in their relationship. Paul was a manual worker. He described his childhood as happy; he always felt good with his parents and enjoyed a lot of personal freedom. But his parent's divorce, which happened while he was going through puberty, had a powerful affect on him. He became independent at an early age and as a plumber was soon standing on his own two feet.

Monika described a much harder childhood. Her relationship with her mother was very fraught. After enquiring further, it turned out that her mother was sent by her mother to the countryside during the war and so they were separated for a long time.

Talking before the constellation, Monika complained bitterly about her husband. He neglected her, was always working and also made lots of mistakes, which she then had to iron out. Confronted with these accusations Paul is defenceless and counters by describing his stressful and exhausting life as a manual worker. For his wife's sake he would be prepared to give up his business and look for another job if that would help.

As expected the constellation showed that the solution to the couple's relationship problems lay elsewhere. I first asked Monika and Paul to place representatives in the constellation for the relevant parts from their adulthood and childhood. It quickly became apparent that Monika's childhood part is carrying the childhood anger and separation anxieties of her mother, which stopped

Monika and her mother from being able to develop a stable bond. The constellation suggested that Monika's mother was not sent to the countryside purely because of the war, but indicated a deeply disturbed bond between the mother and the grandmother.

Monika therefore expects something from her husband, which he is unable to give her: a replacement for maternal love, affection and attention. At the same time, she complains that he, like her mother, is not there for her, something her mother had also said of her mother. The emotionally contaminated conflict between the mother and the grandmother has thus been unconsciously transferred to their relationship.

Why, then, did Monika seek out a husband like Paul, who so clearly finds it hard to stand by her? The situation becomes clearer when Paul places a representative for his mother in the constellation. Monika's neglected childhood part tries to lean against Paul's mother' representative, something Paul's childhood part, however, views with great suspicion and jealousy. Monika's needy part has discovered the supportive mother in Paul's soul.

And why did Paul choose Monika to be his partner? The answer to this seemingly lies in Monika's survival part, which represents a challenge for Paul's adulthood part (this makes Monika an interesting woman to him). The constellation also revealed that Paul's childhood part is interested in the traumatised part of Monika's mother. Paul's childhood part thus senses in his own mother a part of her that is in need of help and which he would like to help.

By dealing with their inner parts, which are heavily burdened and superimposed with the feelings of their respective mothers, Monika and Paul are better able to integrate their childhood and adult parts and need no longer look for the solution to their own emotional problems in each other. Monika needs to free herself from her mother's abandonment trauma in order not to destroy her relationship through these inherited trauma feelings and Paul must recognise that he bears no responsibility for his mother's misfortune, a feeling which, on the one hand, draws him towards Monika, but at the same time hinders him from getting involved emotionally with her on a deeper level. In the course of the constellation process both manage to take steps forward in their emotional integration. They were therefore able to come together as a couple again.

The female as idealised mother

Men whose mothers grew up in a bonding trauma situation, often instinctively seek out partners who also suffered bonding trauma as children. Insofar as they have perfected the art of suppressing their traumatic experiences with their own mothers, they feel strong enough to tolerate patiently the multiple sufferings of their female partners. They are always on hand to play the role of the saviour. They patiently compensate for the chaos caused by the traumatised elements of their female partners, which increasingly emerge during their relationship and marriage. For example, they may adopt their partner's children from her previous failed marriage; they are financially very generous, or they may tolerate the inability of the partner to keep a tidy home, because she is sometimes completely incapable of taking decisions due to the splits in her soul. They are unable to see the reality of the situation and cling tightly to the moments when their partner shows her accommodating 'I'll-do-anything-to-please-you' survival side, learned in childhood and which can be outwardly charming and seductive. Despite experiences to the contrary, they see this as reflecting their partner's true nature, just as when they were children they consciously only noticed their mother's occasional 'wonderful' side.

You're the evil one!

In discussions with social workers, psychological assessors or divorce judges, that this kind of couple are likely to have at some time, the woman is often able to show her adapted 'sunny' part. This is because the situation is increasingly sliding out of control for the man, due, for example, to the wife's conflict with the children. Because of his idealisations and inability to say anything negative about his wife, the husband struggles in vain to make clear that she is a completely different person at home where she tyrannises him and the children. In such cases, custody decisions are often awarded in favour of the mother. If the assessors and judges have little understanding of the effects of personality splits, they will often view the woman as the victim of a dominating male, instead of identifying the perpetrator part within the woman. Ironically the formal administrative assistance therefore may be paving the way for the children of these couples to become anorexic girls or violent and sexually aggressive boys. It would be much clearer to name the root cause of the evil in such entangled family structures, if the mothers were advised to seek immediate therapeutic help with their trauma. This would help make clear to them who the 'evil ones' really are, against whom their survival self is blindly fighting and whom they see in their husbands and partners. In many cases these are the fathers who abused them as children. Similarly, the husband should also be advised to seek therapeutic help, so that he is able to understand better why he so naively loves and is so committed to such a deeply traumatised woman.

The man who loves and never leaves me

For many women there exists the idea that through their love they will be able to save a man who continues to show the extent of his own splits through alcohol abuse, violence and aggressive behaviour towards her and the children. Such women base their illusions on the moments when their husbands tell them they are the only people who understand them and when they act like kind, sweet young boys, are attentive or behave in a seductive manner. Their partners do not see the fact that at any moment he may become violent and drink himself senseless. They keep on giving another chance to their partners' 'good and nice' parts. Why? Because they possess this same element in themselves, which keeps hoping for attention from their own mother or father, and will put up with violence and abuse, refusing to give up on the illusion that it can be achieved by self-sacrificing love. Not wanting to see their own trauma, they are also blind to that of their partner. Psychological literature uses the term 'co-dependency' to describe this behaviour (Kolitzus, 2000).

"I must be grateful to him!"

One of my clients went to a group run by Alcoholics Anonymous for relatives because of her husband's alcohol use. During this therapy, the cause of her co-dependency was established as being her entanglement with the fate of her mother, who was sent away during the Second World War, aged only nine, and never saw her parents again. She was bound to the part of her mother's soul that preserved the feeling of displacement, helplessness and fear. As a result, and despite her attractive appearance, communication skills and intellectual ability, she had no sense of self-worth. She undervalued herself and was happy and grateful when her husband accepted her as his wife. She didn't really love him but accepted his proposal of marriage because of his persistent devotion to her. When during therapy she dealt with her entanglement with her mother, understood her traumatisation and was able to free herself from her entanglement, she was able to accept her own abandoned and frightened child within her soul. She became increasingly self-confident and followed her own path more in her marriage.

6.5 Entanglements in Psychotherapy

The relationship between psychotherapists and their clients can also become symbiotically entangled and end up in a symbiotic dead end. One of the most common problems arises when the therapist tries to change the survival elements of a client and overcome their 'defensive strategies'. This results in futile confrontations, since generally the client's survival self can mobilise significantly more energy than the healthy self of the therapist can. In a polite situation, the survival part of the client rejects all the therapist's attempts to bring about a change in its survival strategies with a "Yes, but that won't work!" If the therapist herself then ends up in survival mode — because, for example, she feels power-less or becomes angry — this can lead to entanglements and unhelpful transference.

With psychotherapists who strongly take on a helping role, there is a tendency to protect the client from his trauma feel-ings. Here the therapist may change the subject, comfort the client or try to calm him down whenever he starts to feel his fear, anger or pain, i.e. his trauma feelings. In this instance the therapist is reacting from her own survival self, which also wants to prevent her own trauma from surfacing. Since she is also afraid of losing control if her trauma parts surface, she also suppresses these in her client and thus enters into a form of coalition with the client's survival self. In these cases, the therapist and client both need each other in order to avoid coming into contact with their respective splits.

It can also occur that a client will sense that he cannot burden his therapist with his really difficult life experiences, fearing that they would overwhelm her, as his own parents were overwhelmed before. Consequently there is not a lot that can happen in the therapy and it is likely to become long drawn out and tiring.

There are a variety of therapy situations that carry the seeds of entanglement within them. For example:

- When parents send their children to a psychotherapist without being prepared to deal with their own psychological problems, there is a danger that the therapist will side with the parents in making the child the problem.
- Also if parents undergo therapy only in order to help their children this neither supports the child's disentanglement from his parents, nor are they clearly devoting themselves to resolving their own splits – again they focus on someone else and avoid dealing properly with their own problems.
- Sometimes women start psychotherapy saying they want to solve their husband's or partner's problem, even though he has made it very clear that he doesn't want to deal with them. What these women want is understandable, but in my experience a therapy based on this focus also allows the female to suppress the splits in her own soul and to look for the cause of what's wrong in her husband.

"What can I do for my traumatised son?"

In a seminar a mother wanted to know if she needed to do something for her son, who had recently suffered a serious accident at work. The constellation showed that a part of her own soul that was traumatised in childhood was trying to cling to that part of her son that had been traumatised by the accident. This woman's traumatised part felt it wasn't being noticed and supported by its own survival part. That the traumatised part of the mother was now also clinging to her son was too much for both the son's traumatised and survival parts. The required therapeutic step consisted of making the entanglement visible and showing the mother that she needs to take the time and space to be able to look after herself better. The more she does for herself, the more she will help her son, who will then be able to concentrate all his energies on becoming well again.

"I'm worried the client will kill herself"

During a supervision seminar, a counsellor expressed his fear that one of his female clients might kill herself. From a constellation it became clear that the counsellor's own trauma part was stranded helplessly between the client's survival and traumatised parts, making it even harder for them to come into contact. It was only when he recognised his own fear of death, which had been with him since childhood (among other things, his father had narrowly escaped being shot in the war), that the way became free for his client also to face more openly her ideas of the possibility of salvation through death. The client then realised that death would not solve her loneliness. This constellation showed what actually lay behind the client's suicidal thoughts: a desire for contact with another living being. She will be helped more if the counsellor recognises this need behind her suicidal thoughts and makes her aware of it instead of panicking.

6.6 Entanglements in Social Work

In many areas of their work, social workers have to deal with people who have splits in their souls and as a result are always suffering extreme social distress and getting entangled in unsolvable conflicts. In addition, their clients are often far from recognising their own problems and requesting any kind of psychotherapy or counselling. Their survival selves instead look for the solution to their problems almost exclusively in the outside world so shielding themselves against any confrontation with the actual traumatisation and split.

I found the following example in a magazine (Brigitte

9/2005) and have edited it slightly for presentation here. In my opinion, this case history describes very well the situation of a woman who, due to the traumatisation suffered in childhood, generates an enormous amount of family chaos around her leading to the involvement of many different social workers and the courts. The splits in her own personality are also reflected in the behaviour of those meant to help her and her children.

"I'm a good mother!"

Mrs H is 26 years old and the mother of five children from three different fathers. The child welfare office had applied to the custody court to have six-year-old Sandra, Mrs H's second child, placed with a foster family. A psychological assessor had decided that Mrs H was not fit to be a parent to all her children. Mrs H found this unfair and tried to fight the decision with all means at her disposal. She claimed that: 'I love my children and my children love me. I'm a good mother. I am bringing them up so that they won't be still hanging onto my coat tails at aged 30 or 40. They should be friendly towards other people, but not trust them too much.'

Mrs H had her first child, Tobias, while aged 17. Her five children are now aged nine, six, five, three and one. Mrs H is married today to the father of her two youngest children. All seven of them live in a run-down council flat on the edge of a village.

Mrs H is a chain smoker and has a typical smoker's cough. She went to a 'special needs' school herself, just as her son Tobias now goes to a school for children with learning difficulties. As her son was about to set off for the football pitch with the social worker sent by the welfare office to supervise the family, his mother asked him: 'What happened to your cough?' She told the social worker that Tobias liked to feign illness so he wouldn't have to go to school.

Mrs H was the oldest of five brothers and sisters. Her father was a builder and her mother worked as a cleaning lady. As far as the child welfare office was aware Mrs H's mother was an alcoholic and her father drank excessively and frequently. At aged six, Mrs H went into what was called a 'home for difficult children'. She returned home a year later. She doesn't remember much of her childhood.

When Mrs H was pregnant with her first child, her mother put pressure on her to have an abortion. The social worker assigned to the family at the time advised her to give up the child for adoption. However, Mrs H wanted to have the child and bring it up herself. After giving birth, she sometimes left her son with her parents so she could work as an apprentice cook, something she abandoned after only one year. Two years later she threw out her boyfriend, the father of the child, because he was always drunk at the weekends.

Together with her son Tobias, she moved out of her parents' place to live in a larger town. There she got involved with an older man. Again she left her son with her parents. When she wanted to take him back six months later, her parents refused to give him back. As a result she 'abducted' her own child from her parents' flat. Her parents informed the police, which eventually led to Tobias being placed by the child welfare office with a foster family before returning to his mother.

Mrs H again became pregnant and within two years had brought two girls into the world: Sandra and Annabell. A few weeks before the birth of her second daughter she also threw out the father of these children. She said: 'I found out that this man was playing around with animals' (having sex with animals).

The father of the two girls was allowed visiting rights by the court once every two weeks. On these weekends, Mrs H would sometimes also send her son Tobias to the girls' father. Six months later she found out from one of the children that this man, the father of the two girls, had been sexually abusing them. When she told the child welfare office, they didn't believe her. According to Mrs H's statement, the 'woman at the welfare office' said to her at the time, 'You're one of those mothers who throw their children in the rubbish bin!' — to which Mrs H reacted, 'So I tipped the table over in front of her!' The children had to keep on going to the father. It was only when another woman reported the girls' father to the police for the sexual abuse of her own children that he was arrested and later sentenced to three years in prison.

When Mrs H gets involved with another much older man, she quickly ends up pregnant again, and two boys, Martin and Dennis, are born within a short time of each other. In this new family, which moves to a small village, it is Sandra who must fight for her place most of all. The teachers at the nursery school notice 'haematomas at different stages' spread over the entire body of the four-year-old. To this Mrs H protests: 'I don't kick my child. At most she gets a slap on the bottom or a clip around the ear.' A psychiatrist, who made a diagnosis of Sandra, wrote among other things that: 'Sandra still wets her bed. She empties the fridge at night and roams around the village. She drowned her brother's rabbit in the shower.' According to statements from Sandra, it is her stepfather that has been so brutally hitting her. Mrs H said of Sandra: "This child is always lying. She always wants to be the centre of attention and have everything to herself. She only wanted to wash Tobias' rabbit." Sandra is placed with a foster family, who sends her back again a year later, because their adopted child didn't get on with Sandra.

The social worker assigned by the welfare office to spend 20 hours a week with the family as a supervisor evaluated Mrs H as being 'alert and authentic'. She wanted to show her by her own example that there are other ways of treating children than always reacting aggressively. She said: 'I'm trying to broaden Mrs H's perspective. I want to strengthen her self-confidence'. She repeatedly took Mrs H away from the family for half a day to give her a sense of herself. She also once took Sandra home with her for the weekend.

Mrs H wanted the child welfare office to leave her in peace for good. She doesn't want anyone ever again interfering with her family. She said: 'Sandra and I are now getting closer. I used to push her away when she wanted to give me a kiss. I don't do that anymore.'

At the custody hearing Mrs H says of the squalid conditions in her flat that: 'I can only tidy up when the children are not there.' As to the bruise on Martin's forehead she says, 'He hits his head against the bed at night. Annabell used to do that, my husband too.'

In the end the court rules that Sandra should be sent to live with a foster family as soon as possible. The judge orders Mrs H and her husband to undergo family therapy. He threatens her that if she refuses to do so she will also lose her other children. "

This story clearly demonstrates how, in bonding trauma situations, the victims of one generation become the perpetrators of the next. Mrs H passes on the neglect and violence she experienced in her own childhood onto her own children and, armed with her defiantly independent survival self, avoids recognising the reality of her life. Her survival part idealises her totally chaotic situation. She is incapable of empathising with her children, as that would require contact with her split-off trauma, which would endanger her. The only option available to her, therefore, is to bring up her children according to the strategy dictated by her own survival self – i.e. despite all her own needs, to separate and become independent from her mother as soon as possible, to expect nothing from her, and outwardly to be submissive while internally remaining deeply mistrustful of all adults. Mrs H also directs her mistrust, developed in childhood from her alcohol-dependent mother and father, towards her children. She doesn't believe them when something hurts them, she hits them, denies the severity and insensitivity with which she mistreats her children, accuses her children of lying and blames them for their problems. She sees in her children all the negative characteristics her survival self is unable to see in herself. Her deluded ability to love seeks affection and support from older men, but she is incapable of consciously seeing their violent and inappropriate behaviour and is unable to protect her children from them, because to do so would mean coming into contact with the traumatising experiences of violence and neglect in her own childhood. She is incapable of this. Her main survival strategy here involves rapidly separating from them, bringing her relationships to sudden endings. She does not learn from her negative experiences and soon starts another relationship with another traumatised man.

She doesn't see the interventions of the child welfare office as helpful to her – on the contrary, she sees them as attacks on her established form of existence, which is made up of her survival strategies for adapting to the many splits in her soul. She defends herself using every means available, even physically in emergency situations such as when the child welfare office tries to thwart her survival strategy because of the danger posed to the child. When she gives birth to her children, she is probably able to an extent to embrace the traumatised parts of her soul as a self-comforting strategy, and partially feign an appearance of normality. At least she's not alone. She's not really a mother to her children, but instead searches for a mother for her own traumatised and abandoned inner child. This explains why she always has one more child when the others become too old for this kind of twisted mothering and increasingly start to cause her problems. If one of her children comes too close to the wounded part of her soul, she feels threatened and pushes the child away even becoming violent.

As a result, the interventions by the child welfare office, social workers and judges do not have the desired result, as long as the root of the problem is not addressed, i.e. the splits in Mrs H's soul. When a child is taken away from a woman who has suffered bonding trauma and is placed in custody, she will have another child quickly, because her emotionally weakened survival self is unaware of the responsibility of having children. Indeed, the ability for self-reflection is massively restricted for people who have experienced bonding trauma for fear of what will emerge within them if they try to deal with it.

So anyone from outside who tries to intervene in a family environment that has been affected by violence, abuse, incest and addiction for generations is right in believing that they are dealing with a survival system that is kept functional through splitting. The central figure of the entangled relationship chaos in such cases is usually the mother who always attracts men with abusive tendencies also having suffered bonding trauma. Also the children have to be part of this system. In their emotional dependence they cannot escape the pull of love mixed with violence, and in a relatively short time must develop both the attitudes of victim and of abuser. For those who intervene, supervise, establish boundaries or provide support there is always the risk that they too will become entangled in the system of the people involved.

As we saw in this case many professionals tried to take control away from Mrs H. They recognise the abusive component in her. Accusatory 'you-messages' (see Schulz von Thun, 1992), as in the case of this child welfare officer ("You are the type of mother who…") serve only to provoke a person's survival self. This survival self defends itself all the more vehemently against this insight into the reality of the person's life and mobilises all its powers of resistance, directing all the bottled up feelings of hate against the helper. Establishing limits without becoming entangled is only possible using 'I-messages', for example with the statement: "I am representing here the public interest and we will intervene here to stop your children falling into bad ways and being mistreated by anyone. As long as I am working with this family, this will never happen again. I recognise that there are parts of you that are unable to see things this way".

Specialists working with such cases, such as the social

workers acting as supervisors, may be very sensitive to the client's childhood and their resulting needy or wounded trauma parts. However, this places them in danger of only seeing the client as a victim and playing down the abusive element. The 'alert' aspect of Mrs H is, at best, the mistrusting, observing survival element, while the part of Mrs H that is 'authentic' cannot be ascertained from the case report. The social workers' wanting to be a model of a proper and violence-free upbringing is not sufficient.

So in social institutions, the splits in a client's soul are often reflected in those of the team of helpers. Some will only see the abuser and survival parts and push for monitoring and punitive measures. Others will only experience the victim and trauma parts and want to offer the client and their family system increasing support and help. It can even happen that members of psycho-social professional groups, when ignorant of dissociative disorders and personality splits, experience the victim element of the client as abusive and the abuser element as victimised. This is also seen clearly in this case study: when Mrs H draws attention to the abuse of her children by her ex-husband and asks for help, nobody at the child welfare office believed her. On the other hand, her unfeeling and aggressive educational methods are not pointed out to her by the social workers, who instead regard her with pity.

A way out of these unhealthy entanglements between social workers and clients is, in my opinion, offered by viewing both the victim and abusive elements of the client together, addressing them properly and appropriately through counselling and legal measures. It is of little help to work only with the psychologically disturbed children by putting them in special day centres, homes or foster families or implementing educational support. Children are too symbiotically entangled with their parents, especially their mothers. It is also of limited use to try and act as a role model to the mother in bringing up her children in the hope that she will develop maternal skills as a result. Without clearly showing these mothers that their own traumatic childhood experiences and the resulting splits are present in *everything* they do – (even when they try to hide it from themselves and others by preserving an image of normality) and restricting their survival strategies (which are damaging both to themselves and others), encouraging them to undergo proper therapeutic treatment to enable them to deal with the trauma-induced splits, nothing will change. In professional institutions, the team of helpers should be able to see clearly what is going on psychologically with a traumatised mother and how the splits are already affecting the development of her children, splitting them as well. The members of such a professional team need to be able to support each other fully in this task, developing the personal and professional confidence and courage required to confront such mothers and fathers with the reality of their traumas, reflecting their survival elements openly, setting clear boundaries for the abusive elements and offering support to the victimised elements. If this is not done their children will not escape the presence of splits in their own souls. Daughters of mothers and fathers who have suffered bonding trauma most likely will become the next generation of confused mothers, and aggressive fathers.

6.7 Delusional Entanglements

In the mirror that is his mother, the child discovers the foundations for his psychological identity and a sense of who he is. If the mother's soul is a mirror distorted by split-off and entangled parts of her soul, however, the child will have no clear point of reference for his own core identity. Because the mother herself does not understand her own feelings, she is unable to distinguish between hers and those of her offspring. The children are also unable to learn which feelings are their own and which belong to their mother. They fail to recognise themselves in their emotionally entangled mother. The child's identity is confused because their mother is confused. In contact with his mother, a child absorbs all the disruption in which the mother's soul is entangled.

Physical contact with a sexually traumatised mother is disturbing. Physical intimacy such as hugging is confused with sexual feelings, and the mother often sees in the child someone who excited her sexually and was violent towards her as a child. The child must therefore protect himself from his mother and retreat from her, despite wanting nothing more than to be close to her. The result of this is a split between one part of the child's soul that is desperately seeking the mother's love, and another part that is very cautious because of her chaotic and highly sexualised feelings and behaviour. The alternative would be either to surrender to the feelings of abandonment or to be become entangled in the mother's sexual trauma. Intimacy can only occur if the child gives up his desire to achieve his own delimited identity. Paradoxically, this means the child can only obtain a sense of identity through the mother by losing touch with his own reality.

When the child does engage with the mother's traumatised soul, he must accept that what his mother sees and feels as she looks at him is someone completely different; she sees someone who physically and sexually abused her. The child identifies himself with the mother, and therefore with the entangled victim and abuser parts of her soul. Thus, through contact with his mother, a reflection is created in the child's soul of both the abuser and the victim. It is now both rapist and rape victim in one person.

When part of the child adopts this reflection as his identity, he becomes crazy and confused, not knowing who he is. This may cause uncertainty as to the child's sexual identity, since an abused girl will also carry a reflection of the male abuser in a part of her soul and is unable to understand if this part belongs to her or not.

People who had such bonding experiences feel out of control in their confusion. They are unable to trust their feelings or know really who they are – in psychiatric terminology this is the component of the schizophrenic. In the model of splits of the soul this corresponds to a form of a survival self with a strong desire for cognitive clarity since any emotional intimacy puts them close to 'psychotic' delusional, states, which to them seem totally real. In my theory this corresponds with the activation of traumatic feelings originating through symbiotic contact with the mother.

Sexualised lack of relationships

To illustrate the kind of deep psychological insecurity bonding system trauma can cause, I have selected some notes a client left with me. He had had many psychotic episodes during which he would imagine himself manically on the one hand, as a man no woman could resist, and on the other with paranoia as a potential child abuser and murderer. The background to his family history, from what was reconstructed over a number of constellations, consisted in his grandmother supposedly having had extramarital affairs and apparently having murdered a child born of one of these affairs, a sister to my client's mother; and his mother had been sexually abused by her father.

The client also remembered being sexually abused as a child by his father. "I'm sitting in the cafe and starting to take notes. As always, I write down all my feelings and thoughts. Today I feel hate for what I perceive as ugly people and as disgusting men. The disgust is sexual and fat. At the same time, I'm fascinated by some men. Cool and creative and masculine, visibly strong men. Sometimes a whole month passes without my having sexual feelings about men; then they come again. Despite my sexual feelings for men being an issue for a long time now, the thought of leading a gay or bisexual life is not really acceptable to me. I don't want it; I'm not female after all. Also, I continue to have sexual feelings for women. But I always feel insecure when I find men attractive. Three or four years back, homosexuality would somehow have made sense to me. Especially after smoking dope, I would feel this exaggerated, slightly crazy admiration for other boys. But now I'm more comfortable with myself, I'm able to leave others be; before I would have found them either horrible or great.

"But maybe homosexuality has nothing to do with admiration and it's a matter of sexual feelings instead – but that doesn't make things any better for me. Sometimes I have a bad conscience, because I'm so obsessed with the issue of sexuality, and there are plenty more important things in life.

"For two to three months now I've been seeing a girl. Hey, when I think about that, I feel better. She's a really cool girl. Sometimes I feel madly in love. Other times I feel disgust and hate. On the one hand, I'm happy that I've fallen in love with a girl (in a way I've never felt before); on the other hand, I still feel unsure whether it's not just something else (friendship, lust, inherited feelings of love from the incest in my family). When I kiss this girl, when she kisses me, I lose awareness of my body, and I find the physical contact uncomfortable. Sometimes, when I've had something to drink, I stop to think for a minute, and then I enjoy the contact. I also don't feel much during sex. I think my sexuality is very weak at the moment. Sometimes I'm happy with it like this, as I'd be afraid of a strong, powerful sexuality. Since my second psychotic episode, I've been afraid to sleep with a girl because I was worried I'd become violent in the heat of sexual arousal. But now, thank God, I don't think so often about this during sex.

"I don't have a bad conscience towards the girl because I feel and think so many strange and bad things, which would definitely shock and repel her, since I'm honest when it comes to the feeling I have now

"My basic feeling can usually be described as follows: I have no relationship to the world. I go for a walk, I sit in a cafe, I talk with friends, I eat with my family, I have an appointment with my therapist during which I experience many different emotional states, I'm angry, I'm psyched up, I'm a bit sad, and then I'm also in love. But there's no real feeling, no certainty, no inner peace. Everything flutters and shines, as if I'm unable to respond to the life around me. There are some faces that trigger something in me, but that's all twisted and sick.

"I try to hold on to things: smoking, drinking coffee and talking about my problems; I cling on to painting, making music, writing. But I can't hold on to people. But then maybe that's also not true. I still don't know what it would be like to interact properly with myself and the people around me."

A bonding trauma situation essentially renders a person incapable of having relationships, because it stands in the way of authentic feelings and emotional intimacy. The survival self is caught up in reflections and contemplation, the trauma self is in the middle of the chaos of fear, anger, mistrust, sexual arousal, and feelings of shame and guilt. Sexuality as the source of lustful encounters between man and woman comes with the idea that this sexuality has caused harm and been the cause of rapes, incest, and illegitimate children and their disposal. Sexual desire is confused as to what it should be directed towards; it can apply equally to men, women and children, all at the same time. It is indistinguishable from loving affection. Equally, there is no difference between parental love and love in a partnership. The survival self therefore keeps as great a distance as possible from interpersonal relationships, for it is afraid of dragging the trauma self into the abyss of the psychosis.

For the client quoted above, it was, among other things, a very important realisation to learn that his psychotic experiences were triggered by interpersonal intimacy. This increasingly helped him find a way to escape the many splits in his soul.

Manic Love

This example is an excerpt from a man's description of a manic episode: "Love, I felt love, a limitless love for J, for the children, for E, for my pupils and colleagues. I felt a love that couldn't be understood rationally. At the same time my thoughts began to race: who was I, what is the world, what is life? Everything had its meaning, and order. Good and bad were abolished. I wrote confusing texts about healing, also a couple of songs. I was out of synch with normality – but what was normal? Who was I? I was haunted by the idea that I had a special calling. Am I perhaps a reincarnation of Jesus? Is it my calling to be the president of the United States? I started drawing up a list of leaders in the staff room. But then I'd soon drop such thoughts. A lot came and went.

"The contact between me and my children, my partner and my mentally handicapped pupils was intense. In lessons and when with them I was able to concentrate in a way I'd never known before. I was so incredibly alert, but then, during the breaks, I would feel exhausted from all the concentration and my manic thoughts unconnected with the lessons. One good experience from school was the performance at the Christmas party. I was a priest in the nativity play. Before going on stage I sat down in a neighbouring room and prayed for strength. Afterwards I was able to give a strong performance in the play. Some of my colleagues found me strange; others gave me the feedback that I'd played my role very well, like a real priest!

"In the weeks running up to Christmas, an amazing amount of things went on inside me. I remember how, at the beginning, I would note down my characteristics, what I'm like, on index cards. It was if a new ordering of my life were about to begin. My religious feelings had a strong influence on me. I had a powerful urge to attend church regularly, and I said my prayers. I read the Bible with fresh eyes.

"My partner found it all a bit suspicious. At home the mineral water crates were piling up, because another of my special perceptions had been that I could identify the effects of different mineral waters on my emotional balance. 'Steinsieker'[6] encouraged simple reflection when my thoughts were racing too much, 'Marienbrunnen' gave me tranquillity and strength, 'Christinenbrunnen' was refreshing, stimulating when I felt tired and weak. I consciously chose the type of water and developed a 'mineral water theory', which I sent to a well-known homeopath. He confirmed categorically what my sense had been telling me – it was well known that mineral water had certain healing effects. I felt encouraged by this confirmation of my perceptions, but admit that my 'great findings' were old hat."

In their psychotic phases, people entangled in a bonding system trauma will live out their confused feelings. These intense feelings – their mania is mostly about illusionary love – drive them to confused thoughts. Since they don't understand the origin of these feelings, which stem from past traumatisations in their family, they look for explanations in their current experience. Under the influence of these feelings, they manufacture all kinds of illusory benefits in their immediate present. They sense that something really intense is happening in them, but they can't find the key to the solution of the riddle, which the bonding with their parents or grandparents buried somewhere deep inside their souls. In their manic phases, they search feverishly for this key and in so doing run a high risk of jeopardising what their lives have been up until now. They can also bring misfortune on others. Only the truth about what really lies behind their intense feelings can calm them and bring a permanent stop to their craziness. Frequently

[6] These are types of mineral water in Germany.

symptoms of manic love often include incestuous relationships that result in children; or relationships between high-status men and low-status and dependent girls and women that give rise to children whose origin is then hidden or who are disposed of. Manic love is an attempt to compensate for an extreme lack of love.

7

Living in Survival Mode

There are many ways we can choose to deal with our internal splits and blockages, some more conscious and others less so. This is the world of the survival self, that I will try and give a brief picture of in this chapter. After a traumatic experience some people spend most of their lives in survival mode.

7.1 Hyperactivity

Afraid of re-connecting with their trauma, people with splits in their souls try and protect themselves from the idea that the problems they experience in their lives are the result of traumatisation by developing survival strategies. They seek solutions to the problems from the past in the present, creating illusions of a happier future. Unable or unwilling to address what is inside them, they pin their hopes for a better future on attempting to bring about changes in the outside world. In previous chapters I have described the many different forms of interpersonal entanglements that result from these strategies, giving rise to conflicts in relationships and in the educational, social and political spheres. These survival strategies can actually trigger wars in families and between nations. The survival self sees strategies that avoid confronting the deep emotional pain as the only form of existence possible, as a protection and vindication of the person in conflict situations, and this is the reason why society and political institutions are built up on survival strategies. It would be interesting to do a closer study of the particular collective traumas that cause entire societies to resort to extreme strategies of avoidance, control, compensation and illusion.

Supporting traumatised people in their attempts to change their environment, other people or society does not in the end help them. A woman who complains of her husband or partner's violent behaviour will even so stay with him as long as the relationship complies with the needs of her psychological splits and the resulting illusions. If she were supported to leave this partner, without having changed something within herself, she would most likely move on to another partner with whom she would experience the same relationship difficulties. Similarly, traumatised parents will not be any better off if they are given advice about how to bring up their hyperactive, aggressive or drug-using children, or if attempts are made to 'heal' the children. Traumatised parents often use their children as an outlet for the psychological pressure they feel, projecting their own trauma feelings onto their children. Additionally, in their dependency, children willingly accept this burden, thereby relieving their parents. Similarly, as long as people who complain of bullying at work do not see their own contribution to the problem, which may even have caused the bullying in the first place, they will make no progress. With any psychological crisis there is always the chance to change something internally, but this means having the courage to get to know and accept the state of one's own soul and to feel the pain. Only then will the pressure on the survival self to be outwardly hyperactive gradually ease.

"I'm not given a hearing"

A woman, whose husband had been sadistically torturing their child since it was small, came to me for therapeutic advice as to how she should deal with the situation. She had already seen many doctors, psychologists and lawyers to organise support against her husband, but had always experienced rejection and sometimes humiliation. She wrote to members of parliament, had meetings with local politicians, contacted the police and the office of the public prosecutor because she suspected that her husband had not only tortured and abused his own child, but other children too, and was still doing so. Everywhere she went her pleas fell on deaf ears, her concerns and needs not given a hearing. Her charge against her husband for child abuse was rejected by the public prosecutor.

I felt a lot of sympathy for her heavy fate, and her sense of impotence was strong. My sense also was that there must be something in her own soul that led her to get involved with this man and marry him in the first place. It did not seem to me to be just chance. When she spoke about him, she wasn't just very afraid of and angry with him; she would keep thinking about how he could be helped to stop being an abuser.

Indeed, in the subsequent therapeutic consultations her own life story became clearer, a story that was quite incredible. During the civil war in her country, as a baby within an ethnic minority, she was stolen from her biological mother by a military officer, and given to his wife as consolation for a miscarriage, and she grew up believing that these people were her parents. Her whole picture of her family and her entire past was stood on its head. With this new and painful realisation, however, she felt much more at ease and could understand what it was that had been puzzling her for her whole life about her (supposed) parents and siblings. As a result she was able to adopt a clearer stance in her behaviour towards the authorities and social organisations. She could recognise more clearly from whom she could expect to receive help, support and understanding for her situation and from whom not; and who, on the contrary, were even then continuing to try to exploit her for their own interests. She realised that she had seen in her husband a similarly helpless being in his soul as she had concealed in her own soul. Without this unconscious coalition between the traumatised childhood part of her own soul with that of her ex-husband, she was now much more capable of taking action against him. She increasingly came to recognise what was essential and important to her in her life.

7.2 Suppressing Symptoms

Problems that originate from splits in the soul express themselves through symptoms such as feelings of restlessness, insomnia, anxiety, despondency, confusion, etc. as well as countless different physical symptoms. Like physical illnesses, psychic disorders are the means of expression of the split-off trauma-self. The survival self therefore tries to suppress and dispel these symptoms, whose origins it doesn't understand.

Flight into drugs

Drug use is the most prevalent method of covering rising trauma feelings. Day-to-day drugs, like coffee, cigarettes and alcohol are for the survival self the simplest means of obtaining short-term relief when traumatised personality parts make their presence felt. They dampen and conceal nervousness, fear, loneliness, inner emptiness, despair, hopelessness or confusion. The active substances in drugs only serve temporarily however; in the long run the effects become increasingly diminished as the metabolism of the body and brain becomes used to them and neutralises their effects. As a result, there is a tendency for the survival self to increase the dosage. Drug addiction of some kind is almost inevitable when trauma is in the background. When everyday drugs are no longer enough to suppress the symptoms that threaten the survival self, high potency drugs are only a small step away.

Drug use can also be a way of making oneself independent of intimate relationships, for by intimate relationships it is highly likely that the trauma feelings will be aroused. For example, instead of persisting in futile conflicts with parents and enduring parents' ongoing disputes, many adolescents accept friends' offers to get high on marihuana, even knowing that this may damage their brains and cause their school performance to suffer. They see no other means of escaping their problems.

This was the case with Martin, for example. He was a highly sensitive boy, and one could see how much he longed for a warm relationship with his mother, who was cold and inaccessible. Of his father he said that he had tried to win his attention and recognition, but without result; his father would only yell and explode at the slightest incident.

A drug offers a substitute for the good feelings we typically strive for as humans: happiness, contentment, the feeling of being loved and valued, being able to experience oneself and feel alive. The more distanced the survival self becomes from intimate relationships by the use of drugs, the greater the dependence on the drugs. Consequently, it is impossible for a therapist to persuade someone from addiction if one doesn't understand what the drug is a substitute for. When a client came to understand that her addiction to chocolate originated from the fact that she was very lonely as a child and took refuge in sweets, she was then able to embrace her neglected inner child, keeping her addicted survival part at bay using the healthy part of her soul. No one will desist from addiction to work and gambling, for example, unless he is able to see clearly the purpose of the behaviour within his psychological structure. With workaholism, for example, trauma-based anxiety and feelings of anger and grief are suppressed by the survival self by constant activity.

"She worked for two!"

"My grandmother did the work of two men. That meant something on a farm". That's how a seminar participant described her grandmother. At first this sentence could be understood to mean that her grandmother's labours on the farm were the equivalent of the work done by two men. However, the constellation suggested that the grandmother had passed her children off to her husband as his, and that instead they may have been the children of her lover, the other man. So it seemed that the mother of the participant might have had a different father than had been believed so far. The sentence "The grandmother did the work of two men" seemed to take on a completely different meaning for the client. There had indeed been two men for whom the grandmother 'worked': the cheated husband and her secret lover. The seminar participant had always had a very loving bond with her grandmother, and after the constellation, as this family secret came to light, she said that she felt relieved and freer. By her survival strategies, she had also spent her whole life working hard, almost to the point of physical breakdown, always trying to be a 'good girl' and not trusting of men. Her daughter, who had suffered several psychotic episodes, during the first had imagined herself as a great actress; by her delusional behaviour she had unconsciously revealed the deception, exposing the grandmother as an actress in her deception of her husband.

7.3 Eliminating Illnesses

The survival self wants to get rid of illnesses quickly, and expects doctors and therapists to be able to cure them immediately. But if we assume that symptoms of illnesses are in fact symptoms of the traumatised part, we can see that the removal of the symptom can only be successful if the trauma is addressed. The trauma self, representing the memory of trauma experiences, essentially controls the entire body, so illnesses that result from traumas are software rather than hardware problems. It is not the hardware of the computer that needs repairing, but the programs that control the body and its organ functions that must be changed and rewritten.

Traditional medicine supports the survival self's attempt to rid itself of its split-off life experiences by elevating the status of symptoms that indicate a traumatisation to the status of purely physical illness. Without an understanding of the background to the symptoms and their deep, biographical significance for an individual, the complaints presented by a client are understood indiscriminately as treatable physical illnesses. Viewed logically, this means that there is little differentiation between the consequences, conditions and causes of a phenomenon. Every symptom is in principle simultaneously cause, condition and consequence. The goal of treatment therefore becomes freedom from symptoms. Achieving this requires the use of:

- medication to reduce pain, lower blood pressure, reduce fear, alter depressive moods, curb confused thoughts, etc;
- operations that remove the suspected source of the symptoms;
- physical therapy to try and alleviate the symptoms.

Medical treatment is often life saving because the traumatic splits have been affecting the body for so long that it has lost its ability to balance and manage itself. So in the short term conventional medicine is indeed able to change symptoms.

Pain, pressure, inflammation, fever, fear, confusion are all reduced or eliminated temporarily following treatment. In the long term, however, symptoms based on underlying traumatic experiences do not prove successfully treatable. With the increasing duration of treatment, what were originally temporary conditions are likely to become chronic. The longer medication is taken, the more extensive are the side effects, which means that another medication must be taken to compensate for the side effects of the first. It is not only the mentally ill, who undergo long-term treatment with psychotherapeutic drugs, and end up in these infinite medicinally-induced loops. People with neurodermatitis, rheumatism and asthma, for example, are familiar with this ever increasing spiral of medical treatment.

The suppression of a symptom can also result in that symptom being replaced by another. Physical pain can seem easier to bear than psychological pain. When I personally feel physical pain I have become accustomed to contemplating what traumatic conflict it might symbolise. Constellations can help us perceive the language of symptoms more clearly. In such cases a client may choose a representative for his or her symptom. Some illness symptoms turn out to be the survival self attempting to suppress the memory of trauma.

If the body undergoes an intensive treatment of physical symptoms that represent the secret expression of the person's traumatic experiences, there is a risk that the defensive mechanisms will break down and the traumatic memory will be set free. The person's consciousness will then be overrun by the hitherto suppressed trauma experiences.

"The body and the hot air balloon"

A patient told me that she became extremely suicidal after having been to a Chiropractor whose treatment had relaxed her tensed up and twisted spine. However, her unconscious traumatic experiences had caused so many splits within her that she had almost entirely lost the feeling of her body and had, so to speak, given her entire body over to her trauma self. Her image of the situation was that "my soul is hanging in the sky like a hot air balloon and below it lies my body connected to the hot air balloon by a thin cord." After her physical treatment the suppressed trauma feelings held in her numbed body flooded her consciousness and overwhelmed her. To her despairing survival self, committing suicide or going mad seemed to be the only escape when the suppression of the traumatic memories was no longer possible.

Undoubtedly cancer has many different causes; however with patients that come to me for therapeutic help it is sometimes possible to indentify clear connections between the cancer symptoms and the splits and entanglements in their souls. From my observations, bonding trauma and bonding system trauma increase the likelihood of severe physical illness among those who cannot openly express their feelings of fear, anger and grief and emotional pain within the family, instead suppressing them deep inside. An aggressive survival part, for example, that constantly fights internally will physically destroy itself in the process.

Medical procedures performed on vital organs are drastic interventions. With organs that come in pairs, such as the kidneys, it is possible that the remaining, healthy organ will compensate for the lost function of the damaged organ that is removed in the operation. However, without an understanding of the traumatic background to the organ failure, this hope can be deceptive, as the example below makes clear. Whether a heart operation can really solve the problem of the underlying trauma is extremely questionable. I clearly remember this case of a man who came to one of my seminars with a heart problem.

"I'm close to tearing apart!"

Mr F is a craftsman with his own company. For him a 60-hour working week is not uncommon. He had his first heart operation four years previously. His wife is very worried about him; she fears he will have another heart attack and so she convinced him to attend my seminar. He spends the first two days of the seminar sitting on his chair silently, uncommunicative. He observes everything keenly, but is not yet willing to take on representations. On the third day he found the courage to do a constellation for himself. The representative for his heart immediately had a feeling of being unable to breathe and of being torn in two directions. His survival part began going round and round in a circle, until finally collapsing on the floor in exhaustion.

The constellation showed that the background to the strain on Mr F's heart was connected with his father's loss of his homeland during the war. In addition, his mother had lost her brother also during the war. A deep, heavy feeling of grief lay over the representations of the maternal and paternal systems of origin. With part of his soul, Mr F was drawn into his parent's maelstrom of grief. The other part of him was looking around desperately for a way out of this oppressive family climate, without finding one. Consequently, in his survival self, he could only continue turning in circles faster and faster until exhausted. I suggested Mr F place a representative for his parents' emotional pain in the constellation without himself getting drawn into their whirlpool of despair and grief. On the next day of the seminar, Mr F felt as if he had been saved.

8
Inner Healing

As inside, so also outside

I understand the term 'inner healing' to mean a process that looks for solutions from within the soul, not in the outside world. Inner healing means no longer being dependent on what others do or expect of you. Those who follow a path of inner healing are confident that their external problems will be solved when an inner willingness exists. The healthy self will then no longer be pressurised into acting by the survival self. The path of inner healing even views external problems first and foremost as an opportunity to understand oneself better, and to enquire as to why the soul might currently seem in need of a particular problem. The process of coming to terms with splits in the soul, and becoming free of them is neither easy nor comfortable a path to follow. Ultimately, however, it may prove to be the shortest and most effective path.

In my experience, there are different processes involved in the step-by-step movement towards a state of inner healing.

8.1 Recognising Splits

First and foremost are the recognition and acceptance of the fact of splits in the soul. A characteristic feature of a split soul is that the separated parts no longer have any connection with each other; people who have splits in their souls can only perceive, feel, think and act with consciousness in one part of their soul at a time. They can only be conscious in a survival part, or in another part of themselves that has managed to remain healthy. Becoming aware of the splits and recognising the daily situations that trigger the changes from one personality to another is an important first step on the path to inner healing.

In the following example a patient describes her experience after a therapy session in which we worked on the internal perpetrator and victim parts that were irreconcilably opposed to each other. Her mother had not wanted her since she was conceived through an extra-marital relationship, and the father had impregnated two other women at the same time. The patient survived her mother's attempts to abort her, as well as later attempts to kill her after she was born. However, she had absorbed her mother's destructive energy and the other parts of her soul had to fight this, defending themselves and keeping the self-destructive part at bay. This self-destructive part of her that had merged with the violent and hostile part of the mother – in technical terminology we would speak here of 'perpetrator introjects' (Huber, 2003) – continuously drew attention to the attacks the mother had directed towards her in her childhood.

"It won't kill you. Carry on!"

"At first, after the last session, I had lots of circular thoughts; I wanted to explore and fathom everything out. When I was done, I felt emotions boiling up in me: doubt, anger and destructiveness. I spoke to this protesting part: 'What is it you need? What can I do for you to make you feel better?'

"I rode my bike out into the peaceful countryside to pick blackberries. I was drawn by a steep hillside of gleaming berries. When my container was nearly full, I spotted some more blackberries right up at the top. I climbed up and started picking. Suddenly the container slipped from my hand and I fell over backwards. When I came to and opened my eyes, I was lying on the lower part of the hillside in the wet grass. I checked nothing was broken and was grateful my fall had been cushioned. Still in a daze, I heard a voice within me ordering me to 'Keep on picking while you're still in one piece.' I got up automatically and started picking again. Suddenly I stopped and recognised the situation. The voice inside me was violent and devoid of compassion. I realised that there are many different parts in me: a part that wants to destroy me, another that protects me and another that will abandon my body in an emergency.

"I experienced something similar 25 years ago, when I wrote off my car; a destructive force that had taken over the car gripped me. I was speeding away from a stop sign towards another sign 150 metres away. Then suddenly the car flipped over onto its roof. It was a total wreck. Apart from the shock and some gentle whiplash, I escaped unscathed. I felt the destructive energy as something that came from outside, also like the 'light energy' that protects me.

"I've since discovered some connections. When I was eight-and-half years old, I had to help loading the hay. The trailer was already overloaded when my mother called to me to 'Stamp down the hay at the back so it doesn't fall.' The next moment she drove the tractor forwards and I fell off the back of the trailer hitting the ground hard and gasping for air. My mother came over and said to me: 'It won't kill you. Lie down over there under that tree until the dizziness is gone.' My back hurt for weeks afterwards.

"Aged 35, I sought medical advice for my back pain. The X-ray showed that two vertebrae in the thoracic area were wedged together. The doctor said: 'You must have suffered a heavy fall in your childhood.'

"As a child I was full of questions about the world

around me. Today I have the same curiosity about my inner world. How can I trust myself when one part of me wants to harm or kill me? There's another part of me that trusts blindly and so betrays me. That part is foolish and stupid. How then can I trust others? I have the feeling there are lots of small cracks and splits embedded in the larger split between heart and mind."

Bonding trauma in particular gives rise to a complex structure of dissociations and split off parts. The constellations method helps a lot to encourage recognition of the different components of the soul. It provides a kind of X-ray image that highlights the structure of the soul. By selecting a representative for each split, patients are able to see themselves from the outside and witness the interactions of the various components. Seeing things from this observer perspective encourages the development of a new level of consciousness, something that is needed later when integrating the different parts of the soul.

8.2 Understanding the Split-off Parts

In my experience, the constellations method also lends itself superbly to a more intense process of getting to know the individual parts of the personality. The representatives provide the perceptions, feelings and thoughts of the individual parts, giving them expression and a voice. Patients are thus able to see what affects the individual parts and how much or how little contact there is between them. It is precisely in these deeper, fundamental splits that they are able to see just how completely separate from one another the traumatised and survival parts are, and how little notice they take of each other. As a rule, the survival part ignores the traumatised part, turns away from it, rejects it, labels it a malingerer, considers it pointless and dangerous to deal with, and is afraid that it will do uncontrollable things. Understandably, the survival self is strongly opposed to and critical of any psychotherapy that works to reveal these things.

In most cases, the traumatised parts are locked away in their own world where they have no contact with any of the other parts, concerned only with themselves. When represented in a constellation they may freeze, shiver or stagger while gazing at a fixed point on the floor or in the distance. They may stop and stare as if wrapped in cotton wool, feel vulnerable or lie curled up on the floor in desperation. They are each trapped in their own trauma-induced film. Everything I have read about traumatised states in the specialist literature or have observed directly with traumatised people, I have witnessed in the representatives used in constellations.

Fearful and Frozen

According to his doctor's assessment a tumour had been developing in Hermann's brain for over 15 years. After the tumour was surgically removed, Hermann continued to have headaches and feel dizzy and lethargic. And his tumour tissue continued to grow. Through a constellation Hermann wanted to find a psychological explanation for the tumour in his head. The part of his soul that was in contact with this tumour turned out to be an early childhood state that had been denied contact with his mother who had been unable to decide whether to keep him or to have an abortion. In addition, in the background there was also a representative for Hermann's grandmother, who had been completely traumatised and frozen with fear by the war and sexual violence. Death seemed to be the only way she could release herself from this feeling of being frozen. Putting a representative for death into the constellation, we could see that the part of Hermann that was in contact with the tumour was magnetically drawn towards it. This part was drawn to death as the only source of support. Hermann, who was sitting in the outer circle watching the constellation, now admitted that he had suffered terrible anxiety all his life and had often considered suicide. When a representative for the healthy part of his grandmother, the part she had abandoned due to traumatisation, was brought in to the constellation, the picture changed. Suddenly real feelings were possible amongst the representatives, and Hermann sitting in the outer circle was also deeply moved by these feelings. He increasingly opened his heart and was then able to cry from deep within his soul, and to make contact with his split-off part so that it could let go of death as its focus.

This process of making the splits visible can also be done in individual therapy. To do this the patient chooses cushions as place markers for the various components. When they then enter the energy field of the different parts, provided they can be open to them, they are able to sense the various perceptions, physical sensations, moods and attitudes of the different parts of their souls.

8.3 Understanding the Structure of the Parts

The phenomenon of the psychological split is difficult to understand; indeed within the personality structure the survival self refuses to see the splits as real. The experience of therapy, and especially constellations, can create a new consciousness and understanding for the healthy parts of the soul of what splits are, how they come about and how they develop over the course of one's life. A deeper understanding of the overall structure of the soul and the cooperation and conflict between the different parts is an important requirement for psychotherapists if they are to help patients resolve these splits. Without this understanding, they may work on only one part and believe that they have achieved a good result, while another part that has remained in the background will undermine the effect of the therapeutic treatment thereby rendering it useless.

Splits in the soul, especially in cases of abuse, can run so deep that patients are unable to discover their inner selves without having an understanding of their overall psychological structure. One of my patients described her discovery process as follows:

"The devil and the angel"

"The most important thing I discovered was that I have a split. I found that out during my therapy. Then something really important came out during a constellation, namely that 'good' and 'bad' are separated in a split. There's no way you can make that assessment from experience. It's simply a case of two things that become separated from each other. And being separated from each other, that's how the problem arises. That is, because there's no consciousness between the two parts.

"My situation was basically to do with my grandfather, with whom I more or less grew up because my mother would have preferred to have killed me. To my grandfather I was the most important and dearest thing in the world, as he was to me. He was the only person I had. But at the same time he inflicted such incredible, ritual abuse on me. All these ritual stories originate with him. He was part of a pseudo-religious group, which is how it happened. The constellation made it clear to me: my grandfather appeared in two ways in the constellation: one was simply wonderful, the one I love, the one I still love today, a great man, and a loveable person, while the other part was terrorizing me. What it means to split became very clear to me: parts being able to co-exist, although they are really mutually exclusive. You might think you can't have the devil and the angel in one. But you can."

Over a number of constellations this patient became more clearly aware of the overall structure of her personality and the cooperation and conflict between the different parts: "For me it's like there's a part in me that's the 'therapist'. She can really open up, take a step back – and then take control all on her own. She's got no problems whatsoever. She's totally healthy. She's really good. And then I have this other part, the one I always call the 'master of daily life' and who can deal with absolutely everything. There's nothing she can't manage, but she also completely cuts the other parts up and keeps them all in. She says, 'Quiet! There're no problems! It's over! Now get moving!' But how the others feel, those that otherwise wouldn't have come to light, that I didn't know before. That's something I found out through the constellation. How bad they feel – that I didn't know before. Even myself, I didn't feel anything like that, because naturally I've got these other two parts into which I could always escape – I could always run away as soon as things got too much for me. And then I left these other poor children down there in the basement and I stopped caring about them. Naturally that was also a survival strategy. But I really didn't know that. I saw it in the constellation for the first time."

8.4 Reconstructing Reality

The reality of an event is divided by the splitting that follows a trauma. Each of the split parts possesses part of this reality; the truth about the trauma must be reconstructed by the healthy part. In many cases, this healthy part has no conscious knowledge of the trauma. The parents' or grandparents' traumas are also only vaguely known to it. The traumatic truth of the person's biography and family history needs to be brought to light in a step by step manner on the path of inner healing.

Where there is a will, and where the parts of the soul that have been blocking the emotional memory of the trauma can be persuaded to cooperate, it is in my experience usually possible in the constellations process to raise to the level of consciousness all the essential facts that contributed to the creation of the splits. This must happen and these facts must become known if a solution to the split is to be found. Often this means that the presence of the survival part, the part that refuses to look at the trauma, will initially only be partially noticed by the healthy part, and for a while consciously ignored. For the traumatised parts of the soul, which express themselves through feelings and physical sensations, this can create a certain amount of free space in which what happened in terms of traumatisation can be expressed. With severe traumatisation this is not possible in one step and multiple therapy sessions and constellations will be required.

It is particularly true in cases of sexual abuse within the family that the actual incidents in question become fully eradicated from the child's consciousness. The survival self is usually left with no conscious memory of the event and no images. For some patients, it may take many years – during which they may undergo extensive conventional and alternative medical treatments and/or conventional psychotherapy that is not able to uncover things – for them to find the courage to deal with the abuse through a constellation. When they succeed in recognising the truth of their sexual abuse at the hands of close relatives, it represents for them a giant step forward on their path of inner healing. This is something that mainly can occur only in stages.

"It feels logical"

"For me it felt very logical to understand that my father abused me when I was a young child. I basically knew that my father had an inclination towards paedophilia, and there were also witnesses and others who experienced it themselves, my sister and my sister-in-law. When I spoke to my mother about it, she was very shocked and defensive. My boyfriend also got really angry, saying it was ridiculous to make such accusations against someone. But I've started seeing things differently. I've now established much more inner distance to my father and I'm also in the process of resolving this abuse issue in my relationships with men. If I don't it will just keep on being repeated."

Secrets and truths

In situations where there is a background of bonding system trauma it is particularly necessary that patients recognise how much their inner lives are influenced by the family secrets. When patients with strong entanglement symptoms start therapy, the crucial secret usually lies somewhere in the darkest unconscious recesses of their souls.

In most cases, it must be assumed that targeted questions, e.g. to the mother or father, are unlikely to yield any useful information about the secret traumas in the family. Either the memory of the traumatic event has also been split-off in the parent so that they can no longer remember it consciously – for example in the case of a mother who was herself abused as a child and has buried the experience deep within her – or the questions the child asks her parents places them under enormous stress, which they defend against using their tried and tested survival strategies: digression, acting as if they don't understand the question or lying; and if the child is not satisfied with this, she may be accused of being crazy or sick, or having been persuaded into believing these things by friends and psychotherapists.

In my work I have only ever experienced a few cases in which questions asked of the parents lead directly to a family secret being revealed. Sometimes it is more the aunts or cousins who may shed light on such a dark chapter in the parents' or grandparents' history. Otherwise, it is better to steer clear of such questions and trust that, during the course of the therapy, all the facts as far as they are useful, will come to light and that a satisfactory solution can be found on this basis.

Constellations in groups are one of the best ways of detecting these traumatic secrets. In many cases it can be seen in a constellation with sufficient clarity that a trauma is present in a patient's bonding system and underlies the various symptoms in question. However, there will always be a certain haziness and lack of clarity that patients must learn to tolerate.

Essentially, it must be enough for patients to receive some explanation for their previously unexplained feelings, something that they can agree to deep down inside. Then they are able to see that something traumatic is at play in their mother or grandmother or that something important has been kept from them – e.g. who their real father is, or that there were other, disowned children and so on. It is not necessary to know each and every detail about what happened in the past in order to live better with a new reality in the present. What is important is the feeling of greater inner coherence.

"I'm a cuckold child"

With one of my patients, herself a therapist, it became clear over many constellations that there was some doubt as to whether the man she knew as her loving father really was her father. Both her parents died long ago and she was finally able to allow some room in her soul for the possibility that she was an illegitimate child of her mother with a different man.

"At first I simply couldn't believe it. Then it was confirmed again in another constellation, albeit with the same group and the same constellations facilitator. I proceeded to tell lots of people, who all reacted differently. The reactions ranged from shock to disbelief. My patients and I learned from this that something that appears unexpectedly simply needs time to be accepted. The feelings of loss and shame and all the things associated with it also have to be accepted. I'm now able to appreciate even more what I learned from the father who brought me up. It's clear to me now why I was always searching for something in my life, couldn't really settle down and was always interested in things to do with the psyche and other people's problems. I also now understand better *why* I did things in my life. It would be easier if my mother was still alive and I could ask her. On the other hand, I accept it the way it is. There's no way I'll have investigations performed, like opening graves to gather genetic material. I'm no longer interested in the verification. I've found my place now. Initially, the revelation left me completely confused. But I've matured personally, something I can pass on to my patients. I've become more sensitive in my work as a therapist. I now have more understanding for my patients."

She then made a statement that seemed very important to me: "It's clear to me now that a problem is not solved just when things come to light. After they come to light, it takes time and good support from the therapist to be able to accept the truth. This involves going through many different processes until acceptance can come."

It can prove effective in constellations to use a representative for 'the truth'. If this representative is introduced into the constellation by the patient's healthy self and not the survival self – and for this reason I ask the patient to name this person but not to assign him or her a fixed position in the constellation – this representative can sense what is wrong and unclear. If patients are not open to the truth, for example if the truth is boycotted by strong and symbiotically entangled survival parts within the person, then this can be understood by how the truth is used or misused differently by others in the family system in the constellations process. In such cases facts may be cleverly denied and reinterpreted, and the truth becomes just as split as the people who treat it like a mere opinion. Those who cannot trust their own healthy feelings will delude themselves as well as others and surrender to the lies of others without a fight. The real truth only comes with the courage to stand by one's own painful feelings.

8.5 Understanding the Survival Parts in Therapy

Now that I had a better understanding of the principles of splitting, it became my goal in every therapy session that my patients make at least one step further towards accepting and overcoming the splits in their soul. It should become clearer to them that the solution to their problems does not lie in living through their survival parts, because to do so strengthens them even further. They must recognise that the healthy parts need to come into contact with the traumatised parts, because a large amount of energy and fundamental potential of the personality are bound up in these parts. Above all, they need access to the emotional qualities bound up within the traumatised parts – i.e. fear, pain, anger, grief, love – in a form that is free of the traumatic experiences.

To this end, the survival parts must allow the healthy parts to turn towards the traumatised parts. This is not easy for the survival parts because, armed as they are with their many strategies, they feel superior to the healthy parts and are convinced that the only way of dealing with the inner turmoil is to keep it at bay and unconscious. For the first steps towards integration, it must suffice for the survival parts to be still and not go into distractions and diversions as soon as the therapy begins to make headway with the trauma part. During this process it is a great achievement if they can be persuaded to resist interfering by their strategies of avoidance, control and compensation. The survival self must come to trust that their special abilities of avoidance are not lost forever and can still be put to good use in a different form in a new overall structure of the soul.

Without a willingness on the part of the survival self for the trauma to be processed, no real inner change can be possible. As a therapist, I do not want to be used by a patient's survival self so that the psychotherapy becomes a consolidation of the split rather than an integration. It is therefore of enormous importance that the patient clearly formulate his or her issue at the start of every therapeutic session. This creates a framework through which to establish to what extent the survival self parts are currently prepared to permit change to occur. If an attempt to bring a split off trauma experience to the surface is begun too early and without the sanction of the survival part, the process of inner healing will not progress.

"The nagging part"

Once when I attempted to bring a patient directly into contact with a traumatised part, where much of his original vitality had been preserved, the whole therapy session became very heavy going. At the end of the session the patient added a cushion to the other parts, naming it his nagging part. This part was not in the slightest bit convinced that psychotherapy could be of any benefit to it. The next day I received an email from the patient explaining what this was about: "Do you remember when I said at the start that I can't go there, because something was still missing and the decision hasn't been taken yet? That's when the nagging part first made its presence felt, and I ignored it. In a sense, the different parts of me were competing for the upper hand. Each one seems to think it's doing what's right and wants the right things. Last night I tried again to give some space to the nagging part in the hope it would eventually settle down and I could continue with the work. But it wasn't enough. I think I'll only be able to access my vitality when the nagging part is more relaxed and more clarified. "

The next day I received the following message from the patient, which shows how, using his growing understanding, he continued to contemplate his different parts and achieve ever deeper insights as a result: "Something about this nagging part is becoming clear to me. It views everything as nonsense, is no longer interested in therapy and is always nagging me. But there's something else behind it: it's a defiant child that wants to have exactly whatever crosses its mind at any given moment. And when it sees that's not going to happen, it does whatever it wants anyway or starts causing trouble. It manipulates me and stops me saying things that are obvious. For example, initially when I said that I couldn't access my vitality because something was missing, I should have insisted on that because this defiant part of me wanted to be seen. It was in my mind, right before me, but I wanted to move on, to make headway, and so I ignored this part. I didn't want to admit to myself that I still wasn't ready to go there, and even less so when I tried to do it all the same. The defiant part wants to be seen, and if this doesn't happen, then it nags at me until it gets some attention. A different part of me doesn't want to see that part and dismisses it ('Keep quiet, don't be annoying – oh no, not .... again!) and carries on as if the defiant part had said nothing. I want to reach precisely that point that I have set out to reach. No diversions, no interruptions and no additional problems. This is a reluctance I have towards doing another ten years of therapy, which is what I have had in my life up to now. I want to see it through, bring it to a satisfactory close, without anyone getting in between. But it just doesn't work like that, and so I reach the stage where the defiant part gets so large and powerful that nothing else is possible.

"The other thing that stayed with me from the last therapy session is the part that is full of vitality. I feel it a little bit here and there today. This morning, when I woke up, I was less depressed, sad, listless and frustrated than usual. I had the thought that it's actually not that important where I work and where I am. It's much more important, who I am, how I feel, how happy I am with myself. Like that funny book called 'If you are happy with yourself, it doesn't matter who you marry', or something similar. That was a new feeling for me."

Defiant behaviour is normal amongst children between 3 and 4 years old. Defiance is an important stage of psychological development in the process of becoming independent of one's parents and in standing up to them. Only when a child insists that he be allowed to do things on his own does he learn to trust in his own abilities and learn from his mistakes. If a child is denied this defiant phase by his traumatised parents, he remains stuck in this early development stage. Failing to develop into adult competence, this defiant part makes a disruptive appearance during later developmental stages, and the person remains defiant, even if no longer actually dependent on the parents. The defiant childhood parts in students, employees and clients/patients experience all teachers, bosses and psychotherapists as if they were the parents who want to restrict them and against whom they must assert themselves – whatever the cost. In this way, many people waste many of their chances in life.

Purely on the grounds that many patients have been unable to go through these natural developmental stages at the appropriate age, the psychotherapist must be extremely cautious in thinking that they know the best solution to their patients' problems. Faced predominantly with defiant, defensive or overly cautious survival parts it is impossible to impose any kind of therapeutic goals. The first task must be to win confidence in the process of inner healing.

8.6 Liberation of the Traumatised Parts

Anything that gives people strength and power will help them deal better with stressful life situations (Eberspächer, 2002). Accordingly the specialist literature uses the term 'resources'. Resources can be:

- Networks of social support (e.g. family members, friends, people in similar life situations)
- Material security (a home, financial income, safety)
- Inner attitude and outlook (e.g. belief in one's own ability to solve problems)

Teachers, pastoral helpers or psychotherapists can become resources for people in psychological distress. Just the presence of another person who listens attentively and is well-disposed towards them can be a very new experience for many people.

Trauma theory has also adopted the concept of inner resources. For a traumatised person to be able to confront his trauma, he must first have his existing resources consolidated and develop new ones. Luise Reddemann, for example, has developed an array of useful exercises that help trauma victims rediscover their inner stability and learn to deal with their own bodies in a way that promotes healing, before they re-encounter the horror of their trauma. (Reddemann, 2001, 2006) Michaela Huber also describes some self-exercises that can be used to find ways out of trauma-induced helplessness (Huber, 2005).

For a time I introduced resources such as 'help', 'support', 'warmth', 'security' and 'love' into patients' constellations. Although this produced a certain amount of relief at the time, in the end it did not lead to stable solutions. I noticed how when a patient placed the resources into the constellation himself, he often placed them so that they would consolidate him even deeper into the split; the resources basically seemed drawn into strengthening the survival parts rather than the traumatised parts. As long as the patient's survival parts commandeer resources they block any process of inner healing.

Consequently I have since stopped using resources in this way in constellations. For the trauma part, the basic resource required in the first steps of change is for the survival parts to keep still, and for the healthy parts to show an interest and the courage to allow change to occur. The challenge of therapeutic practice essentially lies in discovering behind all the different survival parts, the split-off trauma part within a patient with which it is possible to begin a healing process in that moment. In my experience this means finding those trauma parts, which, despite everything, have remained healthy and retained within them something of the original, life-affirming, life-hungry and innocent human soul.

177

The therapeutic process can allow traumatised parts to re-emerge from their exile in the unconscious and return to the light of the conscious. In doing so they can have new experiences, and a connection between the healthy parts and the traumatised parts can be established. This reduces the pressure on the survival self parts, which then become calmer.

8.7 Solutions to the Four Types of Trauma

The difficulties encountered in overcoming splits in the soul are different for the four types of trauma, and so call for different types of solution.

Existential trauma

With existential trauma it is necessary to re-establish the person's trust in external safety. The idea that something life-threatening could happen at any moment must be overcome. The trauma part must also be able to show the original fear, and the tension stored in the body must be released, by fighting resistance, shouting, lashing out or physical trembling, as Peter Levine's theory of 'somatic experiencing' suggests (Levine, 1998). If this is successful, the survival parts can then gradually risk giving up their control strategies of avoiding dangerous situations under all circumstances.

"I'm allowed to defend myself"

I observed something interesting with a patient who established the cause of her panic attacks as the fact that she was almost strangled by her stepfather when aged two. He had grabbed her by the throat and begun squeezing her powerfully. Accordingly her survival part rejected the traumatised childhood part in her, and she remained with fear and stressful feelings. Since as a child she didn't know that this man was not actually her father, and that she was an illegitimate child of her mother's by another man, besides the fear of death, this traumatised child was also in conflict as to whether or not she was allowed to oppose her 'father'. After the fear of death and the bond with her stepfather were separated in this part of her soul, the patient was able to accept her own trauma-tised child unreservedly, who then could release her panic by crying out and defending herself by thrashing about with her hands and feet.

Trauma of loss

The dead are preserved in the soul for different reasons:

- because a death came too soon for it to be dealt with properly by grief (this is particularly true of children who lose a parent or sibling when young)
- because a death induces a state of shock and panic, and grieving cannot take place (e.g. war situations), or
- because there are feelings of guilt towards the dead person, perhaps due to not having stood by him or her sufficiently during their hour of death.

With trauma of loss, the survival self knows rationally that the absent or dead person is no longer there and will not return, but due to the suppression of feelings such as fear, anger and pain, however, it does not feel the full extent of the pain of loss. Consequently the person lost remains alive and present in the soul by means of the images and fantasies of the survival self, even transferring these internal images of the deceased person onto other living people. A partner might then come to replace a dead mother or father; a parent might transfer the image of a child who died young onto a later child; a new partner might replace a previous partner. This does not support real relationships. Firstly the replacement person is not perceived as the person they really are; secondly real intimacy with the replacement person can never be allowed because if it were the traumatised part would become too stimulated and

succumb to a state of retraumatisation. The traumatised self
remains withdrawn in its sorrow and despair, always hoping
that someone will appear who will console it and release it
from its sorrow.

"Mummy is really dead!"

Johanna lost her mother when she was 13 years old. Her
mother contracted cancer and a short while later died.
Johanna was not present at her mother's death; when her
mother was nearing the end, Johanna was taken to her relatives and when she returned home her mother was no longer
there. Her mother's death was hardly ever discussed in the
family, and also there was hardly anyone outside the family
Johanna could show her suffering to. So she split it up inside
her: one part withdrew from the outside world and was in a
state of despair at her mother's absence; another part
distracted itself from the pain by worrying about her two
younger siblings and thought about how it might fill the gap
left by the absent mother. Mostly Johanna was worried
about her younger brother. However his representative in
the constellation did not feel anywhere near as bad as
expected; he had clearly found his own way of getting over
the death of the mother and the excessive care of the survival
part of his sister was even hampering him. When, at my
prompting, the patient finally found the courage to tell her
survival self that there could be no replacement for the dead
mother, the illusions of the survival self collapsed. It was
overcome with pain and felt now for the first time the full
extent of the pain at the death of the mother. The representative for the traumatised part then crept over towards the
survival part from its corner. The representatives for both
parts of Johanna could now face each other and embrace one
another in their joint pain. Johanna herself then went over to
each of the representatives and began to cry bitterly with
them. This was no longer a superficial crying, but a sobbing
from the depths of her soul.

With a loss trauma, the loss must be finally accepted and the illusion that the beloved dead person will one day return dispelled. The living person must recognise that it is pointless not to want to go on living because the beloved person is no longer there. They must free themselves emotionally from the dead person and leave him or her in peace. It often helps to imagine that the dead person probably would not want the living person to stop living or enjoying life on his or her account; it is a useful image that the dead person would be happier when those who once loved him or her are themselves happy.

Bonding trauma

In bonding trauma the child is unable to attune himself to his parents' feelings and, if traumatised, they remain unpredictable to him. One moment his parents are overflowing with feelings of fear, anger, despair, pain or love; the next they are ice-cold. Only by undergoing a split, just as their parents did, are these children able to survive this situation. Parts of the child's self split off in order to be isolated from any feelings of compassion or symbiotic need, or being tossed back and forth by the parents' emotional chaos. To these parts of the self, feelings are something opaque needing to be kept under control so as to prevent the rug from continually being pulled out from under its feet. The idea of showing one's feelings is viewed by these parts of the self as putting oneself at someone else's mercy, which is indeed the case when the self with the symbiotic needs resurfaces, continually allowing itself to be dragged into other people's feelings. Even as an adult, there will always be tendency to fall back into a state of fear, anger or despair as if in contact with the mother or father. The self that experiences symbiotic needs has the same experiences in relationship with partners, its children, friends or colleagues at work as it does with its parents, and always feels overwhelmed and at the limits of its strengths.

It is necessary, therefore, to escape this either/or situation:

either I have emotional contact with another person which gets difficult, overwhelming and, forces me to try and adapt to others, thus finding no inner peace; or I avoid feelings in relationships, but then have no real contact and am left feeling empty, alone and cold inside.

The process of inner healing requires first and foremost the recognition that one's own mother and father were so caught up in their own traumas that they were unable to understand their child properly. They could only see a distorted image of the child through the veil of their own trauma. Children who empathise with their traumatised mothers and fathers will play down their aggressive and violent sides. In the process of healing they therefore need to abandon the illusion that their parents will ever be able to see things as they really are. This is a bitter and sad truth for the children to accept. It is, however, the only truth that actually makes it possible to put a stop to all the pointless efforts to make their parents love them unconditionally. It means finally learning to distance myself from the emotional chaos of my own parents, accepting that they are traumatised and split, trapped inside themselves; being able to be beside them without having to suppress one's own feelings but able to have feelings of one's own, even if these are different from those of the parents. It means learning to differentiate between what belongs to me and what does not. Which feelings were adopted from my parents and which are my own? Which survival parts belong to them and which are mine? What should I react to and what not? What should I take responsibility for and what not? Finally, it means no longer looking for emotional support in the outside world, in other people, but rather finding it within oneself. This all requires, as described above, contact with that part of my soul that originally managed to remain healthy.

In cases of sexual abuse acceptance of the truth – that sexual abuse took place – is very important. During an abuse situation, a process of splitting begins that leaves one part of the soul believing the abuse never took place, or if something did happen then it happened to someone else. Consequently many people who want to find the truth about their abuse go through the following stages in a constellation in order to reverse the split in their souls:

The revealed truth is first experienced at a distance, as if on a stage. The split-off part of the soul is a spectator, confirming to it that everything is just theatre, not real. The next step involves experiencing oneself on the stage as an actor, as yet with no emotional involvement; there is a curtain, which shrouds the perception of the enactment. As the process continues the curtain becomes more and more transparent. When the liberating cry is finally heard, releasing the feelings that have been suppressed for a lifetime, the curtain tears apart and the patient has arrived at her own emotional truth.

From head to heart

The extent to which perception can be split off through traumatic experiences of violence became clear to me in my work with a patient who, since childhood, had been exposed to the most extreme sexual attacks by her father, even forced to sleep with her father in their marital bed by her mother. We began her constellation with what for her was the worst symptom, her racing pulse. The representative for this part could only feel her body between her throat and her hips. One by one in the course of the constellation we added three additional parts of the patient's soul, each of which could also only feel a limited region of their bodies: their legs, abdomen, the neck, throat and facial area, and the upper part of the head. In accessing the feelings of her heart in this way, the patient was able to create a new integrated core for her physical experience. This process made clearly visible how far her rational thinking had become separated from her body and her sensations, and how much she had always denied her emotional and physical needs through her rationality.

In bonding trauma it is also very important that patients find the clarity they need in order to step out of the perpetrator-victim pattern. One of my patients, who was hated by her mother so much that she was almost killed by her, and who was also severely abused by her grandfather, formulated her experience of stepping out of the perpetrator-victim pattern as follows:

> "This is the most important thing, this is the biggest issue of all – the victim-perpetrator issue. The most interesting thing, however, is when you suddenly realise that just as you are a victim, you are also a perpetrator – on a different level, in a different place and with a different history. There's no such thing as being just a perpetrator or just a victim. Both are in you in equal measure: you might live consciously as one and unconsciously as the other. Or you live actively as one and passively as the other, or one overtly aggressive, the other covertly aggressive. But you always have both in you and you always act out both somehow. This was actually by far the most important thing I took away from my therapy, because the issue of my victim role, my God, well... But what's much more important to me is my perpetrator role. That's what counts for me in my life. When I stop being a perpetrator.. then that's crucial, for example in my relationship. It allows my partner to deal properly with the problems we have between us. If I just keep on playing the victim and complaining the whole time about what I have put up with and never come over to his side, then there can't be any real cooperation. That's true not just for my marriage, for example, but also everywhere else. If everyone would only start dealing with their perpetrator roles, there'd be no problems any more. I understand that now."

You can only give up your perpetrator or abuser role when you accept that you actually are a perpetrator. Those who are able to look at what they have made of having originally been a victim of violence and sexual abuse in their lives, also have the courage to free themselves from their internal perpetrator. As long as someone who has been victimised can only see themselves as a victim, they are denying the existence of the perpetrator within, that they are also in fact a perpetrator.

Bonding system trauma

People who are burdened with guilt will only make progress if they deal with the issues openly. It is helpful if they find someone to work with who does not make moral judgements, listens to their story without playing it down, glossing things over or finding excuses for them. The strength needed to change one's life grows out of the courage to stand by one's own feelings of guilt and shame.

For those who have been in a traumatised bonding system as children, the basic solution consists of disconnecting themselves completely from their family of origin. The survival part, which is entangled with the perpetrators in the system, must be prepared to free itself from the lure of craziness, and the misconception that, because others in the family system *see* them as normal behaviours, violence, abuse, drugs etc. *are* actually normal. The symbiotically entangled survival part, having an emotional connection to the other victims in the system, must let go of the idea that they are able to make amends for something in the system; this part must give up showing sympathy towards the victims and the perpetrators in the system, and the illusion that there is help in these feelings. The person must accept the truth of what happened, finding their own way to manage love, sexuality and anger. For children in a traumatised bonding system there is no choice: they can only bond with their entangled parents and reproduce their splits in their own souls at the expense of their identity. Only as an adult can one find the strength to see through and step out of this emotional dynamic that creates so much confusion with one's own identity.

8.8 Liberation from Childhood Dependence

If we don't understand the forces of emotional and psychological bonding, it is incomprehensible why even adults seem unable to separate themselves from their mothers or fathers. While many may manage to do this to a degree, getting their own flat and even their own family, internally they remain fixated on their mothers, and sometimes their fathers too. They will neglect their partners and children, and their thoughts are constantly oriented towards their parents. They sacrifice themselves to this until the day they die, subordinating their lives to their parents' lives.

To me this clarifies a particular characteristic of human existence: we are group creatures, and can only survive as a group. The human species exists in groups – family units, clans, peoples and nations. From the perspective of biological survival, the group is more important than its individual members; so long as a sufficient number of the group survive, the group will continue to exist. In this sense, the forces of bonding help us as individuals, guaranteeing our individual survival within the group. But at the same time these forces also place us at the service of the group, rendering us not just members, but also, in unfavourable circumstances, prisoners of it. In fact the principal of bonding never lets us avoid our responsibility towards the group, even if we try and distance ourselves from it in our minds. On an emotional level the process of releasing the bond can only ever be gradual, and never absolute. The need to belong will always remain on a deeper, unconscious level. In the soul not belonging is experienced as a death sentence.

Especially people with a psychiatric diagnosis such as schizophrenia are incapable of separating from their mothers. Symbiotically these people still cling to their parents, in spite of the fact that they can never really get close to them, and also exactly because they can't get close to them they keep trying.

One of my patients who had recognised the splits in his soul and understood that contact with his mother was the source of his confusion and psychosis, asked me the following question: "Whenever I'm really annoyed, and sick and tired with the whole situation, I have the feeling that one or more parts of me wants to leave my body, split off completely and go to my mother. Naturally, I don't want this to happen. What can I do about it?" The parts inside him that split off early in his childhood development never stay with him when they see that his adult part is not coping with stress and fear. They run away to their primary bonding person, as is totally normal for children. When there they experience the usual dose of entanglement.

As a therapist one is keen to help the patient get what he or she so clearly did not get in their childhood. This is why so much effort was, and still is, made in traditional family constellations to try and establish good contact between the representatives for the mother and her child. However, this should not be mistaken for reality. The reality is that it was not possible for some people during the symbiotic phase of their life, to be physically, emotionally and energetically nurtured and sustained by their traumatised mother. It is nonetheless possible to enable patients to come into closer contact with their own inner selves, to accept their own needs, understand their desire for acceptance by their mother, and to understand the mother's blockage. Patients' souls can be opened towards whatever small amount of real love actually did exist, and they can be shown how, despite everything, their souls contain in their early split-off parts the power and vigour they need in their lives.

While one of my main goals in constellations in my earlier work as a therapist was to establish contact between the symbiotically needy child and his mother, I now view this approach more critically. If the mother is still alive, patients will often be full of expectation that their relationship with their mother will change. But because the mother herself must undergo therapy in order to overcome the splits that hinder a purely loving relationship with her child, disappointment is to be expected. Because of the splits in her own soul, the mother will always ensure that her child cannot confide in her fully. The symbiotic phase for mother and child is long since over, and the chance of creating such a loving bond is gone. It is a childish illusion to believe it possible to turn back the clock.

By using representatives to fill the role of the mother and

her split soul, patients can get a clearer idea of why they had such extreme conflicts with their mothers. They can learn to accept their mother the way she is, together with the splits in her soul, and realise that they themselves are not to blame and that there is nothing they can do to release their mother from the splits in her soul. They must separate themselves from their mother's trauma feelings so that they can be at one with themselves and their own feelings.

"I accept my not being accepted!"

One of my patients had spent her whole life in despair at not being wanted by her mother. It was a decisive step for her during therapy finally to accept that her mother had not wanted her. After she became willing to accept this pain and was able to say to herself: "I accept myself as a child, whose mother never accepted me", she wrote me the following in a letter: "I know now what bonding looks like, I now have an idea what it is about. I know what I saw. I now have the experience; I can stand on my own two feet and feel it. I can stand alone in the world, without fear of going under or ending up in the psychiatric ward. I can trust my feelings, they are right for me. What I feel, feels right. The truth does no harm, it sets you free if it is expressed and felt in love."

In my experience, the kind of crying one does when accepting childhood loneliness sounds very different to the crying of one who hopes that the mother will return after all. The former is a deep, violent and heart-breaking crying. And it stops after a strong bout. On the other hand depressive crying is less deep, more miserable and wailing, and goes on and on. It rarely stops, and always starts up anew when the despair resurfaces. When people reach the deepest point of pain, it is then that they find themselves. The illusion makes room for reality and this newly created space can be filled with new life.

Whoever is fully at one with their own pain will create deeper connections with others than through their persistent efforts to be recognised, accepted and to belong. They themselves become a centre towards which others are drawn. For everyone essentially has the need to find peace in his or her own soul.

"I'm no longer my mother's best friend"

Renouncing the Sisyphean task of winning the mother by becoming, as it is known among daughters, a 'best friend', even to one's own mother, can sometimes help contact with other family members, for example siblings. Asked about the most important result of her therapy, one of my patients answered: "I've been able to get away from the entanglement with my mother. But as a result we have virtually no contact any more – though there was some contact before, as I always used to be her best friend, and she always saw me and related to me as her mother. Once I stopped being that, and instead started being the daughter role, and refused to look after her like she always wanted, she initially became very aggressive. It was incredible. She began ranting and raging, and then I said to her: 'You've always mistaken me for your mother.' Then she had a fit, a real fit of rage. After that I had little contact with her for a long time. She tried to re-establish the old arrangement using aggression; it was completely terrible for me. I always thought that when I did some constellations my relationship with my mother would improve. But that's not at all what happened. Things are very, very distant now. There's nothing more that can be done. In the meantime we've started showing each other some respect. She leaves me much more in peace than before. She's stopped interfering in my life. This is actually very convenient. But the warmth, the familiar warmth or whatever it was, that's completely gone. And that's something I don't really like. My mother is just pottering along now. I let go of her and no longer feel guilty about always having to help her.

"As a result of this my relationship with my brother is much, much better. We're the best of friends now. That turned out really great. I gained something there that was new to me. By dealing with my mother I've come closer to my brother."

Escaping from an unhealthy symbiosis with parents is a long process on the path of inner healing. As suppressed pain, together with fear, are the main source of a split, it is only through pain that we can disengage from entangled symbiotic childhood bonding with our parents. Only by allowing the suppressed feelings of fear, anger, shame and pain to surface can split-off parts connect with present experience and the healthy parts of the soul.

8.9 Fusion or Side by Side?

When traumatisation is recognised and the split-off parts of the personality increasingly become familiar with, understand and accept each other, the question arises as to whether the split between the parts is still necessary, or whether it is possible to fuse them into one unified self. In many cases this seems achievable; in other cases, the split-off parts seem to be side by side in a state of conscious co-existence. Freed from its jail, the trauma part can have new experiences; the survival part, which previously always had to be active and on its guard, is more often able to withdraw and leave the playing field to the healthy parts. As in a ball game, the process is best kept flowing when the different parts are always passing the ball back and forth. Therapy sessions thus often feature two parts speaking alternately, with both, each from its own standpoint, approaching a new, common identity that conforms better and better to the fears and growth requirements of both sides. An 'either-or' situation can become an 'as well as' situation on many levels. Like a zip, the survival self and the trauma self parts can join together and close the split 'tooth by tooth', and healthy feelings can increasingly start to inform actions.

8.10 Living Instead of Surviving

When someone becomes free of his traumatic split and his symbiotic dependencies, he will eventually feel the need to live life differently from before. He will notice when things are not right and start looking for a new personal and professional orientation. He will make new friends and acquaintances, sort out existing relationships or approach his old job with a new outlook. His childhood desire to help his mother often creates the idea that he must urgently help others, perhaps as a doctor, psychologist, social worker or nurse. It is therefore only logical that by giving up this desire, his professional motivation may be brought into crisis, creating the need for a professional reorientation. This can be very beneficial in terms of developing a truly professional attitude within the caring professions, that gives personal responsibility to patients. He is able to protect himself from patients' attempts to entice him into entanglement by means of blatant displays of their needs or by threats of rejection or physical violence.

"I can detach myself now"

In relation to the above, a patient said during an interview: "I'm an alternative practitioner and I also do therapeutic work. I have discovered that I took up this profession in order to help my mother. I went into the caring profession in order to find a solution for her. When I detached myself from her, so that I no longer felt the need to help her, I lost all my interest in helping others. So my professional life has collapsed. I really need to find my footing again. But slowly, slowly, it's coming. I'm much more detached from my patients now. I give them much more personal responsibility; I'm much less caring, which makes some of them really resent me. But I've learned to detach myself properly. And I also like that my constellations work is much easier. I'm moving increasingly away from homeopathy, which requires you to delve so incredibly deeply into people's lives and protect them so much. And when their situation worsens for a while, you have to be there for them. Even at night! And this is getting too much for me. I prefer having someone in front of me with his problem. Naturally, I'm still there for him afterwards. And I'm very responsible in my work, that's something I always hear in feedback. But I can't go on like it was before."

Up until now, the survival self did not want to look back at what had happened. For this reason it set its sights on an empty, distant future and stuck to this illusion. The trauma self remained in the powerlessness of the past and was fixated on what had happened. However, by retreating it retained in one part of it something that remained healthy despite everything. This gave room for the hope that some means of escape could exist if the parts that remained healthy as well as the traumatised parts could come closer and support each other. This allows both to enter the present together and to do what is *now* possible despite everything. This explains the returning of the person's original vitality.

"A wonderful feeling"

A patient, who had been sexually abused as a child by her grandfather as well as a friend of the family, came to the following conclusion about her long journey of freeing herself from the splits in her soul step by step. "My problem in the last constellation was to understand why I have such great anger in me and why it is so important to me to be grown up and to make my own decisions. After the constellation, I drove over to the house of the former friend of the family simply to test my feelings again, to

see whether it was true or not. Then I visited my grandfather's grave and – yes, it was true! All the grief and all
the pain, which was always there, I could understand it all
more now. It was always there, but I could never understand it. Now it all made more sense. I don't want to say
that the pain and grief were nice, but it had a purpose.
What I feel at this moment is peace and normality in a
positive sense. The constant slog and uneasiness are
gone. Now I have a totally different relationship to my
mother.

"The reason for the last constellation was actually my
job, as I've always had massive problems in my professional life because I always said 'yes' to things I didn't
want, and then would feel horribly disappointed. And I'd
even berate myself for doing something that was totally
inexplicable. Now that's completely gone. Professionally,
I no longer have any problems with my employer. And
now new career prospects are opening up. I'm quite clear
about what I'm worth financially. Everything's under
control! I'm overjoyed – so much has happened. I'm
happy and want to take it further. I can see all the possibilities and notice that life is just starting. I'm no longer
just surviving. It's such a wonderful feeling!"

9

The Therapeutic Use of Constellations

9.1 From Family Constellations to Trauma Constellations

The controversy surrounding family constellations in Germany, which has at times been intense, has affected me in recent years; it has allowed me to gain greater clarity about family constellations. Regardless of any philosophical superstructure and mode of practice in the tradition of Bert Hellinger, for me the constellations method has always remained an extremely valuable tool with which to gain new insights into the life of the human soul. I therefore continue to be interested in improving my understanding of the essence of this method and contributing to its further development.

The constellations method has been part of my own personal development and professional journey as a psychologist and psychotherapist since 1994. I began to accumulate experience with the constellations method by practising in the classic family constellations tradition. This form of family constellations showed me the fundamental importance of bonding with one's biological parents, and the extent to which this determines one's fate in life. It opened my eyes to the multi-generational effects of emotional bonding, which stores the history of a family over at least three or four generations. In my experience, this makes family constellations a useful therapeutic method with which to reveal the web of mutual dependencies in which we all exist from birth onwards. Family constellations allow us to see how this web of bonds influences and shapes each and every one of us in our deepest psychological core.

Increasingly, however, I have come to realise that the problems for which people seek therapeutic help nearly always have traumatic origins. In my experience, people are interested in family constellations because they have relationship conflicts in their family of origin, with their parents or siblings, or because they no longer see eye to eye with their partners or children in their current family. Usually bonding disorders in relation to one's own parents lie at the heart of these relationship conflicts, which in turn are often due to one's parents' personally experienced traumatic experiences. In many families the parents' traumatic experiences result in bonding trauma situations, where the parents' trauma is reflected in the child's psychological structure, with a high probability of repeated traumatisations in the subsequent generation.

While in a classic family constellation we find signs of personal trauma along with traumas taken on from the patient's family system, these are not addressed directly or treated as traumas. The goal of a classic family constellation appears to be more an attempt to (re)activate the family bonding system as an emotional resource for the patient, thus attempting to meet their unsatisfied symbiotic needs. In providing patients with a clear understanding of the 'ordering' of interpersonal relationships in a family – according to the succession of the generations, the relationship between man and woman based on love and mutual respect of each other's differences, the superiority of parents and the sequence of births in a family – they gain healing images which they can use to find their place in the relational system of their family of origin, thereby achieving an inner balance.

I see now that while this is a well-intentioned idea, it doesn't help people make real progress with their emotional problems. Helping them gain insights into the rules of relationships based on mutual respect only touches the surface of their problems, and this preoccupation with external events in a family can even distract patients from their own inner problems. Based on my model of the splits in the soul – i.e. the trauma self, the healthy self and the survival self – we could even say that the survival self is happy with any form of therapy in which the actual trauma is *not* addressed; it can thus live under the illusion that the current relationship problems can be solved without the survival part having to confront its own traumatisation.

Like most family constellations facilitators in the beginning of the constellations movement, I was still totally ignorant about trauma theory and was unable to recognise trauma and the symptoms of trauma in a constellation – even when, from my current perspective, they were so clearly displayed in the behaviour of the representatives. As a result I had a tendency to subordinate individual problems to those of the group. I know today that this can lead to a deepening of the splits in the patient's soul, particularly if the family system (as in a bonding trauma and bonding system trauma) does not turn out to be a resource, but rather the cause of the traumatisation. To ask the patient, as the child of entangled and violent parents, to 'accept his parents', 'take things on where they left off', or 'bow down before his parents' is essentially staging a retraumatisation for the patient. Requesting such a thing is to idealise the parents and ignore the violence that originated with them.

Facilitators dealing with the phenomenon of emotional trauma who are aware of its significance, no longer work with the same goals as in the classic family constellation, instead creatively use the vast potential of the constellations method to achieve healing from trauma, as Johannes B. Schmidt describes in his extremely readable book (Schmidt, 2006). Instead of family constellations, we can speak of trauma constellations in cases where a patient's traumatic experiences become the focal point of the therapeutic work.

9.2 The Complexity of Constellations

To me 'constellations' are just as fascinating as any enigmatic phenomena. At first sight they seem easy to put into practice. On closer inspection, however, they turn out to be highly complex procedures. They are made up of the following elements:

- the people participating in the constellation: the facilitator, the patient, the people who agree to take on representations and the rest of the group observing the process;
- the theoretical assumptions, ideas and objectives of the facilitator using this method in whatever capacity or role – e.g. as a counsellor, therapist, supervisor, spiritual teacher or healer;
- the methodological approach; and
- the different situational contexts (seminar groups, organisations, public space etc.) in which constellations take place.

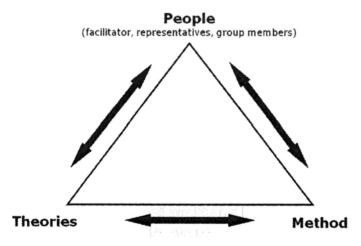

People
(facilitator, representatives, group members)

Theories   **Method**

Figure 11: The interaction between theory, method and the people in the constellations process

As the above diagram should make clear, the people, theory and methodological approach in a constellation are all mutually interconnected. As human beings, we all have different ideas, interests and goals and therefore also use the tools available to us in completely different ways.

The personality of constellation facilitators is in my opinion an important factor that can affect the constellation process. Depending on their philosophical, psychological and sociological assumptions, historical knowledge, professional qualifications and expertise, level of personal development and the extent to which they themselves are still trapped in their own splits, a constellation can take an entirely different course. The philosophical conceptual models devised by Bert Hellinger (who made a major contribution to the development of the constellation method and helped popularise it internationally) are therefore just *one* of countless different ways of approaching the constellations method. Bert Hellinger follows his own path in his use of the method (Hellinger and ten Hövel, 2005), to an extent also followed and practised by others (Weber, 1998, 2001) but also viewed critically by many (Goldner, 2003; Haas, 2005). To describe constellations essentially as 'Hellinger's method' would only make sense if every constellation facilitator were to follow Bert Hellinger's constructs and application of the constellations method exactly as he has done through each of his developmental phases of the work. For example, Hellinger describes his latest development as working with the 'Movements of the Spirit-Mind' (Hellinger, 2007); here he retreats further from public and scientific discourse and adopts the position of an enlightened healer.

The constellations community is currently witnessing what, in my opinion, is the necessary separation of the constellations method from its focus on the personality of Bert Hellinger, along with an appreciation of the merits of his work and a critical analysis of his biases (Nelles, 2007). There is a debate surrounding the facilitator's own past: "The accusations that have often been levelled at systemic family constellations – as being patriarchal, chauvinistic, reactionary, irrational, esoteric, magical/mystical, ritualistic, religious, fatalistic or unscientific – contain an element of truth, not because we are intentionally biased, but because we are blind to our bias." (Gruen, 2007) If the attitudes enumerated by Gruen originate from the survival self, they will not change by appealing to them; the underlying traumas need to be addressed first.

9.3 The Practice of Trauma Constellations

I now facilitate constellations on the basis of the principles of bonding, trauma and splitting as described in this book. This type of constellation therefore has only a little in common with classic family constellations and the so-called movements of the spirit-mind. I often begin a constellation with one or two split parts of the patient's soul and then see how the process develops from there. The constellation is meant to help patients understand where the splits in their soul come from and how they can learn to accept and overcome them. It is not a repetition of the entanglement or a deepening of the split in the soul, but rather the removal of the split from the soul, which in my opinion should be the main goal of the therapy. Patients' symbiotically entangled parts must learn how to free them from the trauma feelings inherited from the parents, thereby finding stability within themselves. Healthy parts and traumatised parts of the soul should be able to merge into a new emotional entity so that the strain is removed from the survival self that forces the person to resort to avoidance, control, compensation and delusional strategies.

Practically speaking, the essential simplicity of the constellations process means that it is relatively easy to describe. Basically I establish an agreement in advance with the group I'm working with in which I stipulate the following points:

- Participants know that their participation in the seminar is their own responsibility.
- I accept therapeutic responsibility for the duration of the seminar.
- If patients require further therapeutic help after the seminar, it is their responsibility to find this.

- Each participant decides for him or herself if they want to take on a representation in another's constellation.
- If someone in a representation realises that the role is becoming too much for them, he or she can step out of the role at any time.
- Each representative is obliged in their role to refrain from committing any acts of violence against other seminar participants.
- Anyone leaving the seminar prematurely will communicate his or her intention to me, as the seminar facilitator, as well as the entire group.

In my view this ensures a sufficiently transparent and clearly defined space for the activities that will take place in the group. It establishes and limits competencies and responsibilities. The group should be a *safe place*, which is of great importance when working with trauma.

If a patient (in what follows I will use the male form, though naturally men and women are meant equally) in a group expresses his willingness to do a constellation for himself, I ask him about his problem and what would be a good result for him. In doing so I note whether, when formulating his problem for the constellation, he is residing in a healthy part of his personality. If he is in a survival self, I will try to build a bridge to a healthy part of his soul. If this fails, it is generally better not to do a constellation with this patient at this time, because from experience I know that strong survival parts can impede change and, after a certain point, the constellation will only go round in circles and become tiring.

If I sense that I am dealing with healthy parts of the soul that are open to change, I suggest to the patient that he choose representatives from the group for various personality components, people and symptoms. The patient chooses these representatives and places them in the room according to his sense of the relationships between them. He then returns to his seat next to me and together we follow the constellation as it develops. I give the representatives time to tune into their roles and wait until they move or say something. I give them no guidelines and I do not censor what they say during the constellation. I take their movements, words and behaviour to be expressions of something the meaning of which can only be understood after it has become clear what is really at stake. Where, in order to gain greater clarity, I deem it important to 'feed ' additional representatives for people or parts of the soul into the constellation process, I ask the patient to select the representatives and add them to the constellation. Sometimes I talk to the patient to obtain additional information or to make sure I understand his issue. I always keep an eye on him during the constellation, observing how he reacts to what is happening. I try to maintain simultaneous contact with the patient and the represented system. This enables me to be receptive to what the representatives say and whatever else the patient and entire group may want to communicate during the constellation.

As the patient's emotional conflict gradually becomes clear through the experiences of the representatives, I try, by suggesting phrases aimed at one of the traumatised parts, to bring the patient into more intensive resonance with what is happening in the constellation, and so to the origins of the split in his soul. If this process is on the right track – and thus far split-off memories of traumatisation have become clearer and the entanglement of various parts of the patient with his parents, grandparents etc. have become more transparent – then the patient himself can join the constellation. He is then able to continue with the process of emotional change already begun while observing from outside the constellation. Step by step, I work with the patient on a solution to his inner turmoil. This should gradually allow new centres of emotional integration to form. From my experience, a patient will make the most progress if he has the courage to delve deeper into his personal pain and so release his emotional blocks. During this phase all the representatives remain in their roles. The constellation can be brought to an end when the patient feels his problem, which he formulated at the outset, has been resolved.

I then ask all the people involved in the constellation to go back to their seat and let the process fade out gradually. This should give the patient the necessary space and time for the new emotional patterns to take hold within him. After a short while, I ask the patient to release the representatives from their roles by thanking them for their efforts and calling them by their names. At this point the patient often expresses a desire to withdraw from the group for a while in order to give the emotional events he has just experienced further space for change. From experience I know that therapeutic interventions into traumatic events can be demanding and exhausting for the patient, and it is therefore advisable that he take a break to recover.

To me, as the facilitator, there are a number of good arguments in favour of not intervening directly in the constellations process. One of the main reasons is that if I act on his behalf and seek a solution for him by manipulating his internal system, I could become entangled with him, especially with his survival-self parts. Using my understanding and overview, I guide the constellations process, which I see not as a reflection of *actual* reality as such, but as a reflection of the patient's *emotional* reality. Responsibility for any change to this emotional reality remains with the patient himself. I find it a delicate balancing act not to be drawn into the patient's split emotional system and so not becoming just another figure in his entangled and traumatised bonding structure, and at the same time, not cutting myself off from the patient's system and so, as far as possible, I must use my presence and competence to create the space the patient needs to develop his self-healing energies.

9.4 Methodological Aspects of Constellations

Despite the considerable differences in application of the constellations method by different constellations facilitators, is there something we might call the essence of the constellation method? In my opinion the essence of the method consists in the attempt, with the aid of another person, to understand a person's deep emotional structure. What I mean by this will perhaps become clearer if we review some of the other methods normally used to understand the problem of someone seeking psychological help:

- There is the assessment conversation, in which the therapist gauges the patient's psychological state. This is done based on the patient's statements and the understanding and experience of the therapist in fitting the patient's case into a general diagnostic schema.
- There are the questionnaires patients complete so their behaviour and ways of experiencing can be weighted and assessed in comparison to so-called normal criteria.
- There are psychological measurement parameters, from simple pulse measurements to complex brain images, which are deemed to allow conclusions to be drawn about the patient's psychological problem.
- Depending on their training, therapists may also use dreams, body language, facial expressions, gestures or voice prints as diagnostic clues to the patient's hidden problems. In hypnotherapy, for example, the patient is put into a trance-like state in order to gain access to his unconscious.

What is entirely new about the constellation method is that it is not the patient and his self-disclosures, or the therapist and his diagnostic procedures and therapeutic techniques, which aim to raise the patient's hidden emotional conflict to a conscious level. Rather, it is another person entirely, often unknown to the patient, who provides clarity about the patient's inner life. This approach does not require that the people acting as representatives in the constellation know the patient.

If we consider how unusual this procedure is in comparison with the traditional diagnostic approach of psychology, it is little wonder that many people have found cause to question it and that many professionals consider it to be 'controversial'. It runs against our conventional understanding, our familiar way of viewing the world and human beings, that someone can know something personal about us despite our not having mentioned anything specifically or an expert having established it through objective measurement. It looks like unscientific magic and thus can cause discomfort and fear.

There are nonetheless many other psychological methods that share similarities with the constellations method – for example *role-play*. In role-play we assume we are dealing with a fictional re-enactment, a game of pretend, a training ground for behaviours and communication. Jakob Moreno's *psychodrama* is also based on the re-enactment of a family situation. The psychodrama game is meant to open up new perspectives and options for action. Similarly, Virginia Satir's *family reconstruction sculpture* attempts to reveal hidden behavioural patterns in a family (Franke, 1996).

Constellations claim to be able to reveal a client's emotional and hidden reality as well as his most important attachment relationships. Is this assumption justified? Should we assume that, like the client himself, the representatives are able to perceive and authentically reflect what the client's attachment figures feel and think? We might dismiss this suggestion as pure speculation. However, the constellations method would never have become so widespread if the patients doing the constellations didn't experience their personal situations being reflected in the behaviour of their representatives with a significant level of authenticity. Also the vast majority of people who offer to be representatives in constellations do not seem to feel they are just participating in a mere stage show, but rather, during the constellation they really do feel they are being possessed by something coming from outside of them. The assumption that constellations can reflect a sufficiently reliable image of a patient's emotional reality can at least be posited as plausible working hypothesis.

According to traditional ideas of how information is exchanged between people – predominantly verbally and consciously – the constellations phenomenon should not really exist. To date no theory has been devised that even partially explains how complete strangers can suddenly gain access to another human being's most intimate feelings, and how the history of a family system can be revealed with astonishing accuracy through the experiences of the representatives. The frequently quoted idea derived from the theory of the English biologist Rupert Sheldrake that constellations are 'morphogenetic fields' (Sheldrake, 1999) that induce 'knowing fields' is, in my opinion, unsatisfactory. Indeed, it does not stem from Rupert Sheldrake's own experience with constellations – the term 'field' was tacked on afterwards as a potentially plausible explanation for the constellations phenomenon (Galarza, 2006). Attempts to shed light on the constellations phenomenon using scientific speculation from the field of quantum physics are also only in their early stages, and we cannot tell how much clarity this may eventually provide (Schneider, 2007).

While in the following subchapter I will suggest the existence of a deep connection between the constellations method and so-called mirror neurons, I am in no way claiming to be able to explain the mysteries of the constellations method in this way. It does, however, prove interesting to establish a relationship between an exciting new discovery from the field of brain research and the similarly fascinating phenomenon of the constellations method.

9.5 Mirror Neurons

Where the eyes meet, you come into being. *Hilde Domin*

My attention was first drawn to 'mirror neurons' by a book by Joachim Bauer, a professor of psychoneuroimmunology in Freiburg. In his book, entitled 'Warum ich fühle, was du fühlst' ('Why I Feel What You Feel'), Bauer explains in a very clear fashion what mirror neurons are and the different functions they correspond to in human development: from the intuitive learning of simple movements to the ability to find one's way in social communities (Bauer, 2005).

The existence of mirror neurons was proven by a research group from the University of Parma (Rizzolatti, Fadiga, Fogassi and Gallese, 2002; Rizzolatti, Fogassi and Gallese, 2007). They discovered that certain nerves in the brains of monkeys that control some of the animals' highly specific movements also transmit impulses when a monkey observes another monkey performing one of these special movements. That is to say that there is neuronal activity in precisely the same region of the brain that is responsible for controlling the special movement, even if the monkey is not performing the movement itself. The movement is simulated in the mind when the monkey sees another animal performing it. "Nerve cells that are capable of implementing a certain program in one's own body and are also active when one observes or otherwise experiences how another individual in reality implements this program, are known as mirror neurons." (Bauer, 2005)

This is not only true of visual observation. Listening and speaking about a certain action can also trigger the resonance phenomenon: the special nerve cells in the brain begin to fire and in so doing show that they have been stimulated. Through mirror neurons, therefore, we are continually in contact with what is happening around us. The mirroring of other people's activity in us occurs simultaneously, involuntarily and with no pause for thought.

Mirror neurons also seem to come into play when we empathise with other people's feelings. We all know what it is like to be infected by someone else's fear, to grimace when we watch someone sink their teeth into a lemon, to feel ashamed when someone else is ashamed, to laugh when someone else laughs or even to feel pain when we see someone suffering. To run alongside others, to laugh with them, to clap along with them, to fall into raptures with them is fundamentally easier than trying to block these action impulses. We can observe this clearly in football stadia, beer tents or carnival processions, and we can also experience it for ourselves, too.

A further characteristic of mirror neurons is that they "add the observed parts of a scene to an expected general scene" (ibid). Thus mirror neurons also seem to provide a supporting basis for intuition. As the vast majority of these action sequences correspond with the experiences of all members of a social community, according to Bauer mirror neurons permit the formation of a common intersubjective actional and semantic sphere. "Intuitive ideas can develop in someone even without reaching consciousness. For example: when you have a bad feeling but don't know why. This, among other reasons, is because we can have subliminal perceptions, i.e. not consciously registered, which activate mirror neurons in us." (ibid)

Mirror neurons are not only there to simulate the movements of other people within ourselves, allowing us to be better in tune with them; they can also activate other people's bodily sensations and feelings within us. This leads to a direct understanding of other people's perceptions and feelings. We feel sick when we see someone else who feels sick; we grab our own hand in shock when we see someone cut his or her finger with a knife. The discovery of mirror neurons has given a scientific foundation to the phenomena of sympathy and empathy. "The system of mirror neurons provides us with the neurobiological basis for mutual emotional understanding. When we experience the feelings of another person, the nerve cell networks start to resonate, to vibrate, and this allows the other person's feelings to replicate in our own emotional experience." (ibid) This mirroring appears to resemble a copying process.

It is possible that the system of mirror neurons forms the basis for the symbiotic side of our human existence, our dependence on attention and recognition, our deep longing to belong and our community-spirit, our exceptional ability to empathise and corresponding willingness to do everything to try and help others.

In this context Bauer points out that "people in a state of close emotional attachment" are able to mirror each other particularly well and understand each other intuitively, something which affects the other person. The closer the relationship with another person, the more profound the corresponding mirroring: "the resonance pattern loved ones elicit in us soon becomes a permanent fixture. A dynamic inner picture of this person is created made up of his or her vital qualities, longings and emotions. Having access to this kind of inner representation of a loved one means having a kind of extra person within you." (ibid)

The fact that emotionally close people are able to mirror each other so intensely acquires a special meaning in the context of bonding theory. The scientific research initiated by John Bowlby into mother-child bonding shows how emotionally interwoven the relationship between mother and child is (Bowlby, 2001). During our first years of development we are in a state of emotional symbiotic unity with our mothers. This is something I have discussed frequently in this book. In terms of mirror neurons, we can say that mother and child mirror each other reciprocally. The mother mirrors the child within herself and the child does the same with his mother. This provides the child with the basic building block he needs for his own psychological development. By mirroring his mother, the child gains access to the other people also mirrored in the mother's soul, for example the child's father, even if he is no longer alive, his brothers and sisters, the mother's parents and their parents. The child gains access to all of his ancestors mirrored in his mother's soul, to the good and the bad things that have occurred in the family system into which he is born.

If the mother is incapable of adequately mirroring the child, because her mirroring system is not functioning properly due to her own traumatic experiences, the child is then only able to mirror a chaotic image of his mother's emotional structure. This lays the foundations for bonding disorders in the mother-child relationship and subsequent emotional development problems in the child. Bauer also believes "that fear, tension and stress massively reduce the firing rate of mirror neurons. As soon as pressure and fear are generated, everything dependent on the system of mirror neurons dies away, i.e. the ability to empathise, understand others and perceive subtleties." (ibid) A traumatized mother is therefore not able adequately to mirror her child's needs within her. For her the child, especially when she is in a survival mode, becomes a screen onto which she can project her own emotional confusion. Conversely, the child then resonates with the split-off traumatised experiences of his mother and falls into a state of confusion, for he is no longer able to distinguish clearly between what belongs to him and what to his mother.

The existence of 'perpetrator introjects', which become established in the child's soul when he or she becomes the victim of violence, mistreatment and abuse, are easier to explain in terms of the existence of mirror neurons. In these situations the child can only mirror the behavioural patterns and intense feelings coming from the perpetrator in himself.

Mirror neurons clearly establish such close connections between members of a socially active species that the question arises as to how can there be any room for individuality. However, our brain also seems to have laid the foundations for this. The existence of the two halves of the brain presumably makes a major contribution to the development of individuality and the liberation of the individual from just his or her group existence. "The problem of how the brain differentiates between self and not-self is yet to be fully solved. However, the previous data, presented among others by Jean Decety's research team, shows the following: the brain stores the picture it has of itself and of those it has created of other people in the two different hemispheres [of the brain]. When the self makes plans, has intentions or carries out an action the left side of the brain takes control. Our own actions are represented in the left side of the brain. Pictures of other people, on the other hand, are stored in the right side of the brain. In the 'collection of bodies' in the right side of the brain, we also will even find a picture of our own body, but only as long as the self is not acting. As soon as the self becomes an actor, the left side comes into play." (ibid) If we assume that the left side of the brain is a later product of evolution, this would make individuality an evolutionary acquisition that allows us humans to break free from our herd instinct, and extricate ourselves from our symbiotic resonance with our respective group.

The cited findings about the workings of mirror neurons and the different functions of the two sides of the brain in my opinion provide a good place to start when trying to understand how representatives in a constellation are consistently capable of grasping a patient's unconscious emotional states without losing their own sense of self in the process, as well as why they are able to differentiate between the acquired feelings of the role and their own feelings, and then afterwards step out of the representation with relatively few problems. From childhood onwards, we are able to mirror the people around us while at the same time constructing our own identities. To do so we require no special teaching or training. This explains why people taking on representations for the first time in a constellation, provided they don't freeze up from their inhibitions, do so just as well as those who have been representatives many times before.

The mirrored perception of other people's emotional states could also be of particular importance in the choosing of representatives for a constellation. Aided by mirror neurons, patients intuitively and unconsciously sense the similarities between themselves and other seminar participants and choose representatives accordingly.

Fortunately, it is not only an ability to mirror other people that we develop from childhood onwards; we also develop counter-strategies that allow us to protect our innermost self from the all too inquisitive mirror neurons of others. We appear to be able to steer and control how much of ourselves we reveal, to whom we open ourselves up and to whom we close ourselves off. We can see this phenomenon clearly during constellations. In my experience, representatives are only able to feel what a client is willing to share. If he starts closing himself off or switching to a dissociated state, the representatives' source of information will dry up.

It seems common from my observations, and also to be expected in light of the theory of splits, that a patient will switch back and forth during a constellation between the different parts of his soul. In this sense the representatives can be said to be more or less 'online' during a constellation, depending on which of the different mental states the patient finds himself in most at a given moment. This finely tuned interplay between the representatives in a constellation and the patient is also seen when the representatives experience an immediate sense of relief when, after momentarily falling back into survival self state, the patient relaxes his emotional blocking and again enables a clear emotional mirroring of his emotional states.

A further statement in Joachim Bauer's book about mirror neurons particularly appealed to me: "From a neurobiological perspective, we have every reason to believe that no device or biochemical method will ever become available that can understand and influence another human being's emotional state as well as can be achieved by people themselves. " (ibid) The longer I work with the constellation method, the more I become convinced there is no better way to understand and distinguish between a patient's emotional states than through constellations i.e. by the mirroring of a human being through another human being. The representative is similarly the best measuring system, as it were, for understanding someone else's emotional constitution. In my opinion, no therapist, counsellor or even scientist is able – whether by use of questions, initial conversations, questionnaires or measurements of brain activity – to obtain such specific, complex and precise information about why a patient is suffering from anxiety, depression or even psychotic states of confusion as is possible with a constellation. There is no faster way for a therapist to get to the heart of mental illnesses than to become a representative for someone suffering from a mental disorder. It is not a supposedly objective view of the patient from the outside, but rather the most precise grasping of his inner perspective that helps us to understand what he is really suffering from. Thanks to mirror neurons, almost all people seem to possess this ability to understand other people from their inner perspectives.

It comes as no surprise to me then that, from this perspective, Joachim Bauer also became aware of and recognised the value of family constellations. "Constellations and in this case family constellations are highly effective procedures in which a patient and other fellow-patients who act as representatives for his loved ones are arranged – like figures – in what seems like an intuitively meaningful way. When they are 'brought to life' by the questions and instructions of the therapist, these arrangements evoke an intensive resonance effect in all the participants (not just the patients but also in the representatives in the constellation). As a result, massive emotional reactions can occur. Only psychotherapists or specially trained family therapists are capable of managing this process responsibly." (ibid) If this is true, it should serve as a call to all the established fields of psychotherapy to recognise the great potential of constellations and to use them for the benefit of their patients.

Of course, mirror neurons cannot explain everything about the insights and fascinating observations made over the years by constellation facilitators and representatives when working with constellations. In my opinion, however, the discovery of mirror neurons may well represent the foundation of scientific understanding and further research into the constellations phenomenon.

9.6 Mirroring and Resonance Phenomena

According to these findings, the classic family constellation will negate the advantage of the constellations method if the facilitator interrupts the mirroring processes too quickly and hastily imposes his or her notions and ideas as to how the solution might look for the patient. If he or she is relatively quick to provide fairly uniform schemas as solution pictures and standardised solution statements, then the process of mirroring will not develop sufficiently for a significant resonance process to be triggered in the patient.

The so-called 'movements of the spirit-mind', the later development of the classic family constellation by Bert Hellinger begun around 1998, may well allow the free movement and expression by the representatives, thus resulting in a mirroring of the patient's emotional reality uninterrupted by the facilitator. However, this approach lacks the structure that makes it possible to understand what is going on; something of the traumatic background in the patient's soul is indeed indicated in the movements of the representatives, but this is not understood in its full context. As a result, after doing constellations of this kind many patients are left with a number of unanswered questions and consequently switch back into their survival modes, in which they are unable to understand the brief appearance of the traumatisation and splits in the soul.

In my opinion, a constellation should therefore serve two purposes:

- On the one hand it should allow the patient to see himself as clearly as possible during the constellations procedure. The representatives should provide the clearest possible mirror of his soul for him to look into. In this mirror he must be able to rediscover himself with all his various different parts, including unconscious parts.
- On the other hand, the process must take place in such a way that the most intense resonance possible is created between the patient and the representatives in the constellation and is maintained throughout the entire constellation. Between the patient and the representatives there must be a continual exchange of information, both verbal and non-verbal.

I would therefore describe constellations as a mirroring-resonance method mediated by human representatives. But what does this mean in terms of the successful implementation of a constellation?

- Only those people and parts of the soul that are relevant to the patient's current problem should be placed in the constellation. As a constellations facilitator, I should therefore understand from the outset what the patient's basic problem is, so that I can then suggest the most suitable 'starting constellation'.
- The representatives should be capable of performing their mirroring function at an optimal level. They must be completely free to express everything they feel and think in their roles.
- The constellations facilitator should not place him or herself above the representatives and tell them what to do, what to think and feel. To avoid interfering with the mirroring process he or she must not censor the representatives' statements.
- The patient must be fundamentally willing for the resonance between himself and the constellation to take place. He must realise that everything depends on him in terms of what things come to light during a constellation and which developmental step is currently possible for him.
- The facilitator must not decide on behalf of the patient how deep the resonance process should go. The constellations facilitator can only create the optimal conditions for the resonance process.

Placing a mirror in front of someone who is not willing to look into it leads nowhere; it only strengthens his anxiety, and therefore the resistance of his survival parts to any change in his emotional structure. A constellation will not yield worthwhile results if a patient claims to be ready for a constellation but a resonance with the representatives fails to occur because his survival parts block access to his traumatised parts and the painful memories contained therein. This kind of constellation can only produce artificial results and will be frustrating for all involved. The less the representatives are connected with the patient's soul, due to his current blocking of the resonance phenomenon, the greater the risk they will only mirror things from their own souls. This kind of constellation is not worth the effort. Only when mirroring and resonance exist in equal measure is a constellation able to move step by step towards that point where something fundamental changes in the soul.

In this sense constellations have the same qualities that you would expect of all other sound therapeutic methods. Only when patients feel they have been understood at the very deepest level do they show the courage and trust to substitute their survival strategies for healthier ways of life.

10

Research Project on the Constellations Method

There are very few scientific studies on the methodology of constellations work. Mainstream science tends to remain silent in discussions about how the constellations method should be evaluated. Studies that investigate the constellations phenomenon using scientific methods come to results that predominantly support the effectiveness of the method (Franke, 1996; Höppner, 2001; Pänzinger, 2004; Schlötter, 2005; Schwer, 2004; Mraz, 2006; Sethi, 2010). Additional and more comprehensive studies that could assess constellations as useful and reliable methods for coaching and psychotherapy are still lacking.

10.1 Research Questions

In 2005 I initiated a research project on constellations in Munich. I was particularly keen to formulate research questions from my own experience with the method that will arise when one works with this method intensively. Three main questions crystallised from this process:

1. How exactly does a constellation work?
2. Can the representatives reliably mirror the psychological structure of the person who is doing the constellation?

3. Have events that emerge during a constellation as expressed by the representatives actually occurred, and how do the patients deal with such new information?

The research team included Katharina Anane, Eva Baier, Christina Freund, Carla Kraus, Liesel Krüger, Sabine Metz, Cäcilia Pänzinger, Monika Stumpf und Josef Telake. In addition to conducting her own interviews, Claudia Härter also coordinated the collection of empirical data and the transcription of many interviews.

How exactly does a constellation work?

In researching this first question we wanted to discover how the patients themselves experience the constellation. Why do some people come to do a constellation in the first place and what do they hope to achieve? So the first part of the questionnaire was as follows:

In this part of the questionnaire we would like to learn how people who do a constellation experience the constellation and what they get from doing the constellation.

1. How many constellations have you done for yourself?
2. For what reason did you do constellations for yourself?
3. When you think about the last constellation you did, how helpful do you think it was?
4. Was there anything that you did not find helpful?
5. When you are doing a constellation, where do you focus particular attention?
6. What do you pay particular attention to in the representative who represents you?
7. What do you pay particular attention to in the other representatives?
8. What did the representatives express that was particularly important for you?
9. Did anything completely new come to light for you?

10. What was important for you when you went into the constellation yourself?
11. What role does the facilitator play for you?
12. What role does the group have for you?
13. Does the situation as a whole play a role for you?
14. Can the representatives mirror reliably?

Can the representatives reliably mirror the psychological structure of the person doing the constellation?

The second focus was concerned with the question of whether a representative can mirror someone's main characteristics when the person is not known to them and if so how. There is a legitimate doubt as to whether the representative can really detect and express what belongs to the patient, or whether they might only be expressing their own feelings and ideas. How reliable is the constellations method? How can the psychological structure of a patient be mirrored in the remarks made by a representative? Where is it unclear? In order to collect criteria we interviewed people who have already had experience with constellations. Part 2 of the questionnaire contained the following 27 questions:

1. How many times have you been a representative in a constellation?
2. What do you think, feel or experience when a participant is naming their issue at the beginning of a constellation?
3. At which point do you feel that you will be selected for a role?
4. Do you take on the role spontaneously?
5. Are there situations in which you decline taking on a role?
6. How do you go into the circle?
7. What helps you to feel your way into the role of the representative?
8. How much time do you need to get into the role of the representative and to empathize with it?

9. How do you recognise that you are fully in the role of the representative?

10. How do you recognise that as a representative you are being taken over by something that does not belong to you?

11. Do you feel that you stay in the role throughout the whole constellation?

12. Can you control how deeply you allow yourself to go into the role?

13. Are there moments in which you find it difficult to differentiate between what is and what is not yours?

14. When that happens, how do you become certain again?

15. As a representative are you able to distinguish whether your own experience gets confused with that of the role you are in?

16. When you are in the role of a representative, do you think of connections with your own issues?

17. How do you stay in contact with the facilitator of the constellation?

18. Does the facilitation of the constellation influence you in deciding how deeply you commit to the role of a representative?

19. What gives you a sense of safety in this respect, and what unsettles you?

20. When you are in the role of a representative, do you find you begin to wish you could help the person who is doing the constellation?

21. Do you find that you censor what you are expressing in any way?

22. When you are released from the role, can you return immediately to your own identity?

23. What helps you to release yourself from the role of the representative?

24. Have you ever felt unable to release yourself from the role of a representative in a constellation?

25. How long have you stayed in such a role?

26. Do you have a sense of why you couldn't step out of the role immediately?
27. What insights have you gained about your own psychological/emotional processes from being a representative?

New insights through constellations

The third research focus looked at how information that emerges in a constellation that is new for the patient is dealt with. A constellation can be very revealing. Thus it is not unusual for events from the family system or history of the patient to be shown that previously were not in the client's conscious awareness. This could be a suppressed sexual abuse of the patient, a rape of the mother, the suspicion that a father might be someone else than the person known as father, a secret child of the parents, a murder in the family and many other events. The question then is how does a patient deal with such new and often shocking information? Does he doubt or trust it? Does he begin to investigate further to be sure? Part 3 of our questionnaire went as follows:

"In this part of the questionnaire we are particularly interested in what happens when something new comes to light for the constellator in the course of a constellation, for example:

- That he has (half) siblings who were unknown to him until this point,
- That he or one of his parents has a different father or even different mother than originally thought,
- That there has been incest or sexual abuse in the family
- That possibly someone in the family is guilty of something serious or carries (some) responsibility for the death of another family member or other serious deeds.

You have made yourself available for this interview because something came up in one of your constellations that was new and surprising for you.

1. How long ago was the constellation that is relevant for this interview?
2. What was your issue in the relevant constellation?
3. What new information came to light in this constellation?
4. Did you experience the constellation as consistent?
5. Immediately after the constellation, how did you deal with there being completely new facts that cropped up?
6. Did you research afterwards to confirm or negate the new information?
7. If so, how did you do this?
8. What results did your research yield?
9. Did any subsequent constellation show up something different or confirm the new information?
10. Have you shared the results of the constellation(s) or your research with anyone else?
11. How did that person react?
12. What changes have resulted for you to date from this constellation?
13. How are you currently dealing with this situation?

We supplemented the thread of the interview described above with three general questions about the interviewee, thus giving a total of 54 questions.

1. How old are you?
2. How long have you had contact with the constellations method?
3. The gender of the interviewee.

The feasibility of the questionnaire was tested in several runs and corrected in some points before the main study began.

10.2 Spot Test and Execution of the Surveys

To answer the three main questions of the research project, the project group decided to carry out interviews with people who had already done several constellations for themselves and who, in other constellations had frequently taken a role as a representative. The intention was to assemble a wealth of experience in constellations gathered over many years by numerous people. A concrete target group for the interviews was made up of people who had done constellations in my seminars and who had accumulated many experiences as representatives. People who had only done one constellation or who had hardly taken part as representatives were only interviewed as exceptions. Thus this was a very selective sample. The results of the study cannot be applied directly to other forms of constellations based on different theoretical premises, methodological guidelines and interventions on the part of the facilitator.

Of the 71 participants in the study the following number answered

- Part 1 of the questionnaire (Why do I do constellations for myself and how do I experience them?) – 62
- Part 2 of the questionnaire (What do I experience in the role of a representative?) – 58
- Part 3 of the questionnaire (How do I deal with new information from my constellation?) – 50

The average age of the interviewees was 46 years in a range from 21 to 78 years. 50 people were female and 21 male. At the time of the study the interviewees on average had already had six years contact with constellations work over a period of from 1 to 25 years.

The interviews took place between May 2005 and March 2006. Eight women and one man conducted the interviews. The interviewers could choose whether to record the interviews and transcribe them later, or whether to enter them straight onto the computer. Some interviews were by telephone, but most were in person.

10.3 How Patients Experience Constellations

The following are selected results from the study. I have listed the answers to individual questions, summarised them into subgroups and commented on them subsequently. As we are concerned here with the spectrum of possible answers, no further quantitative evaluations were carried out. The statements of the interviewees are mostly presented in their original wording and only in a few places cleaned up for this written presentation, for better readability.

Why does someone do a constellation?

The 62 people who answered the first part of our questionnaire had done on average 6 constellations of their own in a range from one (10 people) to ten (1 person). Only constellations done in groups were included, not those done as part of individual therapy sessions.

The following answers were given to the question as to why someone does a constellation for himself or herself. I have attempted to organise them according to various dimensions:

General wishes with regard to themselves:

- To improve my quality of life
- To develop myself
- To manage my problems better and resolve them on an emotional level
- To support my internal development

To change patterns of experience and behaviour:

- In doing constellations I am looking for solutions for repetitive patterns of behaviour, which cause me pain and make me unhappy, so that I can break these patterns.
- I would like to change patterns that limit me.
- I want to heal my soul and come out of my traumas and behavioural triggers

The hope of revealing and understanding things that are more hidden about themselves:

- To know more of what I really want and what prevents me from knowing this. Sometimes I have feelings that I cannot account for.
- To learn about aspects of myself that I cannot get to rationally.
- To overcome my past so that I can live with it.
- To clarify, order, reveal and reconcile difficult things
- To reveal things in my family which are secret, things that nobody talks about, but that I have inklings about in my feelings and dreams.
- To gain clarity about my own mistakes and my family entanglements.
- To gain a new perspective when I look at the representatives in the constellation, so that I don't cling to difficult things that influence my life.
- I hope to get information by working in a group that is not available in individual therapy.

Conflicts with other people:

- To deal with conflicts with my parents and not to pass these onto my children.
- To resolve difficult issues about my mother.
- To learn more about my deceased brothers and to appreciate them more.
- To change my relationship with my partner.
- To solve my difficulties with men and understand why I didn't want children of my own.
- I started because things weren't going well for my son. When I realised my own part and the part my family had played, I started more and more to deal with my own issues.
- First I came because there were blocks in my own life so there was no way forward, and because things were

getting worse for my children. Every constellation took me a step further, opened my eyes and brought me closer to myself, to my feelings and to my centre, and so brought me closer to my children as well.
- I would like to have my uncertainties about my family confirmed.

Physical illnesses:

- My physical illness was the main thing initially; I wanted to get to the bottom of it so that it would heal.
- To find the cause for my anxiety and for my longing for death.

Finding causes:

- I won't get any peace until I get to the bottom of my problems.
- I would like to identify deeper causes and connections, so that I can gradually develop into the person I really am.

Professional advancement:

- I would like to get clearer in making decisions.
- As a therapist I use constellations as a supervision technique, to understand counter-transference.

Working with a new therapy method:

- I couldn't get any further with traditional therapy. I had got to a certain point and couldn't get further. With the constellations I was able to move on.
- The constellations method gave me a way of understanding my problem in a way I couldn't by putting things into words; things simply could not be expressed in language. And moving to a solution that I can continue to work with, where I have the feeling that I am taking further little steps.

- At first I wanted a method to help me progress personally. The more I worked with this method, the more it became the most effective therapy for me to overcome the trauma that I have experienced.

The answers to these questions show that the motives that lead people to seek help through constellations are congruent with those that lead people to seek out therapeutic support in general. Often these include the wish to find solutions for general problems with living, the wish to progress personally in life and resolve relationship problems with parents, partners, children or work colleagues. Frequently it is stressed that the path of internal change is sought for one's own development. When someone goes deeper into their relationship processes through constellations work, it brings them closer to themselves and to the issues in their family system that had been obscure and shrouded in mystery. The search for hidden or obscure causes in relationship conflicts are often cited as a specific criterion for choosing the constellations method. Constellations are, for some, a path of progress where they have come up against limits with other therapy methods because some problems could not be expressed or resolved through language alone. The specific link of my work with the idea of traumatisation is also mentioned as a motive for the interviewees' choice of constellations.

How is the process of one's own constellation experienced?

The following gives an overview of the various replies describing how the interviewees in our sample experience the process of their own constellations.

- I check the representatives out to see to what extent I experience something as genuine or not. I pay attention to posture, gesture, expression and speech.
- I pay attention to the energy: where is it in the constellation? What is the posture of the representatives like?

- I take in everything that is going on and try to categorise it. I look at whether my representative is congruent in his reactions, posture, impulses and speech with my own perception. Where do I see myself and where not?

Paying attention to verbal comments:

- I pay attention to the interactions between the representatives.
- The interaction between my representative and the other people in the constellation must have an authentic feel for me. I must be able to understand them.
- I try to notice everything, including the position of the representatives and the messages they are giving me. I attempt to achieve an internal resonance in myself, so that memories return and I feel, yes, this is what it's like.

Paying attention to feelings:

- I pay particular attention to my own feelings and to the feelings that the representatives mirror.
- I pay attention to feelings. Feelings that simply come from nowhere – those are the ones I trust completely. I don't like it if some image or other gets interpreted into feelings.
- When someone feels something for me on my behalf that I haven't been able to feel before, then sometimes I am able to feel it to some degree. When I sense this inside me, then I have the feeling that something inside me has connected again. And then I can feel more again.

Special comments:

- I try to recognise myself in my representative.
- I focus on my main representative and on the representatives for people where I think there is still a secret or a block or entanglement.

Taking in the whole shape:

- I pay attention to the whole constellation and how it develops without focusing on anything in particular.
- I trust that I will take everything in, even if my head is slower than the rest of me, which really does take it all in.
- I don't control, I don't observe, I don't write anything down, I just let it happen. I don't try to manipulate this deep image of my soul.

Taking in solution images:

- I pay attention to see if a new image emerges for me through the constellation, a solution image with which I can identify and detach from other images.

One's own internal attitude:

- I try to be as honest as possible with myself.
- In moments where a constellation gets stuck I try to open up the space inside myself more, so that a solution can emerge.

Body language, expressions, gestures, speech, interaction between representatives – there are various individual markers to which one can orient oneself in one's own constellation. Feelings are frequently named as criteria for whether a patient can feel happy with his or her constellation.

There seem to be two main positions from which patients observe their constellations: one group watches the constellation very precisely and checks whether they recognise their own narrative in the facial expressions, gestures, postures and speech of the representatives. They try to differentiate as to whether certain expressions of the representatives are similar to the person represented, especially in those cases where they know the person. Some, on the other hand, try to be as open as possible to whatever comes up in the constellation, without judging it. Almost all the interviewees said that they pay more attention to their own feelings than to what is being said. Here it is clear that the wish is to search beyond rational under-standing into areas of their own emotional life that have been suppressed and split off.

Only in a very few cases were the interviewees conscious that they were observing the process from their own splits and so alternating between different emotional states. Only one interviewee referred to emotional splits, which are logically present throughout the constellation process: "I am right in it emotionally and simply feel everything that is going on at any moment. And then of course I simply slide into the split. One dissociates again. But I don't do it on purpose – it simply happens." Another interviewee notices himself going into this process of dissociating into a survival state that controls and avoids the trauma feelings. He tries to control this dissociation so as to allow emotional information that might give access to the traumatised parts within him to flow to the representatives: "I focussed on staying in connection with the representatives. I opened myself in order to give the representatives the oppor-tunity to feel and sense and be open to receive the information. I was completely absorbed in opening myself up, in being with myself, and whenever I cut myself off, I was conscious of tracing my way back so that I could open myself again."

As the constellations facilitator I sit close to the patient. In this way I can clearly see that most patients shift between various ego-states during a constellation. Whenever I notice that a patient has got stuck in a controlling survival state, I try to re-establish contact with his healthy ego states and, with utmost care, move his rejected traumatised parts a little more into the foreground.

The patient finds it very helpful to have contact with me as the constellation facilitator and to notice that I am simultane-ously observing both the patient and the constellation. One interviewee put it this way: "It was always exciting to be drawn into what was happening by the facilitator. I was able to add things and remark on what was going on, and then the facili-tator agreed that what I felt was happening was happening."

The role of the facilitator:

The role of the constellations facilitator was described as follows by the interviewees:

- He needs to have a calm appearance and attitude.
- He needs delicacy of feeling, intuition and empathy.
- He must really want to help me personally, and not just because I am a participant who has paid for a constellation.
- He must not feel any sympathy for me, just empathy.
- He must give me the feeling that I am not alone, that there is someone who is looking after me.
- He must accept all of me, including my shadow sides.
- He must let me keep my dignity.

Professional qualities:

- He holds the central and most important role.
- He is my companion during the constellation, and understands me and my issue.
- He must have a lot of experience.
- He must be a professional who doesn't rely on dogma.
- He should hold a neutral position.
- He must be competent in both a human and professional sense.
- He must ensure safety and holding for the constellation.
- He decides which people and feelings are brought into the constellation. If he omits to bring in something important, there may be no resolution.
- I must feel comfortable with his facilitation of the constellation.
- He must be supportive, helpful, establish positive boundaries, and intervene if necessary to prevent me from being retraumatised.
- He must recognise my fears and must not dominate me or the process.
- He must be able to distinguish between what is important

and what is not important. The patient's questions must always be in the foreground and must not be overpowered by secondary issues.

- He must be competent in interpreting ambiguous images.
- It is important that he provides the right phrases to be said that can have a deep effect and so lead to a resolution and positive end of the constellation.
- He must give the constellation enough time to evolve and at no point create the impression of wanting to achieve a specific outcome.
- He must open up the space and keep control of the direction so that I can trust his interventions. He must know what he is doing and simultaneously be open to solutions that nobody expected.
- At the end of a constellation he must give me a theme that I can continue to develop.

Self-reflection of the facilitator:

- The facilitator must give clear direction to me to pay attention at certain points in the constellation. He must not have the same blind spots as me.
- He must not act himself so much but hold the space open for possibilities.
- He must know himself and be flexible; he must have done his own work for himself.

The requirements made of a facilitator therefore are congruent with the profile expected of a good therapist: professional competence, the ability to engage with people and to resolve his own issues. The interviewees think that a facilitator must be able to understand what is taking place in a constellation, that it is making sense in a way that unfolds gradually, step by step, whilst having its own internal logic. He must be able to distinguish what is important from what is unimportant, then he can make specific interventions at the appropriate moment, for example to help the patient to resolve entangled relationships, or to come into closer contact with his split-off traumatised parts.

Patients expect neither expressions of sympathy for nor shock about their life history, and do not want any overly keen attempts to help them. They need someone who will provide a framework, someone who will accompany them patiently and non-judgmentally through a process that is usually full of fear and shame, when they open themselves and allow feelings to arise that they would normally suppress and keep hidden from others. The fear of uncontrolled re-traumatisation is also present here, and emphasises the need for the facilitator to know what he is doing. Patients notice when the facilitator is more concerned with his own issues than with theirs. Almost all the interviewees emphasised that trust in the facilitator is of primary importance. They would not do a constellation with someone they don't trust, don't know or about whom they have not already heard positive feedback. One interviewee stressed that her trust in me as a facilitator was reinforced by having witnessed me doing a constellation for myself. She said: "I believe that only those people who have done this work for themselves and who continue to work on themselves can facilitate a constellation well."

The role of the group:

The group has a particular role in a constellation. The representatives are selected from the group, and those who are not playing a role as a representative in a constellation are supporting the process as a whole. The interviewees made the following statements regarding the significance of the group:

- The group must be large enough to allow for more complex constellations.
- In a large group it helps if a certain percentage of participants has had previous constellation experience.
- The group must support the whole process. There must be a mutual giving and taking and a feeling of belonging.

- There must be no troublemaker who does not fit in the group.
- I must feel able to trust the others in the group. It helps to know them in advance.
- I must feel accepted by the group.
- The group must support me so that I can reveal myself.
- I need an atmosphere where I feel protected.
- The group atmosphere is very healing when grief and strong feelings arise.
- It doesn't make any difference whether individual members of the group are representatives or sit in the outer circle. Everyone contributes to my feeling of being supported throughout the constellation.
- In the group I can see that my own issues are not as absurd as I always thought. Other people have similar problems and I'm not alone with such experiences.
- The group is like a womb, it nourishes and cares for us as we are born and can breathe and live independently.
- It is sufficient to share the deep experiences with the group during a seminar. Further contact afterwards is not necessary. I have high expectations of the group. It must provide me with a sense of safety and trust.

Some of the interviewees stressed that they like it if the group contains many people who have already done constellations. Others prefer being able to choose representatives who are not so experienced in constellations work. This shows a certain anxiety that people experienced in constellations work might bring their own views and prejudices to play. The group suspends the anonymity in which many people normally live with their problems. A constellations group reveals that many other people suffer from similar symptoms and in similar situations.

One interviewee reflected that the perception of a group and its participants has something to do with how far people have already progressed in their own development: "Whenever I was in a group where there were participants who got on my nerves, then that always had something to do with my own issues. The group mirrors my own internal world. There are some people that I really like and others I don't like so much. For me that means that I still have parts in me which I accept and recognise and other parts which I don't accept and don't recognise and which have a difficult time being part of me. Recently I have only been in groups where I get on with everyone. Of course, there are some people I prefer and others that I like less and I have less to do with. But I can't say there are any who make life really difficult for me. That just doesn't happen for me any more. And in that respect the group is something really important. It reflects a huge amount for me. I find that wonderful.

Other general conditions:

According to our interviewees, there are a number of external conditions that seem favourable for constellations groups. These include:

Environmental conditions:

- There must be quiet (no traffic noise); it must be possible to concentrate; the room must be big enough, warm and light.
- The chairs must be comfortable so that sitting for a long time doesn't become torture.
- The room itself isn't important to me.

Provisions:

- I like having my physical well-being attended to.
- We need an atmosphere where we can feel comfortable and welcome.

Time conditions:

- Agreements on punctuality and cooperation must be respected by everybody.
- There must be enough time available.
- The needs of those doing a constellation must be forefront.

- If it lasts for several days there comes a point when it's been long enough to have done the job; if it only lasts for an evening, there's something missing.
- It helps to take a day off after a weekend of constellations to be able to carry on working on one's own constellation in peace.

Protected space:

- Complete confidentiality is of paramount importance.

Relevance:

- Doing a constellation makes sense when I am really ready for it and not if I'm just doing it out of curiosity.

Most interviewees agree on the external conditions for a constellations seminar. It is the job of the facilitator and the seminar organisers to optimise these conditions. The people who are doing constellations for themselves have the responsibility of preparing themselves fully for a constellation and of providing enough opportunity for them to let the constellation continue to unfold.

10.4 How Reliably can Representatives Mirror Issues?

We designed a collection of 27 questions to sort very precisely how well representatives can differentiate between their own issues and the issues of their representation. 58 people answered this part of the questionnaire. We grouped the frequency of experiences in representations. The following general pattern emerged:

Frequency of representations	Number of interviewees
1 to 10	8
20 to 50	13
50 to 100	15
100 to 200	24

The following presents a detailed analysis of four questions:

- How does someone come across in his role as a representative?
- How does he notice that he is being taken over by issues that are not his?
- How can he differentiate between what are and what are not his own issues?
- What helps him to step out of the representation?

Coming across in one's role as a representative:

The participants in a constellations seminar often sense whether they are going to be chosen for this constellation and this role: "When someone presents their issue, one often feels that there is something terrifying about it. I listen very carefully. I can tell from the way I feel that I am resonating with the issue, sometimes I feel I'm being drawn in, that it has something to do with me. Or I get a feeling of excitement that something is resonating with me." Occasionally there are group participants who feel themselves into a role while the patient is telling their story, or who get the feeling of playing a role in the course of a constellation. "I am strongly emotionally engaged, either right from the beginning or during the process. And when it comes to representing a person, or when I get a sudden feeling and don't get chosen, then I start pawing the ground and silently saying 'Please take me, I really want to play a role'".

Usually participants do not reject taking on a role as representative. Even when it means taking on a difficult role (e.g. that of a perpetrator) they tend to be prepared to take it on. One interviewee said she would only reject a role if she knew the client really well and if she were asked to take on a major role (mother, daughter, sister): "I wouldn't feel very free for something new, because I already know so much about her story." It seems to be important that one is specifically chosen for a particular role: "It's important for me to be chosen directly and clearly as a representative, otherwise it just becomes arbitrary."

I have grouped the answers regarding how those people chosen get prepared for a representation and how they come across in the role:

Immediacy of getting into the role:

- I don't have any warm-up phase. I get into the role right away.
- I used to take quite a long time, but now I go into it from the moment I am invited to take on the role.
- I wait until feelings start developing. Sometimes they are there right away, sometimes not. That depends on the role and on whether it is important for the constellation.

Physical contact:

- Usually I stand with my legs quite far apart so I have good grounding. I use my body as an instrument.
- I go into role when the person doing the constellation touches me, perhaps takes another look at me, and when I feel that she really means it.
- Physical contact is important for me. If someone does a constellation rather hesitantly, I take longer to get into the role.
- I sense a lot through the hands of the person doing the constellation.
- I get into role straight away except when something is not right about the issue or if energy is lacking or is withdrawn from me.

Freeing oneself internally:

- I free myself up before every constellation and try to focus on my feelings when I stand in my position.
- I empty myself internally at the beginning, like in autogenic training.
- I have to close my eyes and take a few deep breaths, I

open my crown chakra very consciously and then I can free myself very quickly.

- I close my eyes and feel where I am being drawn and whether I am getting any sensations of warmth or cold. Then the feelings usually start to arise.
- I close my eyes to filter out the external, and feel inside myself. I need a while to get into role.
- I think one puts one's own personality into a kind of waiting room and then fills oneself with this representation.
- Speak little and pay attention to and experience one's feelings.

Going into a trance:

- I experience myself in the constellations circle and feel a particular connection to the others. The larger external circle is just a blurred background.
- It's a state in which everything disappears. Then I go into a different state.

Most of the interviewees report that they first try to make themselves internally free for the representation, to let go of their own feelings and thoughts and switch off as soon as they go into the constellations circle. They want to be present for the constellation and allow themselves to go with it rather than to be agents themselves as would be the case, for example, in a role-play or theatre play. Some use images such as "I feel like a vessel which opens and is filled with information" or "I am a radio with receiver antennae" or "I open something like a 360° radar" or "It's like flicking a switch". Some take off their shoes, take their wallets out of their pockets or put down their spectacles to mark the transition between ordinary participant and representation, and give themselves a good position and ground themselves.

Most of the interviewees thought that their going into a particular role had something to do with the role itself.

Sometimes it happens apparently in a fraction of a second as soon as someone is chosen as a representative and is still sitting in the circle, and sometimes it can take up to five minutes; there are some roles which only develop slowly. It can be that someone in a role does not feel anything at first; the interviewees experience this as being part of the role too, particularly if they know that there are parts of the person that feel nothing, that block feelings and represent a defence against traumatic feelings.

For many the decisive process is paying attention to feelings in the body. For some, important information is transmitted through the hands of the person doing the constellation. Basic physical sensations such as warmth or coldness can constitute entry points for the process of becoming a representative.

In long constellations the focus of the constellation may shift away from a particular representative and the latter may occasionally feel that they are no longer in role, but: "if the role should require it, I can get back into it right away."

Being taken over by something that is alien to oneself

The following list provides some information about how inter-viewees differentiate between their own sensitivities and 'alien' emotions that 'belong' to the person being represented:

Physical symptoms:

- New and unfamiliar physical symptoms such as legs buckling, pain, aggressive feelings or a desire for a person I felt neutral about before.
- I get frightened, get goose pimples, I get hot, I want to sit down, I feel a weight on my shoulders.

Unusual emotional states:

- When I get the feeling that something I'm sensing actually exists in reality, although I usually think that it's nonsense.

- I was in the role of a mother who couldn't help laughing, although what was happening around her was extremely tragic. But I couldn't help behaving that way, although I tried to suppress the laughter. It didn't work. I felt totally mad. I personally felt extremely embarrassed.
- Once I took on the role of a man who had been declared dead as a result of an epidemic during a war. Then he sat upright in his coffin and carried on living. When he returned home after the war, he beat his wife and children. That was the problem. When I was in this role, I couldn't feel anything any more. Nothing. And I knew I had to lash out, I had to lash out to get any kind of a chance to feel anything at all. Lashing out was simply the last chance to feel myself. That made a very deep impression on me.
- For example, I burst into tears, although I didn't really know anything about the situation.
- When I'm in the role, sometimes there's the feeling that there is a mad force beside or behind me.

Unusual behaviours:

- When I suddenly do things I wouldn't normally do as myself.
- When I sense a different posture, and that I'm no longer myself. I think differently, I feel differently, I move differently.
- When I suddenly have an impulse to move. I have to carry out a physical movement that I actually don't want to carry out.

Images that intrude:

- When feelings and images develop on their own without my thinking about them or thinking about anything in particular, but they simply flow through me and out of me.

- When I freeze or suddenly have feelings or no feelings, when I feel drawn to someone in the constellation or feel rejected by them. When sudden thoughts, images and feelings arise.
- I see either images or a landscape of my own, or I am overwhelmed by floods of feelings that don't really have anything to do with my normal situation as it was when I was sitting in the circle before.

Unusual relational experiences:

- I experience relationship with people who are strangers, even though I don't know them, and I feel as I would if I were a child, a husband, a father, according to what the role is.

Energetic perception:

- Because I have emptied myself beforehand, I know that it is something that is not to do with me that is coming into me now.
- I notice in the energy that it's a different, second kind of energy in me. I am not only myself, but have received something else in addition. And I can separate that out.

The interviewees who realised that they were in a representation most clearly were those who noticed something surfacing in them that did not belong to their own realm of experience, and that either fundamentally did not fit or was not congruent with their state just before the constellation. The most convincing symptom was strong physical feelings that began as soon as they stood in the constellation: "At the beginning of a representation it is mainly physical reactions I feel, like pressure on the chest or in the head. Then come feelings like laughter or grief."

Feeling the impulse to move (to turn, to move towards someone, to run away etc.) plays a significant role. Giving in to an impulse to move convinces the representatives that they have been taken by something that isn't to do with their own life. Surrendering to these movements also means switching off 'one's head': "Before, I wouldn't have allowed myself to make such movements. That would have unsettled me. Now I surrender to the movement and notice that I myself wouldn't move in that way. And that's why I am sure that it's a movement that is not mine. If I continue the movement and switch off my thinking, then that is a sure sign for me. "

According to the theory of psychological/emotional splits it is principally feelings that belong to the traumatised parts of a client that the representatives feel most intensely and that give them the sense of being possessed by something that isn't theirs.

Distinguishing between what belongs to one's self and what is someone else's

How can a representative distinguish between his own emotional issues and those of the client? Some interviewees gave very detailed answers:

Fundamental certainty:

- I have no doubt and I trust that I sense what is contained in the role. I am not dealing with my own issues.
- One is always chosen because a part of one is in the issue. And that in itself allows you to recognise your own part.
- When I am in representation, it's like being in a cinema. I am closer to what is different from me than to what belongs to me.
- I feel emotions that are not mine, and feel a need to do or say things that do not belong to me. I sense that it isn't my issue. My own personality recedes into the background like becoming a spectator who pulls back into the audience. I feel a bit like an interpreter who is translating. I am only the broadcaster or transmitter through which information flows.

Sensing the difference:

- There are always slight differences between one's own issues and alien experiences from the role.
- I sense myself first, then the other energy and so I can tell the difference between myself and the other. If I am uncertain, I can always go back to myself and then distinguish between the two.
- I realise consciously that I'm going into the role with my own issues, and I sense if something that happens touches me personally.

Sensing parallels:

- When I sense parallels to my own issues, I see it and let go of what's mine and concentrate on what belongs to the other.
- As soon as I notice similarities with my own issues, that there is a parallel, the thought then immediately goes away, I can switch off my own issues and am in the role again. However, if I went into a situation that was very close to my own, for example if I had to scream in the role but this is something I can't do for myself in my own life, then my thoughts would stay with my own issues.
- Even when I draw parallels to someone who has suffered sexual abuse, I don't sense parallels all the way along. I once experienced a situation where I was the inner child that the adult ego had been looking for – and immediately I became the adult ego that wanted to go to the inner child. That was like an experience where I realised: oh, that's what it looks like inside you, too. It was like an awakening, and understanding. It is not so much that I say, that's what I am, and I'll just pop it outside this situation. It's more the case that the situation in which I was a representative actually helped me to understand myself better. It was extremely revealing to experience myself in the role. It wasn't so much the parallels that I stumbled

across, as the representative situation that helped me understand myself. And even there it was only details, not the whole.

Switching to and fro:

- I come into contact with something that's already there, but I can also sense my way in and out and ask myself whether it's part of me or part of the role.
- I just need to breathe deeply once or twice and then my own issues recede and the other can be present again. My own issues can recede once I have acknowledged them.
- I notice when my thinking is not exactly alien, but also not familiar to me. When I observe myself in the representation a part of me comments on that from outside and marvels that one can see things a different way, in the way I am just experiencing it or saying it in the representation.

In relation to the other representatives:

- When I feel unsure, I can become sure again by attending to the interactions of the other representatives.
- The reactions of the others show me what's right or not. If I bring in too much of my own issues, I'm perfectly prepared to say: just a moment, there's something not right here for me.
- I mirror in my behaviour whatever the situation is that I experience, regardless of whether I can tell if it's my own issue or foreign to me. First and foremost I mirror. And if I have the feeling that it's to do with me, then I name that, to let the facilitator know what is going on and to get feedback from others in the constellation. Depending on the reactions of others, I clarify whether it is my issue or not. And up till now, even when my issues were running in parallel, what was going on in me was always also relevant to the constellation.

In order to distinguish between what is one's own and what belongs to the role, it is necessary first to develop a sense of what is one's own. Most of the interviewees were confident in sensing what was their own issue. Thus it is possible in a constellation process to switch to and fro between one's own issues and those of the other within the role. Most of the interviewees thought that the role also had something to do with them personally, otherwise they would not have been chosen for it. "I am not certain as to whether everything that one takes on in these representations doesn't also have to do with oneself to some extent. I haven't yet had a role where I could maintain that it had absolutely nothing to do me, that it was completely different. I have always had some point or other where it connected to my own issues." The interviewees do not have any fundamental problem with the parallels between their own processes and those they experience as other in the representations, but rather have at their disposal many ways of separating what is their own from what is not. "Suddenly I realise, oops, that's me there now. Well anyway, at least I have the feeling that I sensed that two things are fusing, conflating, and that one of them is most certainly mine. Then I pull myself together internally and tell myself: well, my issues are going to step back here, now I'm going to do something different and stay in the role. I can see that my issues are getting involved, but if my issue starts gaining ground too much I'm simply not going to allow it." One interviewee said that whenever he felt uncertain he would just wait a while: "When I am uncertain whether I'm bringing in too much of my own issues, I wait a bit and gauge whether an impulse is going to come again. I wait about three times and then I express it."

In particular, physical experiences, rather than images and imaginings, help to reassure most of the representatives enabling them to distinguish between what is theirs and what isn't: "If I get the feeling that I'm getting caught up in images and associations that I have heard about somewhere or read about in some novels, I get cautious and rely on my physical sensations and on the essence of the feelings. I prefer not to get caught up in the images, but to stay with the feeling, because the images sometimes seem somehow superficial and are often too dramatic and deflect from the theme."

The interviewees thus do not seem to want to deny or ignore the part of them that can appear in the role as a representative. When the representative recognises this possibility and sees it happening during a constellation, it loses most of its power to disturb the constellation or put the constellations method under question. Instead it becomes a moment that fosters the development of the whole process. There seems to be a basic tendency not to confuse one's own issues with those of the other, and to be particularly careful not to impose one's own issues on those of the other: "If the role overlaps with my own problems, I tend to hold back with my own judgements and remarks and consider whether it's really about the other person or actually about me. Holding back and waiting enables clarity to re-emerge."

During the constellation process doubts about confusion between what is one's own and what is the other's are often put aside, so that concentration can be given fully to the role. For some interviewees their feelings are the main criteria to inform them as to whether they are still in the role or not. They realise that this is the case when they start looking for solutions at times when a constellation stagnates or gets stuck: "The only thing I would call 'alien' when I am in representation would be my own thought constructs." In such situations the solution is to go back into feeling and sensing again and connect with oneself.

When the person is uncertain, another strategy for testing whether what one feels in the representation is something significant for the role is to orientate oneself to the reactions of the others: "There are things which are so alien to me that I don't trust myself to say them. And sometimes some cue comes from somebody else (another representative) and that confirms it for me. Or, if there is no cue, I turn to the other representatives with my question. If someone says something affirmative, then I feel secure in what I am sensing." Often

246

one only begins to reflect about one's own feelings about the role after a constellation has been completed and one has been released from the role. It seems very important here to have trust in the constellations method as such.

In this section of questions the role of the facilitator again became clear. It was pointed out repeatedly that it is best left to the facilitator and his experience to filter out what can and what cannot support the constellation process. It was felt to be helpful if the facilitator trusted the whole process himself, went with it and did not attempt to enforce his own opinions: "The facilitator must be capable of leading the constellation. I must have the feeling that he trusts the process and shows an interest in the representatives. He must not intervene in a controlling way or try to enforce his own ideas. I must have the feeling that he trusts the process and is willing to go with it. He must open himself completely to the process and lead it at the same time." It seems important to the representatives for the facilitator to be non-judgemental towards them and what they say. That helps them feel safe in taking on the role and expressing all the sensations and impulses that arise in the role.

If particularly deep feelings come up in the role they tend to be interpreted by some interviewees as belonging to them personally. If they wonder whether their own issues are being confused with another's, some tend to turn to the facilitator for clarification. Once they address the issue, some kind of clarity usually ensues which allows the constellation to continue. Should their own issues come too much to the fore, they have the option of stepping out of the role: "When I notice that I can't distinguish what's personal to me and what belongs to the role, I simply step out of it."

If the representatives are to master this task of accurately distinguishing between what is and what isn't theirs, and not confuse their own issues with those of the client, whilst at the same time being able to become deeply involved in the role, they need sufficient space and time, and must not be criticised by the facilitator or by other seminar participants in what they are expressing: "The facilitator is not important to me as such. For me it's only important to be given enough freedom. That should be how he facilitates the constellation and what his motivation is. I have experienced a lot of constellations facilitators. There are facilitators who use the constellation as a stage on which to play 'king'. That is awful. Then there are those who are not confident. That's awful too; I just can't stand it. Then there are those who manipulate like mad. They tell you what to do and what not to do. That's dreadful. You can only go into it really deeply if you have the freedom to move as you like. I must not feel criticised by the facilitator. I think it's catastrophic when that happens." The following answer is similar: "If I can play a part totally as I feel it and don't get pulled up, stopped or criticised, then I think that the constellation can work. I think the facilitator is crucial to the process. And I think that if he doesn't bring love into this work then nothing good can come of it. I am completely convinced about that."

In my function as a facilitator I have come to the conclusion that steering such a complex process cannot be done by control and giving instructions. A constellation is an open process with many degrees of freedom and individual decisions that limit the number of options available. These limitations must arise from the internal logic of the constellated soul-system itself, and that mediates the freedom of choice for the representatives. As a facilitator I trust that the system itself will steer towards a resolution of conflicts in the soul if it is in the first place allowed to unfold in its complexity and not have its variety and liveliness reduced by one-dimensional thinking from the start. For example, how could I decide as facilitator whether remarks made by a representative are a part of his own issues rather than the role he has assumed? Would I not then be imposing my own ideas, my own assumptions? How can I know from the start what the patient's actual inner conflict might be? If I did, would a constellation be necessary at all?

I also often take on representations and ask myself each time whether what I am sensing and how I am behaving in the role has anything to do with the soul structures of the client or not. Intellectually I am never completely certain, but I allow whatever comes up for me in my representation to arise in terms of how my body feels and wants to move.

I had one particular experience that impressed me deeply when I was supposed to take on the role of the survivor part of a patient. There was another representative in the constellation who took on the role of the patient's mother, and one who took on the role of a part of him that was symbiotically attached to the mother. At first I was aware that the part I was representing was trying to make contact with the mother, but in vain. The mother's representative stood with her back towards me and I kept stepping forwards and backwards, but couldn't get nearer to her. Then I felt I had to close my eyes, and then my mouth. I felt more and more isolated and in the dark. My right hand suddenly began to shake. I found I had to breathe harder and harder. The representative for the mother seemed to hear this breathing and reacted defensively. Now she wanted to get away from me (later it transpired that the wheezing reminded her of abuse by her father.) Now in my role I knew that there was no longer any chance of being accepted by the mother. My body started shaking more and more, vibrating and moving. I felt as if I had to free myself of this old way of being which kept me a prisoner in darkness. I fought, moved my arms and legs and shook my body until I could open my eyes and free myself from this paralysed and frozen state. I breathed deeply and gradually turned around, away from the scene with the mother and the part of the patient that was still clinging onto her. I was exhausted, hungry and thirsty. I found something to drink in the room, and that gave me the strength to continue distancing myself from the mother, and eventually I got to a window in the room, which I opened and I leaned out into the fresh air, and it seemed, into the world. It felt like a release; but then I began to feel cold. I began to freeze at the open window. I had distanced myself from the stressful situation with the mother, but I was also desperately alone and lonely and cold. I didn't know how to go on, and I couldn't go back.

In this representation of trying to be in contact with the patient's mother I had gone into a traumatised state and had saved myself by splitting and going into survival mode. The patient whose constellation it was sent me an email that evening: "Many thanks for the constellation today! That was the first time, when I saw the two parts of me, that I felt every sentence, every wheeze, every freezing and every feeling had been understood and experienced, and I felt totally understood. It was unbelievable. Whenever I wheezed, you wheezed and A. (the representative for the other part) did the same when she froze. Right now I feel very sad, but calm and relaxed. Not fighting, not suffering... simply calm and relaxed. Now I understand these parts of myself and understand myself and my feelings in the context of all the women in my past. It suddenly all makes sense."

When several people in a family do a constellation, there is an opportunity to draw comparisons. In one example from our interviews a mother and daughter were able to compare their experiences of doing their own individual, separate constellations: "I spoke to my daughter, who does lots of constellations and my history has always played a major part in them. We exchanged our similar experiences, which was really good for me. Because she has experienced exactly the same as I have in my own constellations. We agreed that the same things were happening."

Wanting to help?

When someone is in a representation, do they feel they want to help the person doing the constellation? Many interviewees answered that they are very familiar with this need to help, but they avoid going into a helper or therapist role while they are representatives. It doesn't serve the person whose constellation it is to have people wanting to help. Some of the interviewees refer to their experiences with other constellations facilitators where they saw the facilitator going into a helper mode: "I have now got over my helper syndrome. But at the beginning, when I first started constellations work, I thought the whole purpose was to help the person doing the constellation. Then I saw that a lot was being staged by the facilitator in the constellations in order to help, and gradually I realised that this didn't help at all, that it was just a performance. And then I felt very unhappy as the representative. Because I had the feeling that I was saying what I felt but also having to create something I didn't feel. And that's not OK. Then I had an argument with the facilitator, who told me to do this and that like this and that in my role. And I said: no, I won't do that because it doesn't feel right. From that moment I realised that it's not about creating a 'help-garden' out of a constellation, but about observing and showing the truth even if the truth is not particularly funny. Since then I decided that I will represent what I feel. And I don't stage anything because it won't help anybody."

Releasing oneself from the representation

Sometimes it happens that a person in the holding circle of a constellation suddenly has a severe reaction and feels as if they are a part of the constellation, although they have not been chosen as a representative. Some people insist on being allowed to join the constellation immediately. This is an ambivalent situation for the constellations facilitator: on the one hand it is true that the participant in the outer circle may sense something that is to do with the constellation, but has not yet been represented; on the other it may be that the constellation has touched something in the participant's own soul history, that he is projecting some of his own issues into the constellation. As a rule I will ask this participant to hold back and to observe what is going on for him. In my experience, participants who join a constellation in such a way may find it difficult to come out of the role at the end of the constellation. When they are released from the role it becomes apparent how much they are stuck in something that belongs to their own family system.

Consequently being released from a representation is a significant element in constellations work. There is a justified fear of getting 'stuck' in a representation. Rituals for being released are a necessary and integral component of my work with constellations. Our interview sample gave us a number of indications about how people experience being released from a representation and what is helpful in that process.

Careful release from the role:

- I come out of the representation straight away because it doesn't belong to me.
- At the end of a constellation I always go back into my own self.

Letting the role taper out:

- Sometimes I don't want to come out of the role. I think I want to stay with this theme for a bit, and then it just goes away.

Being released by the facilitator:

- The facilitator releases me and tells me I am myself again and says my name.
- We shake hands and perhaps give each other a hug. Conversations in the break after the constellation are a great help for me.
- The person doing the constellation must take back everything that belongs to him very earnestly and seriously. He takes what is his and I keep what is mine.

Some methods employed by representatives:

- I release myself from the role.
- Fresh air, going back to one's own place in the circle or leaving the room.

- Breathing, breathing, it's a question of practice.
- I physically go out and move around a bit.
- I shed the role, or imagine taking a shower.
- What helps me to consciously release myself is drinking a lot of water, dusting myself down, taking a step back, and rubbing my face.
- Eating something, especially something sweet, and having a drink.
- I imagine a kind of cleansing glow to release myself internally.
- I take a bow to whatever I have been representing, and I'm myself again right away.

Many representatives can quickly assume the internal perspective of the person they are representing. They can also step out of the representation very quickly. Most of them don't find this particularly problematic according to the interview results. Releasing rituals (the person doing the constellation thanks the representative and calls him by his own name), shaking one's body, thinking one's own thoughts, airing the room and having enough breaks after the constellation are all things the representatives find helpful in releasing themselves from the role.

Going into a representation, and releasing oneself again seems to be a matter of practice according to statements made by our interviewees. The more often one is a representative and the more often one takes part in constellations, the easier it becomes to release oneself from a role.

If someone gets stuck in a role for a long time it usually has something to do with their own story and the events in their family of origin. That is why it is helpful for people to understand this, so that they can emerge easily from the feelings that they feel held in. "The longest time I have been stuck in a role is an hour, until I realised: just a minute, these are actually feelings my mother has. And in the moment where that was verbalised and I told a friend I was talking to, it disappeared – I was myself again."

Occasionally no clear resolution is found in a constellation and the representative can remain in a certain feeling. One interviewee reported: "I felt a huge rage until the next day because the constellation hadn't resolved itself." One interviewee reported a very interesting experience she had in her difficulty in coming out of a representation; her story shows that representatives can represent two aspects of a person simultaneously and thus need to be released from both parts. "I was in the role of a mother. Her ex-husband, that is the father of the person doing the constellation, was also in the constellation. So there were the father and the mother, divorced for over 20 years, I suppose they had a kind of marriage tragedy. The person doing the constellation released me from the role of her mother, as she had put me into that specific role. But I still felt totally in the role of the wife. So it was a kind of double role. Although she had put me in as her mother and released me from that, somehow I couldn't get out of the wife role for another two days. Then I rang the person whose constellations it was and said: 'please release me from the role again on the phone.' She said: 'Yes, I release you from the role of my mother.' And then I said: 'Listen, say her name and tell me: I release you from the role of M.' – her mother was called M. She said: 'I release you from the role of M.' – and then it was gone. So for some reason a split had formed inside me in the constellation and I was released from just one role (the mother) and not from the other (the wife), because nobody had realised what had happened."

Shedding a role can also be difficult if a person who has severe splitting is being represented. "I represented a split personality with a very structured sound part and a very sick soul part. This split preoccupied me and weighed me down for a long time." If only one representative is put in to represent a person who is severely traumatised, the representative can be clearly observed to switch suddenly from one part into the other, for example from the trauma-self into the survival-self. Since coming to understand more about these processes and placing part personalities of people right from the beginning, I am more able to avoid the danger of having representatives switching to and fro between the splits in the person they are representing. It is easier for the representatives then to represent only one part of a split person at a time. I had only just begun this new way of working when we conducted the interviews.

It can be a great contribution to the healing of a person when another puts themselves at their disposal as a representative. The willingness to provide this service might not be as spontaneous and great as I experience it to be in my seminars, were it not that all seminar participants seem to gain from taking on the role of a representative. Altruistic motives and caring for oneself can complement each other: "Why am I a representative? My main motivation is to do something good for myself. Constellations are the only place where I can learn with both head and heart. I don't manage that with other ways of learning. For me it is important to understand with my emotions, it's about linking the head and emotions."

Constellations provide insight into the world of others. They make things accessible to which one previously had no access. According to the statements of many interviewees the constellation is a learning environment par excellence for the inner life of human beings: "it does me good to experience feelings, no matter whether they are negative or positive. I can slip into a role and express what I feel." Representative experiences make psychological illnesses comprehensible: "Then, if I feel totally depressed in the role, I think, ah, so that is how the world looks like for a totally depressed person. That is an amazing experience – as long as you get out of it and don't live in it."

A male interviewee says that his world view and view of human beings has expanded through doing representations: "It is hard to describe, but after a constellations day I feel as if I have shared experiences with a lot of people. As if I have gained some experience and knowledge from all the systems in which I have played a part. After a constellations seminar I have the feeling I have gained as much interpersonal experience as would have taken years otherwise. For example, I was able to understand what depression is like for the first time after a constellation: that grief can be transferred from one person to another. Grasping this experience in an emotional sense – not from a textbook – has been invaluable. I've also learned a lot about interpersonal relationships. That has helped me understand my own emotional life more; I can feel processes that I didn't really understand originally. The experiences I've had in constellations work have been all the more valuable because, although I knew about emotional processes from psychological counsellors, I hadn't experienced them. I was able to experience and feel them through the representations; a great treasure trove of experience! The constellations have also made me more sensitive to interpersonal relationships. I tend to judge less and respect my fellow human beings more. Constellations work has helped me expand my empathic capacity considerably. My basic view of human beings has changed substantially; I see more connections, the bigger picture. When I think about my children this means paying more attention to being authentic, not burying family secrets and avoiding unnecessary burdens for the soul."

Some representatives find it particularly revealing when they are in a role that has something in common with their own parents, whether this is a traumatised mother with whom a child could not connect, or a father who was sexually abusive. "For example, I was in a role which, afterwards, I finally realised was my mother. I didn't notice it while I was in the role. I noticed only afterwards that that was how my mother must have felt. It was especially important for me, because in the role I couldn't get close to the child, because as the mother I was traumatised. And feeling like someone else feels, that's like having insight into the world of feelings, actions and thoughts of another person. It makes me feel empathy and understanding."

According to interviewees, representations also allow access to those parts of one's own soul that have not previously been understood very well. "Sometimes I am in a role where I get the feeling that I'm in one of my split parts. And somehow I get an insight, like: oh, that's the way a part of me reacts. It's a kind of journey into one's own inner self. You can understand yourself a bit better somehow. You can put the pieces of the puzzle together more easily. You simply have more understanding and more insight and more perspective and a better chance to heal."

Representations in constellations seem to provide knowledge that goes far beyond intellectual understanding, because feelings are included right from the start. "I get new dimensions to certain feelings from the representations I do. That leads to deeper knowledge – not intellectual knowledge, but emotional knowledge. I can't formulate it or name it any other way – here's an example: that 'rage' doesn't have just one face, but many faces."

Body, emotion and intellect seem to come together in a special way in this learning process: "For me it's about feelings, about telling the difference between them and about having a language and a consciousness for them, knowledge about what is going on, what belongs to developmental stages, splits and so on. It enables me to have a factual and theoretical knowledge, and to develop emotional knowledge. It's not just about having some theory or other in my head because I've learned it or read about it, but it's because the knowledge, this consciousness, is bound up with feelings and because I have then experienced what splitting is, what trauma is. Without doing representations and observer roles I wouldn't understand the connections between trauma and attachment. If I only heard about it, I wouldn't understand it. Understanding only really comes through feeling it in representations, or when I can experience it in the outer circle as an observer. The theoretical knowledge becomes much more comprehensible for me this way. For example, if the issue is about splitting and I am a split part, and I experience something that another part is ignorant of, or if I can observe from the outer circle how splitting functions, then I can understand it. Otherwise I don't get it. A book wouldn't be enough for me."

10.5 New Information from Constellations

New things come to light in family constellations that tend to be elusive in other therapeutic methods. The particular way that I work with constellations allows those traumatic events in a family system that have been split off from consciousness and represent the root cause of relationship conflicts and symptoms of physical illness to be revealed and understood. Perhaps that is why so many patients who are searching for secrets in their families come to my seminars.

An important question in this work with the constellations method is: can the events that are revealed in the process of a constellation, that may point to suppressed and hidden events that are never talked about and kept secret in the patient or his family system, really have happened as shown in the constellation? The next section addresses how patients deal with such new and often emotional information. Should they take what has appeared in the constellation as fact? Should they let it rest or should they investigate further and gather evidence? Should they search in registration offices or church records? Should they ask their family? Have secret DNA testing done? Confront the members of their family with their new insights or assumptions? Bring charges against perpetrators? Or should they wait and see what their soul does with the information?

Type of new information

50 of the 71 interviewees answered part 3 of our questionnaire and fed back what new information had come up for them in either one or several constellations and how they dealt with this information after the constellation.

The first focus was that in most cases the new information was about sexual abuse. In 17 interviews (34%) the interviews reported that the constellation showed that either they themselves had been sexually abused in their childhood by either their own father or grandfather (8 cases), or that their mother, a sister or their grandmother had been victims of sexual abuse as children. In one case there was information that the grand-mother had been raped by a soldier during the war.

The second focus of new information centred on uncertain identity of a father. This happened in 11 cases (22%) of our sample. For 10 people it concerned their own father, in one case it concerned the client's sister's father. The theme of unclear parenthood applied in one case to the mother's parents, in another case to the great-grandmother's parents (which seemed to be to do with incest) and in a further case to the Jewish bloodline of the family, which had been hidden during the time of National Socialism in Germany.

The third focus centred on the killing of children (9 cases, 18%). In one case on the mother's side there had been a large number of abortions in the family which were never spoken about, and in two other cases children resulting from abusive and incestuous relationships were apparently killed; in two further cases it seemed as though the person's own mother had killed some of her children out of hate and feelings of being overwhelmed.

Dealing with the new information

The following points give examples of case histories of different problem areas in order to show how the people concerned have coped with their new situation.

Abuse within the family system

- *Abuse by the father came to light*
  "At first I was very shaken and unsettled. Very gradually I came to accept it. Now I am not so fearful and am braver in some things in everyday life; I know how to make boundaries and am getting more and more stable. Now I drive on the motorway much more, which is some-thing I wouldn't have done before."

- *Their own abuse and the mother's abuse*
  "I tried to see my mother from the perspective of a traumatised person. That enabled me to have more empathy
  and understanding. In respect to my own sexual abuse I
  try not to project old burdens onto my daughter. And
  from the time of the constellation I wouldn't start any
  more relationships with men that would have led to
  repeated abuse."
- *Abuse by the father*
  "An awful lot happened afterwards. The relationship with
  my mother changed. I would say that we got closer. That
  was a slow process, and six months ago it was still very
  difficult. The relationship with my children has changed
  completely. My children are now much closer to me, and
  they say that themselves. For example, my daughter told
  me a year ago: "Mummy, I am really close to you, but
  not you to me." And now she says: "You're really close
  to me." I can really tell that the burden of my children
  has disappeared. I have a completely different sense of
  intimacy. I used to think I could get really close to
  people, to partners and children. And now I can see that
  I used to have a problem. Since I realised that, well, I
  don't have a partner, but in relation to my children –
  since being able to see things realistically – I've got much
  closer to them. My sense of what a relationship is has
  changed, too. Looking back I can see that my relationships all failed because my 'inner child' kept trying to
  find attachment. My partners, of course, weren't able to
  do that for me."
- *Abuse of the patient's mother*
  "When I asked my mother, she said it wasn't true. A week
  later she said yes, that it was true. That made me trust the
  constellation method more. It also helped me step out of my
  deep confusion a little. At first I only registered everything
  in my head. Now I can look at it with my own authentic feelings, at least from time to time."

- *The patient's sister was abused by their father*
"The days immediately after the constellation were crazy. I think that was the first time in my life that I couldn't sleep. The whole thing was a shock. Afterwards I began to feel better day by day. Now it doesn't bother me any more, it is simply there. It is just the way it was, and now I can say it doesn't play any part in everyday life except when I have contact with my parents. Contact is much more relaxed now. Before there was huge tension between us. That isn't there any more. The relationship itself hasn't changed, but since I know about what happened, it's been easier to be around them. I can deal with it better. It doesn't bother me any more. I couldn't go to my parents if I have a problem. They won't change. But I can deal with it better."
- *Witness of abuse of the patient's sister*
"I often had a lot of trouble with my blood circulation and used to feel faint. During the constellation a situation of abuse came to light where I seemed to have been watching my foster mother abuse my foster sister. The constellation made absolute sense to me and afterwards I felt very relieved."

War trauma

- *The patient's grandmother was raped by a Russian soldier during the war*
"It helps me to understand that my mother was disturbed in early childhood. I needn't take it personally when she has a blackout. I can remove myself in my imagination and what's left is sadness. I don't have to put my own self into question."
- *The patient's mother has been seriously traumatised by her war experiences*
"I kept having conflicts with my boss and realised how that had resulted from my relationship with my mother, and how aimless I am and without direction because my mother rejects parts of me. This is a game I repeated with my bosses. Realising that has been a great relief and I have decided to go into therapy to work through it."

Uncertain parentage

- *The patient's father has a different father*
  "I asked my mother whether that could be true. She told me that it was, and that was why he was in a home and was not accepted either by his mother or his father. The situation was so conclusive and made such sense to me that it felt very cleansing. The result is that I have made peace with my father completely and I know that I still need to work on the feeling of not being wanted, and that my children could be affected by the same feeling. "
- *A suspicion that the patient's father is not their real father*
  "The constellation made sense for me. I haven't done a DNA test to prove or disprove it. My sister was very upset, and my brother said it just confirms what he had felt before anyway. "
- *Forgery of a birth certificate to prove Aryan descent during the era of National Socialism in Germany*
  "I had suspected for a long time that my great-grandfather on my mother's side was Jewish. That was confirmed in the constellations. My mother used to deny it vehemently whenever I asked her. After the constellation she didn't exactly confirm it, but the way she talked about it made me think that it must be true, that he was Jewish. That means that he was not the father named on the papers. We're talking about my great-grandfather on my mother's side. That was in the time of the Third Reich. My mother's father was an SS member, so was her brother, so she had to be Aryan. That's why originally there was no entry in her birth certificate, according to what a relative said – and later what my mother said; originally there was no mention of this on the birth certificate or on the church register. In the Third Reich the different father was entered instead, and he was pure Aryan. But in several constellations it appeared that the one I had thought was the physical father of my grandmother on my mother's side, actually was. And afterwards,

after the constellations, I managed to conclude from various stories that this was indeed true. That is, this Jewish man is my great-grandfather, not the one who was in the records. Then there was some information that two children from this Jewish side of the family survived the Third Reich in my family's cellar. And it was such a relief for me to know that my feelings were right, and not those 'correcting voices' from outside, which used to drive my feelings and my consciousness into a mad corner. That was such a relief and another step for me in trusting myself and my feelings. In principle there are two secrets: that on the one side there was this Jewish father. And then in further constellations it transpired that we have perpetrators, Nazis, in our family. That is my family debt. It's just the way it is. I don't need to fight for the victims and against the perpetrators any more. My job is to keep going into the third position. And now, when I look back over it carefully through all the years I see that it's not about taking a position, winning and keeping that position. It's always a matter of trundling along, because it's easy to throw myself on the side of the victims. And sometimes it's easy to be on the side of the perpetrators. There are both in my family. There are both in me. This victim-perpetrator theme is relevant to me; I have been a victim and I have been a perpetrator. And it's a matter of looking at both of them, sensing both, and then creating something different. That's an exhausting process, but very good, and very valuable. "

Killing of children within the family system

- *Many abortions*
  "There seemed to have been a lot of abortions on my mother's side of the family. I have become more aware of this in conversations with my mother. The relationship has got a bit better, but she still finds it very difficult having guilt feelings and being put under pressure. But I have got a bit freer. "

- *The patient's mother's sister, who was born during the war, died in confused circumstances*
  "The way my grandmother says that she can't remember things tells me that there was something, but she wouldn't say what it was. I get the feeling that it was different from what came up in the constellation. I tried to persuade my mother to work with constellations, but I didn't say anything about my own insight because I thought she would deny it and close up unless she experienced it herself. It made me realise why I felt so uncomfortable with authority and with relationships where I felt dependent and why I reacted so strongly to tyranny. I'm assuming that this discomfort comes from this family history; whenever I feel this discomfort, I ask myself whether it's justified or whether it is connected to this old story."

- *Mother's sister died as a child; her death was not due to natural causes, but she was drowned*
  "I knew I had an aunt with the same name as me and I knew she had died as a small child around the age of two or three. I was told she had died of enteritis. In the constellation it was revealed that she had actually been murdered in water, drowned. This made total sense to me because those drowning experiences were exactly the symptoms I was experiencing. I couldn't wear tight necklaces or tight-necked pullovers because they made me feel choked. And whenever I went in a swimming pool or in the sea I never wanted to go in deep. I could dive, but not properly under water, not so that the water went over my ears because that felt really strange. And then when the representative in the constellation said she had been strangled in the water that made total sense for me. My inner voice said straight away: yes, that's right. It was as if from that moment I understood a lot of my own symptoms and feelings. It made sense for me that some children were simply not allowed to be born and that they were aborted. I'd had this same feeling before, like when I had my first period and kept crying and felt as if

there was this child who wasn't allowed to live. This blood was supposed to be for a child, and I couldn't understand any of it. And after the constellation, when I realised all this, I knew why I had these feelings. It hadn't made any sense before. I've always felt a high regard for children, and after I realised all this I developed even more respect for children, more respect for life, and whenever I see a human being, I see not only what's in front of me but their whole background history."

- *Murder of the mother's sister*
  "It took several constellations for it to make sense and come to light. It also took some time for me to be able to accept it. Then I asked my mother about it, and she denied it. One uncle, my mother's brother, went to see a priest when I told him he had had another sister. He didn't know anything about another sister, so he had a look in the church records, and found some mysterious information about the circumstances of her death, something about a death in a gravel pit. This gravel pit had been owned by the person who, in the constellation, was shown as this sister's murderer. So one part of the family had known of the existence of this sister whilst another part of the family hadn't, and my uncle's spontaneous reaction was: 'Oh, she was murdered.' It made sense to him straight away, and yet this was an entirely spontaneous reaction, without *knowing* that this was a murder. It was his spontaneous reaction when he read about a sister who had died so early and in mysterious circumstances. It was his own reaction, totally his own, without having any other information. My niece is anorexic but since the time I told her mother about this murder she has started eating again, she is much better. My niece's mother discussed it all with a psychologist. Nothing can be proved, but it seems that there are connections. I see it as a confirmation of something I have always felt, and for me it's a real relief to know the reason. Everything used to be fuzzy and now it's clear. And it's much easier for me to deal with it. Before I had no idea how to, or how I was supposed to, deal with my

265

feelings. Things get clearer with time and a bit more solid. I'm calmer, less emotional, and I don't provoke so many conflicts. You get to know your own patterns, and don't fall into them so often. "

- *The patient's grandmother killed her own child*
  "My suspicion that a child had been killed was substantiated. It was somehow reassuring to know it at last. During the constellation I was shocked to the core. Shocked as well about the hints of madness that I had seen in my mother and that I felt connected to also. But in the constellation there was a representative who held these feelings of madness very firmly away from me. I think it was a representative of 'Help'. After the constellation I felt a bit more reassured that my perceptions are not really mad. "

- *The patient's older sister doesn't have the same father and so she herself is her father's oldest daughter. Her mother is also not her grandfather's daughter and her mother's half-sister died in mysterious circumstances.*
  "After the constellation I felt very distressed. I started to do some research and even found the name of my half-sister's biological father. My mother's sisters already knew about all of this, but my mother refused to give me any information. I asked my aunts to tell me the truth. I asked each aunt individually and got the same answer each time. That's how I found out the name of my half-sister's father. But he was already dead. My older sister looks quite different to the rest of us. When we met about two months after the constellation my older sister gave me a hug and said: 'I always had the feeling that you're the oldest of us sisters.' She didn't know anything about my constellation. The outcome of the constellation makes sense for me, and gradually I'm getting calmer and calmer. The mysterious death of my mother's sister was confirmed again in another constellation. All in all my own death wish has lost its hold. Friends tell me that I'm much more relaxed. I'm quite happy now with myself and my life. "

266

Other traumatic events

- *Siblings who were stillborn before the patient's own birth*
"This really moved me deep down and it's been confirmed by other sources. For a few days I had contact with this brother and just showed him my world. I am still moved whenever I mention it. This information was confirmed again in a later constellation. All my siblings were represented, including my stillborn brother."
- *The patient's mother was extremely violent when the patient was a small child*
"I always felt huge tensions in my body. They showed up especially in back pain, nail-biting and grinding my teeth. Through doing the constellation I gave myself permission to protect myself from her. After that I felt very happy inside, my nails are beginning to grow again and I have the confidence to show my feminine side a bit more. I also started one-to-one therapy, and it confirmed to me that my mother had traumatised me with her extreme aggression."

Persistent ambiguity

- For three interviewees the constellation produced more ambiguity than clarity: in two cases it was hinted that the mother's parentage was unclear (Incest? Adopted child?); in one case, according to newspaper reports, there had been a murder in the family. The circumstances of this murder seemed to hint at and influence the patient's current problem, yet had not led to any satisfactory resolution for the patient.

82% of the interviewees in our sample found the new information from their constellations completely congruent, and another 12% found them partially congruent. As has been mentioned, for 6% the new information was not at all congruent. It is an extremely serious matter for patients and their families when something comes to light through a constellation that indicates that people in the family seem to be abusers or even murderers. So it is understandable that the patient's relatives, partners or friends consider it dangerous to accuse another person of having done what was revealed in the constellation. People who have no experience with constellations work particularly tend to reject such new information or consider constellations as a method to be suspect.

The results of this part of our study showed that most of the interviewees dealt very well with situations when new information came to light in their constellation, and when this information activated feelings of guilt and shame. In 94% of the cases in such constellations the interviewees did not plunge into confusion, but managed to extract something positive for themselves from the information. Even if, as in many cases, they didn't have or try to get any additional evidence to give them confirmation, the majority found it a relief to have found an explanation or a justification for trusting their feelings that something was not right in their family. Recognising and accepting this painful past seems to allow patients to develop clarity and the strength to leave this behind them and begin something new. Most of the interviewees in time became reconciled to their own history and their family's history, however painful, horrifying and bad this might have been. They felt much better about their parents and relatives and had better relationships with them than they previously had. This, on the whole positive result has in my opinion to do with the fact that not only are family traumas made conscious in constellations, but healing processes are simultaneously initiated.

Constellations are perhaps one of the few ways that secret truths in one's family can be revealed in one's soul. However, one should not expect constellations to prove something objectively that has happened in a family or in the life of a patient. For example, if it is shown that a child's paternity is ambiguous, it may well be that the child has a different father. However, it might also be the case that the patient's feelings towards his biological father are inhibited because the mother does not love her husband easily, perhaps because she loves

another, or even because she is entangled in an abusive relationship with her own father, so that she sees her father in her
child's father, or even in her own son. If constellations are
broken off too quickly in such cases, then only the first layer
of reality might be revealed, which may be only a fraction of
the truth in such a family system. Where the paternity is
unclear, a DNA test can always be considered of course.

Whenever a constellation throws up a question as to
whether something has taken place in a family or not, in my
opinion the main issue concerns whether the information might
be of benefit for the therapeutic process of the patient. This
benefit is always a subjective matter; that is, the main goal is
for the patient to find resolution for his symptoms, feelings and
internal images, so that he can find a way out of his emotional
and mental confusion and disentangle from the unhealthy
entanglements in his family. In my opinion there is a maximum
amount of objectivity available through allowing the maximum
space for the subjectivity of the patient, so that the person can
develop their feelings, ideas and thoughts in as personal a way
as possible, and so that they can see and feel themselves
mirrored in the constellation. A person will never be able to be
his true self in psychotherapy if he is limited by what he might
think he is supposed to be or do, or by inhibitions, morality,
rules, expectations or well-meant advice about how he should
behave. Only if he feels that the psychotherapist accepts him
completely as he is will he be able to increase gradually his
ability to understand himself and to accept himself as he is,
and be able to take full responsibility for himself and his own
future. A person will only be able differentiate between his
own feelings, ideas and thoughts and those of his ancestors
once he is willing to take responsibility for his own life,
instead of fleeing from something out of fear, rage, defiance or
childish love, or instead of fighting against something,
complaining or wanting to save his parents or anyone else.
Only then will he develop beyond his own fantasies and illusions and arrive at his own reality, regardless of how difficult
his past may have been.

10.6 Summary and Discussion

This research project produced a number of important answers to the questions posed:

- Constellations have a particular significance as a psychotherapeutic method for many people. They are suited in many respects to pick up emotional problems that lead people to psychotherapy, and to illuminate their underlying background and wider context. They surpass one-to-one therapy sessions in enabling diagnosis and offering specific therapeutic interventions. Within a protected frame of reference and safe space they can open up access to emotions that the patient cannot express verbally, that are normally suppressed and only actualised in an uncontrolled manner in crisis situations. They fulfil the need to resolve psychological patterns that have become reified.
- Constellations must be embedded in a suitable framework. Patients and clients have high expectations of a facilitator with regard to professional competence, human empathy and personal clarity.
- The constellations group needs to be able to hold the frequently difficult subject matter in a process of reciprocal giving and taking.
- Representatives often have at their disposal various strategies for going into the role, staying in a role throughout a constellation and coming out of role after the constellation has been completed.
- Feelings in the body and spontaneous impulses to move in the constellation constitute an essential criterion for representatives to notice that they are being taken by experiences from outside themselves.
- Representatives distinguish between what is and what is not their own in various ways. People in representations tend to notice what of their representation is their own material. They are highly sensitive to preventing their

own issues from coming to the fore. Strategies for achieving this vary from person to person.

- The representatives find it important to be able to express everything that comes up for them moment by moment in a representation. This provides a clear division of labour between the representatives and the facilitator.
- The representatives profit in many ways both personally as well as professionally from their experiences in the role.
- Constellations enable psychological content that has remained hidden and split-off to surface; patients experience this as congruent.
- In general patients and clients deal positively with new information that emerges in constellations. It often enables them to resolve feelings that have been vague. Stressful relationships in the family are more readily understood. As a rule old conflicts are not intensified, but rather find sustainable resolution. Patients, with the help of this new information, are able to disengage more easily from unhealthy symbiotic enmeshments with their parents.

The sample of interviewees in the research presented is highly selective. It contains only people who have experienced the kind of constellations work that I practise, and whose developmental process has stretched in some cases over several years. In this respect the results of this study cannot be generalised to other applications of the constellation method.

According to feedback I have received from many of my seminar participants, my way of allowing the patients a great deal of time to develop their issue for a constellation seems to be unusual compared to the majority of other constellations practitioners in the field, as is the freedom that the representatives have to express all their uncensored impulses. I decided on this process because I noticed over time that pre-formed views and opinions or standard guidelines that the patients are assumed to need, or that the representatives are supposed to follow, do not do justice to their emotional processes. In my opinion they even hamper developing the constellations process into a universal and qualitatively valuable tool in therapeutic work. I am convinced that it is only when the highly differentiated emotional processes that are common to us all as human beings are not prematurely interrupted and manipulated, based on incomplete hypotheses, that the constellation method can develop its full potential. This may seem risky to the inexperienced facilitator, but in the end emotional processes cannot be controlled externally or forced into rigid formats. They will only change when they are seen and accepted as they are. This is particularly the case for those emotional aspects of us that I call the survival parts. They must be met with discretion, patience and respectful distance. The facilitator and the group must be prepared equally to subject themselves to the full strength of the traumatised emotional parts of a patient without panicking when they appear and without losing their own sense of safety and boundaries in respect to the patient. In my opinion only then can the apparently impossible succeed: that people can find a way out of their emotional splits even though it may sometimes seem to be awful, hopeless and impossible to do.

Research results alone are not enough to convince a sceptical person, enabling them to decide whether representatives can reliably mirror what goes on in the soul of another during a constellation; only experience as a representative can answer this question. This was my own experience and it seems the same for others who take on a representation for the first time. When one can see that entering a representative role can awaken feelings, thoughts and physical sensations that do not belong to oneself, then one can begin to be confident that such a thing is possible, then one can realise that there might be more things between heaven and earth than one's own understanding had previously allowed.

It can be an all-encompassing experience when someone does a hidden constellation; that is a constellation where the person chooses representatives for parts of his personality or people without telling the individuals or the group who or what they represent. Anyone who has seen a representative behave like the people or personality parts they are supposed to be representing, even without knowing anything about those people or personality parts, finds that all doubts disappear.

As facilitator I have had the privilege of observing the client acutely while they sit beside me. In the course of a constellation he will repeatedly say things like: "Yes, that's just how I feel", "That's just like my mother", "My father always says those words". I seldom experience that a client thinks a representative's behaviour has nothing to do with him or with the person being represented. For example, in one constellation the representative of the patient's mother said: "I have the feeling I'm wearing jewellery everywhere, round my neck, on my fingers ..." The patient answered: "That's right. My mother is a jewellery designer." A more detailed analysis of such observations in practice, as, for example, the astonishing reliability of hidden constellations or the frequency of congruent remarks made by representative during a constellation, is still subject to scrutiny. There is doubtless a great deal of interesting material to research and discover with regard to the constellations method.

11
Looking Forward

I am thankful to be living in Europe in a relatively stable time of peace, after periods of traumatising wars, where we can calmly observe so much of what is in our human hearts and souls, where we can allow ourselves to see these things in a relatively safe atmosphere and reflect on them without the ideological pressure and scrutiny of superior authorities. Unfortunately economic pressures still do not allow many people such a safe place and opportunity to give up their mode of surviving for a freer way of living. In spite of relative affluence and external security there will still be unexpected events of fate in the future. But in contrast to people who were born two or three generations ago, in my opinion there are increasingly realistic ways out of traumatic experiences, if we support each other in accepting bad luck and traumatic shocks in spite of understandable resistance. Traumatic experiences no longer need to be passed unconsciously and inevitably from the parents to the children. If together we observe what traumatic experiences do to us and to all the other people that we respect, value, like and love, then there can be new opportunities for better cooperation. We can learn what is really important in life, and how we can emerge from our splits and have less need to spend time in survival mode; how we can engage on behalf of our own needs without manipulating the needs of others; how we can leave behind the strategies of our survivor parts in order to find a way to our own centre; how we can shape our relationships with other people in a worth-while way, with healthy feelings and an alert spirit anchored in our body. So that we not only survive, but live in the consciousness of the inexhaustible sources of life with all our hearts and all our souls. So that, in spite of all human cruelty, love can continue to be revived in us.

References

Antonovsky, A. (1997). Salutogenese. Dgvt-Verlag, Tübingen.

Antonovsky, A. (1987). Unraveling the Mystery of Health – How People Manage Stress and Stay Well. Jossey-Bass Publishers, San Francisco.

Bauer, J. (2002). Das Gedächtnis des Körpers: Wie Beziehungen und Lebensstile unsere Gene steuern. Eichborn Verlag, Frankfurt/M.

Bauer, J. (2005). Warum ich fühle, was du fühlst. Intuitive Kommunikation und das Geheimnis der Spiegelneurone. Hoffmann und Campe, Hamburg.

Bowlby, J. (2001). Das Glück und die Trauer. Herstellung und Lösung affektiver Bindungen. Klett-Cotta, Stuttgart.

Bowlby, J. (2006a). Bindung. Reinhardt, München.

Bowlby, J. (2006b). Trennung. Reinhardt, München.

Bowlby, J. (2006c). Verlust. Reinhardt, München.

Bowlby, J. (1999). Attachment, Attachment and Loss (Vol. 1, 2nd ed.). Basic Books, New York.

Bowlby, J. (1973). Separation: Anxiety & Anger, Attachment and Loss (Vol. 2), International Psycho-Analytical Library No. 95. Hogarth Press, London.

Bowlby, J. (1980). Loss: Sadness & Depression. Attachment and Loss (vol. 3), International psychoanalytical library no.109. Hogarth Press, London.

Bradshaw, J. (2000). Das Kind in uns. Wie finde ich zu mir selbst. Knaur, München.

Bradshaw. J. (1990). Homecoming. Bantam Books, New York.

276

Brisch, K. H. (1999). Bindungsstörungen. Von der Bindungstheorie zur Therapie. Klett-Cotta, Stuttgart.

Brizendine, L. (2007). Das weibliche Gehirn. Warum Frauen anders sind als Männer. Hoffmann und Campe, Hamburg.

Brizendine, L. (2006). The Female Brain. Morgan Road Books/Random House, New York.

Burford, B. (2010). Geil auf Gewalt. Goldmann, München (English: Among the Thugs. Secker & Warburg, London.)

Casey, J. F. (1997). Ich bin viele. Eine ungewöhnliche Heilungsgeschichte. Rowohlt, Reinbek.

Casey, J. F. (1991). The Flock. Alfred A. Knopf, Inc., New York.

Chase, T. (2002). Aufschrei. Verlag Bastei Lübbe, Munich.

Chase, T. (1987). When Rabbit Howls: by the troops for Truddi Chase, Dutton.

Chopich, E. & Paul, M. (2005). Aussöhnung mit dem inneren Kind. Ullstein, Berlin.

Chopich, E. & Paul, M. (1990). Healing your Aloneness. HarperCollins Publishers, New York.

Damasio, A. (2005). Der Spinoza-Effekt. Wie Gefühle unser Leben bestimmen. List, München.

Damasio, A. (2006). Descartes' Irrtum. Fühlen, Denken und das menschliche Gehirn. List, München.

Eberspächer, H. (2002). Ressource Ich. Der ökonomische Umgang mit Stress. Hanser, München.

Fischer, G. & **Riedesser**, P. (1998). Lehrbuch der Psychotraumatologie. Reinhardt, München.

Fischer, G. (2000). Mehrdimensionale Psychodynamische Traumatherapie – MPTT. Manual zur Behandlung psycho-traumatischer Störungen. Asanger, Heidelberg.

Franke, U. (1996). Systemische Familienaufstellung. Eine Studie zu systemischer Verstrickung und unterbrochener Hinbewegung unter besonderer Berücksichtigung von Angstpatienten. Profil, München.

Freud, S. (1979). Abriss der Psychoanalyse. Das Unbehagen in der Kultur. Fischer Taschenbuch, Frankfurt/M.

Fröhlich, U. (1996). Vater unser in der Hölle. Ein Tatsachenbericht. Kallmeyer'sche Verlagsbuchhandlung, Seelze-Velber.

Galarza, A. V. (2006). Die Hypothese der morphischen Resonanz als wissenschaftliche Basis der Familie-naufstellung. Praxis der Systemaufstellung, 2, 69–71.

Gasch, U. (2007). Traumatisierungsrisiko von polizeilichen

Einsatzkräften vor dem Hintergrund eines berufsbezogenen Selbstverständnisses. Trauma & Gewalt, 2, 70–79.

Glasl, F. (1999). Konfliktmanagement. Paul Haupt, Bern.

Goldner, C. (2003). Der Wille zum Schicksal. Die Heilslehre des Bert Hellinger. Ueberreuter, Wien.

Gruen, H. D. (2007). Die Rückkehr des Schattens. Die Verbindung von Phänomenologie und Wissenschaft in der Spiraldynamik. Praxis der Systemaufstellung, 1, 46–55.

Haas, W. (2005). Familienstellen – Therapie oder Okkultismus. Das Familienstellen nach Hellinger kritisch beleuchtet. Asanger, Kröning.

Hellinger, B. & ten Hövel, G. (2005). Ein langer Weg. Gespräche über Schicksal, Versöhnung und Glück. Kösel, München.

Hellinger, B. (2007). Innenreisen. Erfahrungen, Betrachtungen, Beispiele. Kösel, München.

Herman, J. L. (2003). Die Narben der Gewalt. Traumatische Erfahrungen verstehen und überwinden. Junfermann, Paderborn.

Herman, J. L. (2001) Trauma and Recovery. From domestic abuse to political terror. Pandora, London.

Hinterhuber, H. (2001). Die Seele. Natur- und Kulturgeschichte von Psyche, Geist und Bewusstsein. Springer, Wien.

Holz, S. (2005). Welche Folgen haben psychische Erkrankungen eines Elternteils auf die psychische Entwicklung der Kinder. Fallanalyse bei Müttern mit Borderline-Persönlichkeits-störung. Katholische Stiftungsfachhochschule, München.

Homes, A. M. (2004). Von der Mutter missbraucht. Frauen und die sexuelle Lust am Kind. Books on Demand GmbH, Norderstedt.

Hope, J. (2005). Die Sprache der Seele. Ein visueller Schlüssel zur inneren Welt. Patmos, Düsseldorf.

Höppner, G. (2001). 'Heilt Demut – wo Schicksal wirkt?' Eine Studie zu den Effekten des Familienstellens nach Bert Hellinger. Profil, München.

Huber, M. (1998). Multiple Persönlichkeiten. Überlebende extremer Gewalt. Fischer Taschenbuch, Frankfurt/M.

Huber, M. (2003). Trauma und die Folgen. Trauma und Traumabehandlung, Teil 1. Junfermann, Paderborn.

Huber, M. (2005). Der innere Garten. Ein achtsamer Weg zur persönlichen Veränderung. Junfermann, Paderborn.

Hüther, G. (2005). Biologie der Angst. Vandenhoeck & Ruprecht, Göttingen.

Hüther, G. (2006). Die Macht der inneren Bilder. Wie Visionen das Gehirn, den Menschen und die Welt verändern. Vandenhoeck & Ruprecht, Göttingen.

Ivanov, V. V. (1983). Gerade und ungerade. Die Asymmetrie des Gehirns und der Zeichensysteme. Hirzel, Stuttgart.

Kennell, J. H. (2007). Kontinuierliche Unterstützung während der Geburt: Einflüsse auf Wehen, Entbindung und Mutter-Kind-Interaktion. In: Karl Heinz Brisch und Theodor Hellbrügge (Hrsg.), Die Anfänge der Eltern-Kind-Bindung (S. 157–169). Klett-Cotta, Stuttgart.

Kernberg, O., **Dulz**, B. & **Sachsse**, U. (Hrsg.) (2000). Handbuch der Borderline-Störungen. Schattauer, Stuttgart.

Kind, J. (2000). Zur Entwicklung psychoanalytischer Borderline-Konzepte seit Freud. In: Otto Kernberg, Birger Dulz und Ulrich Sachsse (Hrsg.), Handbuch der Borderline-Störungen (S. 27–44). Schattauer, Stuttgart.

Klaus, M. H. & **Klaus**, P. H. (2003). Das Wunder der ersten Lebenswochen. Mosaik, München.

Kolitzus, H. (2000). Ich befreie mich von deiner Sucht. Hilfen für Angehörige von Suchtkranken. Kösel, München.

Kreisman, J. J. & **Straus**, H. (2002). Ich hasse dich – verlass mich nicht. Die schwarzweiße Welt der Borderline-Persönlichkeit. Kösel, München.

Kreisman, J. J. & Strauss, H. (2004). Sometimes I act Crazy: Living with Borderline Personality Disorder. John Wiley & Sons, Inc. Hoboken, New Jersey.

Krystal, H. (2000). Psychische Widerstandsfähigkeit: Anpassung und Restitution bei Holocaust-Überlebenden. Psyche Sonderheft Trauma, Gewalt und Kollektives Gedächtnis, 840–859.

Levine, P. A. (1997). Waking the Tiger: Healing Trauma. North Atlantic Books, Berkeley, California.

Ludwig, A. M. (1983). The psychobiological functions of dissociation. American Journal of Clinical Hypnosis, 26, 93–99.

Mahler. M. (1972). Symbiose und Individuation. Klett-Cotta, Stuttgart.

Mraz, R. (2006). Nachgeprüft. Ergebnisse einer 10-Jahres-Katamnese aus über 850 Aufstellungen. Praxis der Systemaufstellung, 2, 94–101.

Nelles, W. (2007). Klassisches Familienstellen, Bewegungen der Seele, Bewegungen des Geistes – wohin bewegt sich die

Aufstellungsarbeit. Praxis der Systemaufstellung, 1, 32–45.

Pänzinger, C. (2004). Sind Arbeitsbeziehungsaufstellungen hilfreich in der stationären Kinder- und Jugendhilfe? Zwei Fallstudien über Elternarbeit in SOS-Kinderdorffamilien und Darstellung der Konsequenzen für die Soziale Arbeit. Diplomarbeit: Katholische Stiftungsfachhochschule, München.

Probst, C. (2004). Der plötzliche Tod eines Kindes – kann Trauerbegleitung das Trauma mindern? Gespräche mit Betroffenen und professionellen Helfern. Konsequenzen für die Soziale Arbeit. Katholische Stiftungsfachhochschule, München.

Putnam, F. W. (2003). Diagnose und Behandlung der dissoziativen Identitätsstörung. Junfermann, Paderborn.

Reddemann, L. (2001). Imagination als heilsame Kraft. Zur Behandlung von Traumafolgen mit ressourcenorientierten Verfahren. Klett-Cotta, Stuttgart.

Reddemann, L. (2006). Überlebenskunst. Klett-Cotta, Stuttgart.

Rilke, R M, Rilke's Book of Hours: Love Poems to God, translated by Anita Barrows and Joanna Macy. Riverhead Books, UK.

Rizzolatti, G., Fadiga, L., Fogassi, L. & Gallese, V. (2002). From mirror neurons to imitation: facts and speculations. In Meltzoff, A. & Prinz, W. (eds.), The Imitative Mind. Cambridge University Press, Cambridge.

Rizzolatti, G., Fadiga, L. & Gallese, V. (2007). Spiegel im Gehirn. Spektrum der Wissenschaft, 3, 49–55.

Ruppert, F. (2001). Berufliche Beziehungswelten. Das Aufstellen von Arbeitsbeziehungen in Theorie und Praxis. Carl-Auer-Systeme, Heidelberg.

Ruppert, F. (2002). Verwirrte Seelen. Der verborgene Sinn von Psychosen. Grundzüge einer systemischen Psychotraumatologie. Kösel, München.

Ruppert, F. (2008). Trauma, Bonding and Family Constellations. Green Balloon Publishing, Frome, UK.

Ruppert, F. & Freund, C. (2007). Hyperaktivität und ADHS. Erkenntnisse über die Ur-sachen der Unruhe von Kindern aus zwei Aufstellungsseminaren. Praxis der Systemaufstellung, 1, 74–82.

Rutter, M. (2000). Resilience reconsidered: Conceptual considerations, empirical findings, and policy implications. In Shonkoff, J. P. & Meisels, S. J. (eds.), Handbook of early childhood intervention. Cambridge University Press, Cambridge.

Sander, H. & Johr, B. (2005). BeFreier und Befreite. Krieg,

Vergewaltigung, Kinder. Fischer Taschenbuch, Frankfurt/M.

Saß, H., Wittchen, H.-U. & Zaudig, M. (1998). Diagnostisches und Statistisches Manual Psychischer Störungen. Hogrefe, Göttingen.

Schlötter, P. (2005). Vertraute Sprache und ihre Entdeckung. Systemaufstellungen sind kein Zufallsprodukt – der empirische Nachweis. Carl-Auer-Systeme, Heidelberg.

Schmidbauer, W. (1977). Hilflose Helfer. Rowohlt, Reinbek bei Hamburg.

Schmidt, J. B. (2006). Inner Navigation. Trauma healing and constellation process work as navigational tools for the evolution of our true self. Eigen Verlag, Hamburg.

Schneider, J. (2007). Die Aufstellungsarbeit im Lichte der Quantenphysik. Praxis der Systemaufstellung, 1, 11–25.

Schreiber, F. R. (1995). Sybil: The Classic True Story of a Woman Possessed by Sixteen Personalities. Hatchetts, New York.

Schulz von Thun, F. (1992). Miteinander reden. Störungen und Klärungen. Rowohlt, Hamburg.

Schwartz, R. C. (2004). Systemische Therapie mit der inneren Familie. Klett-Cotta, Stuttgart.

Schwer, B. (2004). Kann die Systemische Psycho-traumatologie Betreuern und Eltern beim Umgang mit hyperaktiven Kindern helfen? Einsichten gewonnen aus Familienaufstellungen an einer Heilpädagogischen Kindertagesstätte. Diplomarbeit Katholische Stiftungsfach-hochschule, München.

Selye, H. (1974). Stress, Bewältigung und Lebensgewinn. Piper, München.

Sethi, Y. (2010). Does the Process of Family Constellations Improve Relationships and Well-being? The Knowing Field International Constellations Journal, Issue 16.

Sheldrake, R. (1999). Das Gedächtnis der Natur. Das Geheimnis der Entstehung der Formen in der Natur. Piper, München.

Sheldrake, R. (1988). The presence of the Past. Times Books, New York.

Spitzer, M. (2005). Nervensachen. Geschichten vom Gehirn. Suhrkamp, Frankfurt/M.

Stevenson, R. L. (1994) The Strange Case of Dr. Jekyll and Mr. Hyde, Penguin Popular Classics, London.

St. Just, A. (2005). Soziales Trauma. Balance finden in einer unsicheren Welt. Kösel, München.

Stone, H. & Stone, S. (2000). Du bist viele. Das 100fache Selbst und seine Entdeckung durch die Voice-Dialogue-Methode. Heyne, München.

Stricevic, J. (2002). Folgen traumatischer Kriegs- und Nachkriegserfahrungen kroatischer Soldaten. Befragung von Betroffenen. Welche Aufgaben ergeben sich daraus für die Soziale Arbeit? Diplomarbeit Katholische Stiftungsfach-hochschule, München.

Ten Hövel (2003). Liebe Mama, böser Papa. Eltern-Kind-Entfremdung nach Trennung und Scheidung: Das PAS-Syndrom. Kösel, München.

Uvnäs-Moberg, K. (2006). Die Bedeutung des Hormons »Oxytocin« für die Entwicklung der Bindung des Kindes und der Anpassungsprozesse der Mutter nach der Geburt. In: K. H. **Brisch** und Th. **Hellbrügge** (Hg.), Die Anfänge der Eltern-Kind-Bindung, Klett-Cotta Verlag, Stuttgart.

Van der Hart, O., **Nijenhuis**, E. & **Steele**, K. (2006). The Haunted Self. Norton Professional Books, New York.

Van der Kolk, B. A., **McFarlane**, A. C. & **Wesaeth**, L. (2000). Traumatic Stress. Grundlagen und Behandlungsansätze. Junfermann, Paderborn.

Vester, F. (1991). Phänomen Stress. dtv, München.

Watzlawick, P., **Beavin**, J. H. & **Jackson**, D. D. (1972). Menschliche Kommunikation. Formen, Störungen, Paradoxien. Huber, Bern.

Weber, G. (Hg.) (1998). Praxis des Familien-Stellens. Beiträge zu systemischen Lösungen nach Bert Hellinger. Carl-Auer-Systeme, Heidelberg.

Weber, G. (Hg.) (2001). Derselbe Wind lässt viele Drachen steigen. Systemische Lösungen im Einklang. Carl-Auer-Systeme, Heidelberg.

Werner, E. E. (2000). Protective factors and individual resilience. In: **Shonkoff**, J. P. and **Meisels**, S. J. (Hrsg.), Handbook of early childhood intervention. Cambridge University Press, Cambridge.

Wittemann, A. (2006). Die Intelligenz der Psyche. Wie wir ihrer inneren Ordnung auf die Spur kommen. Kösel, München.

Wolinsky, S. (1995). Die dunkle Seite des inneren Kindes. Die Vergangenheit loslassen, die Gegenwart leben. Lüchow, Stuttgart.

Index

Green Balloon Publishing

Symbiosis and Autonomy

Symbiotic Trauma - Love Beyond Entanglement

Franz Ruppert

www.greenballoonbooks.co.uk
42 Goring Road, Steyning, West Sussex, BN44 3GF, UK.
Tel: +44 (0) 1903 814489 - info@greenballoonbooks.co.uk

CPSIA information can be obtained
at www.ICGtesting.com
Printed in the USA
LVOW10s1333080817

544249LV00020B/542/P